# 1000
## JAPANESE
## PROVERBS

illiam de Lange

Edited by
Kyōko Suzuki

FLOATING
WORLD
EDITIONS

First edition, 2013
First paperback edition, 2024

Previously published as *A Dictionary of Japanese Proverbs*.

Published by **Floating World Editions**
26 Jack Corner Road, Warren, CT 06777
www.floatingworldeditions.com

ISBN 978-1-953225-07-8

Printed and bound in the U.S.A.

Library of Congress Cataloging-in-Publication Data available upon request.

# Preface

Proverbs are a window into the soul of a people. Such, at least, was the view of the twentieth-century British author Norman Douglas, who stated that in spite of their often apparent triteness, proverbs "embody the concentrated experience of the race." Those who order their lives according to what proverbs teach, he believed, cannot go far wrong. Many would tend to agree with Douglas's view, and over the years his sentiment has found much resonance, so much so that it has almost become a proverb in its own right. It is perhaps no coincidence that the one proverb in the English language to reflect on itself holds that "wise men make proverbs." There is no Japanese equivalent to support this view, yet there can be little doubt that Douglas's sentiments apply to Japan's proverbs in equal, if not greater, measure.

As with so many other aspects of Japanese culture, Japanese proverbs, or *kotowaza* (諺) as they are called in Japan, are an eclectic mix of indigenous and imported wisdoms and insights. Given the huge influence China has had on Japanese culture from a very early time, many of its proverbs are of Chinese origin. Some of these can still be found in their original form of four character compounds, such as 大器晩成 (soon ripe, soon rotten), a proverb attributed to the ancient Chinese philosopher Laozi, or 呉越同舟 (adversity makes strange bedfellows), attributed to the Chinese general Sun Tzu. Many of these ancient and often cryptic proverbs have lost their power in the modern context. They are rarely used by modern-day Japanese speakers, reasons for which only few have been included here. Given their compact and pithy nature, four character compounds, or *yoji-jukugo* (四字熟語), have also been used by the Japanese to coin their own wisdoms. Indeed, they have even been employed to translate proverbs that are Western in origin, as, for instance, in 一石二鳥 (to kill two birds with one stone). Most Chinese proverbs, however, have been adapted to suit Japanese tastes. Over the centuries, they have acquired a (classical) Japanese sentence structure, such as 仇を恩で報ずる (return good for evil) a proverb that is also attributed to Laozi, or 五十歩をもって百歩を笑う (the pot calling the kettle black), a proverb attributed to Mencius.

Many Western proverbs have also made their way into the Japanese

# Preface

language, a few even during the period of seclusion, when Japan's only window on the West was the Dutch factory in Nagasaki. Most proverbs that derive from Western equivalents, however, stem from the periods when Japanese society was forced to open up to the West. First of these was during the Meiji period (1868–1912), when its leaders sought to catch up with the West by adopting and adapting German, English, Dutch, and French institutions and traditions. Another period came in the wake of the Second World War, when, during the American occupation (1945–1952), the Japanese populace became familiar with American ways and manners of speech to an unprecedented degree.

The vast majority of Japanese proverbs, of course, are Japanese in origin. For the foreign student, they are perhaps the most interesting, as they arise from uniquely Japanese situations, concern themselves with Japanese issues, or employ quintessentially Japanese objects and imagery. A good example of the latter is the proverb 餅は餅屋, "for rice cakes, the rice cake shop" (every man to his trade), which features *mochi* (餅), the Japanese rice cake, as well as the rice cake maker, or *mochiya* (餅屋). Another example is 紺屋の白袴, "the dyer's white *hakama*" (the tailor's wife is worst clad), which features both the Japanese dyer, or *kōya* (紺屋), and the *hakama* (袴), or trousered skirt, a traditional garment worn by Japanese men. Another is the wonderfully evocative 居候三杯目にはそっと出し, "spongers put out their bowls for a third helping stealthily," which seems far more sophisticated than the English equivalent (beggars can't be choosers). Other proverbs have their origin in historical events, such as 江戸の敵を長崎で討つ, "to slay Edo's enemies at Nagasaki," which refers to the fierce competition between an owner of a curiosity shop in Osaka and his rivals in Tokyo. Other proverbs, still, are the verbatim words of great historical figures, such as Tokugawa Ieyasu, who in his *Teachings on the Conduct of Life*, continues to reminds his countrymen that 勝つ事ばかり知りて負くる事を知らざれば害其の身に至る, "harm comes to those who know only victory and do not know defeat" (failure teaches success). Ieyasu spoke from personal experience, for in the Battle of Mikatagahara (1572), he and Oda Nobunaga suffered a crushing defeat at the hands of the brilliant warlord Takeda Shingen. It was the hard lessons learned in that frightful encounter that helped galvanize his victory in the far more important Battle of Sekigahara (1600).

Japanese proverbs, then, comprise an incredibly rich and eclectic treasure of the "concentrated experience" of the Japanese race, from the simple lessons of the commoner's daily life, to the profound insights of some of the region's greatest minds. They have been gathered from a wide geographic area and accumulated over a long period of time. There are several thousands of "Japanese" proverbs, and while many of these are essentially sayings and aphorisms, it is no exaggeration to say that the Japanese people have recourse to one of the largest collections of proverbs in the world. As such, they present a fascinating window on the Japanese psyche, as well as the various cultural influences to which those who employ them have been exposed over the centuries.

One of the aims of this dictionary is to give the foreign reader some insight in the origins, as well as the context in which certain proverbs have come into being. Ultimately, however, our aim must be to better understand the Japanese language. If, in the process, we stand to absorb some of the exotic wisdom of the people who speak it, we can only count ourselves richer.

## Symbols

Where relevant, different senses of meaning for each entry are indicated by the symbols ❶ , ❷ , and, on a rare occasion, ❸ . The senses are generally listed with the sense used most frequently appearing first.

Other symbols used throughout this dictionary are listed with their meanings below.

[ ]   : Literal translation
●   : English explanation
◦   : (Rough) English equivalent
✍   : Grammatical or linguistic note
☞   : Historical or other contextual reference
📖   : Reference to literary source
=   : Cross-reference to synonymous proverb
▶   : Cross-reference to related proverb
≠   : Cross-reference to antonymous proverb

# ア

### 愛出ずる者は愛返り、福往く者は福来る

[Those who love receive love; those who bestow (good) fortune receive (good) fortune.] ✍ *Ai* (愛) stands for emotional love and is usually altruistic, whereas *koi* (恋) stands for romantic love, which is often selfish. ● When one loves others, one can expect to be loved in return; when one does good to others one can expect to be treated well in return. ● Love begets love. ● Love is the reward of love. = 愛は愛を生む ♦ 仇も情けも我が身より出る ♦ 魚心有れば水心 ♦ 旅は道連れ世は情け ♦ 問い声良ければいらえ声良い ♦ 情けは人の為ならず ♦ 人は情けの下に立つ

### 愛屋烏に及ぶ

[Love extends to the bird on the roof.] ✍ *Ai* (愛) stands for emotional love and is usually altruistic, whereas *koi* (恋) stands for romantic love, which is often selfish. ● Those who are deeply in love are apt to be enamored of everything that remotely relates to the object of their affection. ● Love me, love my dog. ● He who loves Bertrand loves his dog. ● Love is blind. ♦ 色は思案の外 ♦ 恋は思案の外 ♦ 止めて止まらぬ恋の道 ♦ 惚れた病に薬無し ≠ 坊主憎けりゃ袈裟まで憎い

### 挨拶は時の氏神

[Arbitration may at times be an *ujigami*.] ✍ *Ujigami* (氏神) are the guardian gods or spirits that protect a place connected to the Shintō religion. ● On occasions when tempers flare a soothing word or friendly gesture may help to diffuse the situation. ● Good words cool more than cold water. ● Good words cost naught. ● Good words anoint us, and ill do unjoint us. = 仲裁は時の氏神

### 相手なれば訴訟なし

[If one becomes a partner there will be no lawsuit.] ● As long as one is willing to talk things over one will avoid creating enemies. ● It takes two to make a quarrel. = 相手なれば訴訟なし ♦ 相談は年寄り、喧嘩は若者

**あ**

## 相手の無い喧嘩は出来ない

[A quarrel without an opponent is impossible.] ● Since it takes two parties for a quarrel or dispute to arise one should avoid them simply by not becoming party to them in the first place. ● It takes two to make a quarrel. = 相手なれば訴訟なし ◆ 相談は年寄り、喧嘩は若者

## 愛は愛を生む

[Love brings forth love.] ✍ Ai (愛) stands for emotional love and is usually altruistic, whereas *koi* (恋) stands for romantic love, which is often selfish. ● When one loves one's fellow human beings, one can expect to be loved in return. ● Love begets love. ● Love is the reward of love. = 愛出ずる者は愛返り、福往く者は福来る ◆ 仇も情けも我が身より出る ◆ 魚心有れば水心 ◆ 旅は道連れ世は情け ◆ 問い声良ければいらえ声良い ◆ 情けは人の為ならず ◆ 人は情けの下に立つ

## 愛は宮殿にも藁屋にも住む

[Love dwells in palaces as well as hovels.] ✍ Ai (愛) stands for emotional love and is usually altruistic, whereas *koi* (恋) stands for romantic love, which is often selfish. ● Love is a universal emotion that can affect all of us and may be found at every level of society. ● Love lives in cottages as well as in courts. = 恋に上下の隔て無し

## 愛は小出しにせよ

[Love a little at a time.] ✍ Ai (愛) stands for emotional love and is usually altruistic, whereas *koi* (恋) stands for romantic love, which is often selfish. ● In order to make love last, it is better not to love too passionately. ● Love me little, love me long. ◆ 可愛さ余って憎さ百倍

## 愛は多能で有り、金は万能で有る

[Love is versatile; money is omnipotent.] ✍ Ai (愛) stands for emotional love and is usually altruistic, whereas *koi* (恋) stands for romantic love, which is often selfish. ● Though it is said that love conquers all it is money that rules the world. ● Love does much, money does everything. ◆ 色気より食い気 ◆ 金の切れ目が縁の切れ目 ◆ 地獄の沙汰も金次第

## 会うは別れの始め

[Meeting is the beginning of parting.] ☞ This proverb is firmly rooted in the Buddhist belief in the mutability and transience of life. ● In this fleeting world nothing is constant, and sooner or later the converging roads that caused us to encounter others on our journey through life will inevitably part again. ● To meet is to part. ● Every parting is a little death. ♦ 門松は冥途の旅の一里塚 ♦ 三日見ぬ間の桜

## 秋の鹿は笛に寄る

[The deer of fall are drawn by the flute.] ✍ In former days hunters would use a special flute (or rather a horn) that imitated the mating call of stags to attract and kill a doe. ● Those who are susceptible to the lure of love are vulnerable and easy to exploit. ● Like moths to the flame. = 飛んで火に入る夏の虫

## 商人と屏風は曲がらねば世に立たぬ

[Tradesmen and folding screens will not stand up straight.] ✍ The *byōbu* (屏風), or Japanese folding screen, will only stand up when partially folded. As in English, the adjective *massugu* (真直ぐ), or "straight," has the connotation of being honest and upright. ● Trade will only flourish with a slight degree of dishonesty. ● There is knavery in all trades, but most in tailors. = 商売と屏風は曲がらぬと立たぬ = 屏風と商人は真直ぐにては立たぬもの ♦ 正しき者は艱難多し

## 悪妻は六十年の不作

[A bad wife is a poor harvest for sixty years.] ● When one makes the mistake of marrying an unkind woman one will suffer the consequences for the rest of one's life. ● A bad wife is the shipwreck of a house. ♦ 住に跡へ行くとも、死に跡へ行くな. ♦ 縁と浮世は末を待て ♦ 縁と月日の末を待て

## 悪事千里を走る

[Evil runs a thousand *ri*.] ✍ The *ri* (里) is an ancient Chinese measurement of distance, the equivalent of 0.3 miles. With time, it came to denote the distance one could walk in an hour, and during the Edo period (1600–1867) it was officially defined as 36 *chō*, or about 2.44 miles. Bad habits are easily learned, and as they are often profitable, they tend to spread fast. • Evil spreads fast. • Bad news has wings. • Ill news unsent for never comes too late. • Ill news comes apace. ♦ 蔭徳有れば陽報有り ♦ 好事門を出でず

## 悪銭身に付かず

[Ill-gotten gains do not become one's own.] ● Wealth gained by way of ruse or illegal means is always subject to the effects of revenge and persecution and does not tend to accumulate. • Ill-gotten goods seldom prosper. = 不義の富貴は浮雲の如し ♦ 正直の儲けは身に付く

## 悪に強きは善にも強し

[What is strong in evil is strong in good.] ● Those who are capable or have the power of doing great evil are, once they have turned over a new leaf, also able to do much good. • A strong enemy will make a strong friend.

## 悪人は畳の上では死なれぬ

[The evil do not die on a *tatami*.] ✍ The *tatami* (畳) is a thick mat of woven straw of roughly one hundred and eighty by ninety centimeters, and is the standard measure by which the size of all Japanese rooms are measured. ● Those who lead a life of vice generally do not die peaceful deaths, i.e., within the comfort of their own home. • Evil men do not die in their own beds. • A good life makes a good death. ♦ 身から出た錆 ♦ 刃の錆は刃より出でて刃を腐らす

## 悪法も亦法也

[A bad law is a law nevertheless.] 📖 This proverb is attributed to Socrates. ● Even when a law is generally accepted to be undesirable it will still have to be obeyed. • A law is a law, however undesirable it may be. ♦ 法は人で無い、人は法で無い

## 開けて悔しき玉手箱

[A treasure chest which when opened causes regrets.] ☞ This proverb is derived from the ancient Japanese folk tale of Urashima

Tarō, a simple fisherman prompted by a turtle to leave his village and visit the deep-sea palace of the Dragon King, where he meets and inevitably falls in love with the beautiful sea princess Otohime. As time goes by, however, the fisherman grows homesick and decides to return home. As a parting gift, he is given a chest with the strict injunction not to open it. He returns home safely but his curiosity gets the better of him. On opening the chest a white cloud of smoke escapes, and when the air clears, the fisherman finds that he has aged beyond recognition. ● Used in instances when something much anticipated does not live up to one's expectations. ● Blessed is he who expects nothing. ▶ 当て事と越中 褌 は向こうから外れる ▶ 棒ほど願って針ほど叶う

あ

## 朝謡は貧乏の相

[The morning song is the mark of a pauper.] ☞ Singing usually accompanies merriment and pleasure seeking, in Japan a traditionally nocturnal activity, since in daytime people are hard at work. Consequently, those who have the time to sing at dawn are not hard at work and will, before long, end up poor. ● Those who sing in the morning have too much leisure on their hands and will eventually fall into poverty. ● None but fools and fiddlers sing at their meat. ▶ 稼ぐに追い付く貧乏無し ▶ 勤勉は福の神 ▶ 酒と朝寝は貧乏の近道 ▶ 好きの道には薦被る

## 朝起きは三文の得

[Three *mon* for those who rise early.] ✍ The *mon* (文) was a currency unit derived from the Chinese *wen* that was introduced to Japan during the Muromachi period (1333-1568). It was used up until 1870, when it was replaced with the *yen* (円). ● Those who rise early are considered to be less lazy and will have a longer day to earn a living. ● The first sweep finds the money lost at night. ● The early bird catches the worm. = 早起きは三文の得 ▶ 宵寝朝起き長者の基

## 朝曇りば晴れ、夕曇りは雨

[When it is cloudy in the morning, it will clear up; when it is cloudy in the evening, it will rain.] ● Clouds in the morning are a sign of

5

あ

good weather to come; clouds in the evening are a sign of bad weather to come. ● Cloudy mornings turn to fair evenings. ◆ 夜揚がりの天候は長持ちせぬ

## 浅瀬に仇波

[Rough waves in shallows.] 📖 This proverb is taken from the *Kokinshū*. ● Shallow-minded people are apt to make the greatest fuss about trifling issues. ● Shallow waters give rise to noisy waves. ● Shallow streams make the most din. ◆ 音無き川は水深し ◆ 言葉多き者は品少なし ◆ 静かに流れる川は深い

## 朝虹は雨、夕虹は晴れ

[A rainbow in the morning, rain; a rainbow in the evening, fair.] ● A rainbow in the morning is a sign of bad weather to come; a rainbow in the evening is a sign of fair weather to come. ● A rainbow at morn, put your hook in the corn; a rainbow at eve, put your head in the sheave. = 晩の虹は鎌を研げ、朝の虹は隣へ行くな ◆ 朝焼けは雨、夕焼けは晴れ ◆ 夕焼けは晴れ、朝焼けは雨

## 麻に連るる蓬

[The hemp on which hangs the mugwort.] ✍ Hemp will grow up straight, whereas the mugwort tends to meander. When both grow together, however, the mugwort will follow the hemp. 📖 This proverb is taken from the works of the Chinese Confucianist Xunzi. ● Those with a weak character who associate with someone with a strong character will gradually develop moral firmness. ● With the good we become good. ◆ 強将の下に弱卒無し ◆ 朱に交われば赤くなる ◆ 善人の敵となるとも悪人を友とすな ◆ 白砂は泥に在りて之と皆黒し ◆ 勇将の下に弱卒無し ◆ 良将の下に弱卒無し ≠ 大樹の下に美草無し

## 朝日が西から出る

[The morning sun rises in the west.] ● Used to describe a situation that is utterly unimaginable. ● Pigs will fly. ◆ 石が流れて木の葉が沈む ◆❷ 瓢箪から駒 ◆ 餅の中からの屋根石

### 薊の花も一盛り

[Even the thistle blossom has its spell of prosperity.] ● Even homely women may develop their charm with time. ◆ 女に廃りがない ◆ 鬼も十八、番茶も出花

### 朝焼けは雨、夕焼けは晴れ

[Morning glow, rain; evening glow, clear weather.] ● A red sky in the morning is a sign of bad weather to come; a red sky in the evening is a sign of fair weather to come. • Red sky in the morning, shepherd's warning; red sky at night, shepherd's delight. = 夕焼けは晴れ、朝焼けは雨 ◆ 朝虹は雨、夕虹は晴れ ◆ 晩の虹は鎌を研げ、朝の虹は隣へ行くな

### 朝には紅顔有りて夕べには白骨となる

[Having a rosy face in the morning to become white bones by evening.] ● Life is transient and no one can predict the future or when their moment will come. • Today red, tomorrow dead. • Here today, gone tomorrow. • Today a man; tomorrow none. = 今日有って明日無い身

### 朝に道を聞けば夕べに死すとも可なり

[If one asks how one should live tomorrow, one may die contented tonight.] ● When one has learned the morally right way to live, one may die without regrets, even if one does not have the chance to live accordingly.

### 明日は明日の風が吹く

[Tomorrow, tomorrow's winds will blow.] ● There is no knowing what tomorrow will bring, so there is no use in worrying about future problems. • Tomorrow will take care of itself. • Sufficient unto the day is the evil thereof. = 明日の事は明日案じよ = 今日は今日、明日は明日の風が吹く

### 足に傷持てば笹原走る

[Those with a scar on their foot will run through a plain of bamboo grass.] ☞ This proverb cleverly builds on the expression 足に傷持つ

, the literal meaning of which is "to have a scar on one's foot," but the idiomatic meaning of which is "to have a guilty conscience." Thus, people with a guilty conscience will not be at peace with themselves and always be on tenterhooks. ● One whose foot is injured will not be able to walk leisurely (but be forced to run) through a field of hard and prickly bamboo grass. ● He who is guilty believes all men speak ill of him. ● Quiet conscience sleeps. ● A guilty conscience needs no accuser. = 脛に傷持てば笹原走る

## 預かり物は半分の主

[Those who look after someone's possessions are their owner by half.] ● Those entrusted with the custodianship of the possessions of others are soon tempted to consider them to be partly their own. ● Possession is nine-tenths of the law.

## 明日の事を言えば鬼が笑う

[Talk of tomorrow and the devil will laugh.] ● No one can predict what tomorrow may bring, and to talk of one's expectations for the future is to tempt providence. ● Nobody knows what tomorrow may bring. ● Nobody knows the 'morrow. = 三年先の事を言えば鬼が笑う = 三日先の事を言えば鬼が笑う = 来年の事を言えば鬼が笑う ♦ 一寸先は闇 ♦ 知者も面前に三尺の闇あり ♦ 人の行方と水の流れ ♦ 水の流れと人の末

## 明日の事は明日案じよ

[Let's think about tomorrow's matters tomorrow.] ● There is no knowing what tomorrow will bring, so there is no use in worrying about future problems. ● Tomorrow will take care of itself. ● Sufficient unto the day is the evil thereof. = 明日は明日の風が吹く = 今日は今日、明日は明日の風が吹く

## 明日の百より今日の五十

[Rather today's fifty than tomorrow's one hundred.] ● Rather than wait for an opportunity to make great gains, it is better to seize the opportunity of the moment even if gains are modest. ● A bird in the hand is worth two in the bush. ● Better an egg today than a hen

あ

tomorrow. = 末始終より今の三十 = ❶近火で手を焙れ = 後の千金より今の百文 = 来年の百両より今年の一両 ♦ あの世千日この世の一日 ♦ 大取りより小取り ♦ 聞いた百文より見た一文 ≠ 小節を規る者は栄名を成す能わず ≠ 小利を見れば則ち大事成らず

## 明日は雨人は泥棒

[Tomorrow brings rain; people are robbers.] ● In this world full of dangers it is better to prepare for every kind of eventuality and to trust no one. ● He who trusteth not is not deceived. ● If you trust before you try, you may repent before you die. ● Trust is the mother of deceit. = 人を見たら泥棒と思え = 火を見れば火事と思え ♦ 石橋を叩いて渡る ♦ 転ばぬ先の杖 ♦ 備え有れば憂い無し

## 焦ると損する

[Hurry and you will suffer drawbacks.] ● Doing something in a hurry without much thought or preparation will inevitably lead to failure. ● Patient men win the day. ● Haste makes waste. = 急いては事を仕損じる ♦ 慌てる蟹は穴へ入れぬ ♦ 急がば回れ ♦ 急いた蟹は穴を失う ♦ 短気は損気

## 仇も情けも我が身より出る

[Both evil and good come from oneself.] ● The treatment one receives in life is often the product of one's own actions. If one takes a hostile stance one can expect to make enemies; if one takes a generous stance one can expect to make friends. ● He that soweth good seed shall reap good corn. ● One never loses by doing good turns. ● One good turn deserves another. = 魚心有れば水心 = 問い声良ければいらえ声良い ♦ 愛出ずる者は愛返り、福往く者は福来る ♦ 愛は愛を生む ♦ 旅は道連れ世は情け ♦ 情けは人の為ならず ♦ 人は情けの下に立つ

## 仇を恩で報ずる

[Repay evil with good.] 📖 This proverb is attributed to the Chinese Daoist Laozi. ● When those who are potentially one's opponents are treated with kindness, they will be put under obligation and thus be less inclined to cause one harm. ● Return good for evil.

# 暑さ寒さも彼岸まで

[Both heat and cold last only to the equinoctial week.] ● The summer heat will not last beyond the equinoctial week in autumn; the winter cold will not last beyond the equinoctial week in spring. • No heat or cold lasts over the equinox.

# 暑さ忘れて蔭忘る

[Heat forgotten, shadow forgotten.] ● No sooner has the danger passed than people will have forgotten their fears. Similarly, as soon as the difficulties that caused one to turn to others for help have passed, one will forget the aid given. • Vows made in storms are forgotten in calms. • Danger past and God forgotten. • The peril past, the saint mocked. = 雨晴れて笠を忘る = 喉元過ぎれば熱さを忘れる = 病治りて薬師忘る ▶ 苦しい時の神頼み ▶ 狡兎死して走狗烹らる ▶ 恐い時の仏頼み ▶ 災害は忘れた頃にやって来る ▶ 飛鳥尽きて良弓蔵る

# 羮に懲りて膾を吹く

[Blow on the cold fish salad after learning a lesson from the hot soup.] ● Those who have been frightened or hurt in some situation may act defensively when a similar situation arises, even if their actions are inappropriate. • A scalded cat dreads cold water. = 蛇に噛まれて朽ち縄に怖ず = 火傷した子供は火を恐れる

# 当て事と越中褌は向こうから外れる

[Expectations and loincloths from Etchū are removed from the front.] ✐ The Etchū loincloth is a traditional Japanese garment which is held up by strings that are tied at the front. ● Like the Japanese stringed loincloth, which can easily be removed by someone else who pulls the strings at the front, so one's expectations and hopes may be snatched away by the actions of someone else. • Hope is but the dream of those that wake. ▶ 開けて悔しき玉手箱

# 後の祭

[After the festival.] ● For most things there usually is a right time and place to do them; when they are done too late or in the wrong place they may lose their effect. • A day after the fair. • After meat, mustard. ＝ 六日の菖蒲、十日の菊 ＝ 盆過ぎての鯖商い ♦ 戦を見て矢を矧ぐ ♦ 喧嘩過ぎての棒乳切り ♦ 賊去って張弓 ♦ 賊の後の棒乳切り ♦ 敵を見て矢を矧ぐ ♦ 泥棒を捕らえて縄を綯う ♦ 難に臨んで兵を鋳る ♦ 盗人を見て縄を綯う

## 後は野となれ山となれ

[After (me) let (the place) become a wild plain or a mountain.] ● Used by or with respect to those who wash their hands of something and do not care what happens afterwards. • After me, the deluge. ＝ 末は野となれ山となれ ≠ 立つ鳥跡を濁さず

## あの世千日この世の一日

[Rather one day in this world than a thousand in the next.] ● Rather than behave prudently in the hope of enjoying eternal bliss in a next life, it is better to enjoy to the full the days one is given in this life. Similarly, it is better to seize the opportunity of the moment than hope for better chances in the future. • A bird in the hand is worth two in the bush. • Better an egg today than a hen tomorrow. ＝ 日々是好日 ♦ 明日の百より今日の五十 ♦ 聞いた百文より見た一文 ♦ 末始終より今の三十 ♦❶ 近火で手を焙れ ♦ 後の千金より今の百文 ♦ 来年の百両より今年の一両

## 痘痕も靨

[(When infatuated,) even pockmarks are dimples.] ● When one is in love, even the most negative traits are seen in a favorable light. Used to convey the extent to which one's love for someone affects one's view of them. • Love sees no faults. • Beauty is in the eye of the beholder. • Love is blind. ♦ 恋は盲目 ♦ 惚れた欲目

## 危ない事は怪我の内

[Dangerous things are within the realm of the injurious.] ● If one already knows the outcome may be harmful, it is better not to expose oneself to danger in the first place. ♦ 君子は危うきに近寄らず ♦ 聖人は危うきに近寄らず ♦ 三十六計逃ぐるに如かず ♦ 重宝を抱く者は夜行せず ♦❷ 馬鹿さしじがれば二がえ馬鹿 ≠ 盲蛇に怖じず

**あ**

## 虻蜂取らず

[To catch neither the horsefly nor the wasp.] ● When in one's greed one seeks to obtain two coveted goals, one stands to lose both in the end. ● He who runs after two hares will catch neither. ● Grasp all, lose all. = 一念は継ぐとも二念は継ぐな = 二足の草蛙は履けぬ = 二兎を追う者は一兎をも得ず ◗ 大欲は無欲に似たり

## 阿呆に付ける薬無し

[There is no medicine for curing a fool.] ● Fools are born as fools and no degree of good counsel or punishment will ever make them wise. ● He who is born a fool is never cured. = 馬鹿に付ける薬無し = 惚れ病と馬鹿の治る薬は無い ◗ 三十馬鹿と八月青田は治らない

## 阿呆の一つ覚え

[The fool's one-liner.] ● Those who have limited learning often harp on the same subject, as they have nothing else to say. ● He that knows little often repeats it. = 馬鹿の一つ覚え ◗ 愚者の雄弁は沈黙なり ◗ 沈黙は愚者の機知である ◗ 知る者は言わず言う者は知らず ◗ 雀の千声鶴の一声

## 甘い物に蟻が付く

[Ants stick to sweet things.] ● When there is a profit to be made or pleasure to be had people will soon gather around. ● Like a bear to a honeypot. ◗ 富貴には他人も集まり、貧賎には親戚も離れる

## 雨垂れ石を穿つ

[Raindrops will wear down a stone.] ● If one perseveres in something long enough one will eventually be successful. ● Constant dripping wears away the stone. = 斧を研いで針にする = ❷ 塵も積もれば山と成る = 点滴石をも穿つ ◗ 石の上にも三年 ◗ ❶ 倒れる事は必ず傾く方に有り ◗ 泥棒も十年 ◗ 始めの一歩、末の千里

## 阿弥陀の光も金次第

[The luster of Buddha, too, is in proportion to (the amount of) gold.] ☞ Images and effigies of Buddha are often gilded, so that this proverb could be interpreted quite literally. ● Even the grace of Buddha depends on the amount of money one is willing to contribute to the temple. • No penny, no paternoster. = 金の光は阿弥陀ほど ♦ 地獄の沙汰も金次第 ♦ 釈迦も銭ほど光る ♦ 仏の光より金の光

## 網無くて淵をのぞくな

[Do not face the pool without a net.] ● No task can be accomplished without the right opportunity, preparation, or resources. • Without bait fish are not caught. ♦ 一目の網は以て鳥を得べからず ♦ 差し金無くては雪隠も建たぬ ♦ 種の無い手品は使われぬ

## 網の目に風たまらす

[The wind is not caught in the meshes of a net.] ● Used to describe a futile action, or something that is to no avail. = 籠で水を汲む = 糠に釘 ♦ 馬の耳に念仏 ♦ 蛙の面に水 ♦ 株を守りて兎を待つ ♦ 空吹く風と聞き流す ♦ 猫に小判 ♦ 馬耳東風 ♦ 豚に真珠

## 網の目にさえ恋風がたまる

[The wind of love may even be caught in the meshes of a net.] ✍ Ai (愛) stands for emotional love, which is usually altruistic, whereas koi (恋) stands for romantic love, which is often selfish. ❶ Even cold-hearted people may fall prey to the power of love. • Love makes all hard hearts gentle. ❷ Even women of easy virtue may fall in love.

## 雨が降れば土砂降り

[When it rains it pours.] ☞ This proverb derives from its English equivalent. ● When a number of calamities or hardships lie in store, they often strike at the same time. • It never rains but it pours. = 不幸は重なるもの ♦ 痛い上の針 ♦ 重き馬に上荷打つ ♦ 泣き面に蜂が刺す ♦ 二度ある事は三度ある ♦ ❷ 目の寄る所へ玉が寄る ♦ 弱り目に祟り目

## 雨が降ろうが槍が降ろうが

[Whether it pours down with rain or arrows.] ● Used by those who refuse to abandon their goals no matter what may happen. • Come rain or shine. = 石に齧り付いても

13

## 雨晴れて笠を忘る

[When the rain clears, the umbrella is forgotten.] ● No sooner has a crisis passed or people will have forgotten the danger and neglect the means by which to combat it. ● Vows made in storms are forgotten in calms. ● Danger past and God forgotten. ● The peril past, the saint mocked. = 暑さ忘れて蔭忘る = 喉元過ぎれば熱さを忘れる = 病治りて薬師忘る ◆ 苦しい時の神頼み ◆ 狡兎死して走狗烹らる ◆ 恐い時の仏頼み ◆ 災害は忘れた頃にやって来る ◆ 飛鳥尽きて良弓蔵る

## 雨降って地固まる

[After the rain, the ground gets firm.] ● The lessons and patience learned in the course of great hardships will enhance the enjoyment of the good times that follow. ● After rain comes fair weather. ● Good comes out of evil. ◆ 人間万事塞翁が馬

## 過ちて改めざる是を過ちと謂う

[Not to change one's ways having erred, this is what is called erring.] 📖 This proverb is taken from the *Analects* of Confucius. ● It is not shameful to err, as long as one mends one's ways. Only those who fail to acknowledge their mistakes are truly in the wrong. ● Never too late to mend. ◆ 過ちは改むるに憚る事なかれ ◆ 君子の過ちは日月の食の如し ◆ 地に倒るる者は地によりて立つ

## 過ちは改むるに憚る事なかれ

[Do not hesitate to acknowledge a mistake and to correct it.] 📖 This proverb is taken from the *Analects* of Confucius. ● When one has made a mistake, it is better to own up to it; if one does not, the mistake will go unaddressed and be the cause of yet more ills that could have been avoided. ● Never too late to mend. ◆ 君子の過ちは日月の食の如し ◆ 地に倒るる者は地によりて立つ ◆ 過ちて改めざる是を過ちと謂う

## 有りそうで無いのは金、無さそうで有るのも金

[Where there seems to be money, there isn't; where there seems to be no money, there is.] ● Those whose appearance suggests wealth often have little money; those whose appearance suggests poverty often have plenty of money. ◆ 衣ばかりで和尚は出来ぬ ◆ 数珠ばかりで和尚が出来ぬ ◆ 人肥えたるが故に尊からず

## 蟻の穴から堤も崩れる

[Even an embankment will crumble from an ant hole.] ● The slightest negligence may result in an irreversible loss of the greatest magnitude. Similarly, the greatest of enterprises may come to naught through the tiniest of oversights. ● A small leak will sink a ship. = 大山も蟻穴より崩る ◆ ❷ 蛍火をもって酒弥山を焼く

## 蟻の思いも天に届く

[Even the ideas of ants can reach the heavens.] ● When people with little power act in concert they can achieve great changes. ● Union is strength. = 農民の息も天に昇る = 蚤の息さえ天に上る = 蟇の息さえ天に上る

## 有るが上にも欲しがるのが人情

[It is human nature to crave more than we have.] ● It is human nature that we forget to appreciate what we have and crave what we do not yet possess. ● Much would have more. ◆ 有るは嫌なり、思うは成らず ◆ 一生は尽くれども希望は尽きず ◆ 昨日に優る今日の花 ◆ 千石を得て万石を恨む ◆ 成るは嫌なり、思うは成らず ◆ 隴を得て蜀を望む

## 有るは嫌なり、思うは成らず

[What we have we come to dislike; what we think of does not materialize.] ● Those we have in the palm of our hand we do not like; those we like fail to notice. ● Much would have more. = 成るは嫌なり、思うは成らず ◆ 有るが上にも欲しがるのが人 ◆ 一生は尽くれども希望は尽きず ◆ 昨日に優る今日の花 ◆ 千石を得て万石を恨む ◆ 隴を得て蜀を望む

## 慌てる蟹は穴へ入れぬ

[A hasty crab cannot enter its hole.] ● Doing something in haste is the surest road to failure. ● The hasty angler loses the fish. ● Make haste slowly. ● The long way around is the shortest way home. = 急

いた蟹は穴を失う ▶ 焦ると損する ▶ 急がば回れ ▶ 急いては事を仕損じる ▶ 短気は損気

## 慌てる乞食は貰いが少ない

[The beggar who gets flustered gets only a little.] ● Those who in their greed try to hurry things along will incur the antipathy of others and thus get less than they expected. • There is luck in the last helping.

## 合わぬ蓋有れば合う蓋有り

[If there is a lid that does not fit there is a lid that does.] ❶ Things come in all shapes and sizes, and what is unsuitable in one context may prove suitable in another. ❷ There are many different types of people, and every one is bound to find a partner sometime. • Every shoe fits not every foot. = 割れ鍋に綴じ蓋 ▶ 女に廃りがない

## 会わねば愛しさいや優る

[If one does not meet, one's fondness is all the greater.] ✐ Ai (愛) stands for emotional love and is usually altruistic, whereas koi (恋) stands for romantic love, which is often selfish. ● The love of those who are separated by circumstances is the deepest. • Absence makes the heart grow fonder. ▶ 恋の至極は忍ぶ恋

## 案ずるより生むが易い

[Giving birth is easier than its anticipation.] ● Though something may seem very difficult at first, once one has actually tried it, it may prove less difficult that expected. • All things are difficult before they seem easy.

# イ

## 良い物に安い物無し

[There are no cheap things among good things.] ● Cheap articles often last the shortest time. • Buy cheap and waste your money. • The lion's skin is never cheap. = 安物買いの銭失い

## 家貧しくして孝子顕わる

[A family that falls into poverty produces filial children.] ● The children of a family in financial distress will have to work hard to help keep the money coming in and thus do their filial duty. ◆ 国乱れて忠臣 現わる

## 家を道端に作れば三年成らず

[If one builds a house along the roadside, it will not be finished in three years.] ● If one builds a house along the roadside, many a passer-by will stop to give one advice, causing plans to be changed and the completion of the house to be delayed. If, therefore, one sets out to realize a plan, one should stick to it and not be distracted by unsolicited advice. = 舎を道端に作れば三年にして成らず ◆ 船頭多くて船山に上る

## 戦を見て矢を矧ぐ

[Feathering one's arrows on seeing the battle.] ● To try to remedy a problem when it is too late. ● Lock the stable door after the horse is stolen. ● After death, the doctor. ● After meat, mustard. = 喧嘩過ぎての棒乳切り = 賊去って張弓 = 賊の後の棒乳切り = 敵を見て矢を矧ぐ = 泥棒を捕らえて縄を綯う = 難に臨んで兵を鋳る = 盗人を見て縄を綯う = 火を失して池を掘る ◆ 後の祭 ◆ 六日の菖蒲、十日の菊 ◆ 盆過ぎての鯖商い

## 石が流れて木の葉が沈む

[Stones will flow downstream and leaves will sink.] ● Describes a situation that is utterly unimaginable. ● Pigs will fly. ◆ 朝日が西から出る ◆❷ 瓢箪から駒 ◆ 餅の中からの屋根石

## 石に齧り付けても

[Even if one has to bite into stone.] ● Refers to those who have set their sights on something and refuse to abandon their goal no matter what. ● Come rain or shine. = 雨が降ろうが槍が降ろうが

## 石に立つ矢

[The arrow that penetrates stone.] ☞ This proverb derives from an

い

old folk tale in which a hunter releases his arrow in the assumption he has sighted a tiger. The tiger turns out to be a stone, yet the arrow, released with the intention to pierce, pierces even the stone. ● If one applies oneself to something wholeheartedly there is nothing that one cannot do. ● Faith will move mountains. ● Where there's a will, there's a way. = 一念岩をも徹す = 一念天に通ず = 精神一到何事かならざらん = 為せば成る ◆ 石の上にも三年 ◆ 泥棒も十年

## 石の上にも三年

[Even (sitting) on a stone (should be tried for) three years.] ● To become successful at something one must dedicate oneself to it for an extended period of time. ● Perseverance will win through. = 泥棒も十年 ◆ 雨垂れ石を穿つ ◆ 斧を研いで針にする ◆ ❶ 倒れる事は必ず傾く方に有り ◆ ❷ 塵も積もれば山と成る ◆ 点滴石をも穿つ

## 石橋を叩いて渡る

[Cross a stone bridge by testing it.] ● Take precautions when embarking on a venture that is fraught with risks. ● Look before you leap. ● If you trust before you try, you may repent before you die. ● Trust is the mother of deceit. ◆ 明日は雨人は泥棒 ◆ 転ばぬ先の杖 ◆ 備え有れば憂い無し ◆ 濡れぬ前の傘 ◆ 人を見たら泥棒と思え ◆ 火を見れば火事と思え

## 医者の不養生

[The doctor's negligence of personal health.] ● Those who advise others do not always practice what they preach. ● It is a good doctor who follows his own directions. ◆ 紺屋の白袴 ◆ 駕籠舁き駕籠に乗らず ◆ 大工の掘っ立て ◆ 耕す者は食わず、織る者は着ず

## 伊勢へ七旅熊野へ三度

[Seven times to Ise, three times to Kumano.] ☞ For many centuries, the Shinto shrines at Ise and Kumano have been the destination of countless Japanese pilgrims. The Great Shrine at Ise is dedicated to the sun goddess, Amaterasu Ō-Mikami; and the Three Shrines of Kumano are dedicated to the deity Kumano Gongen, a manifestation of Buddha. ● Used to describe someone's piety.

### 居候 三杯目にはそっと出し

[Spongers put out their bowl for a third helping stealthily.] ● Those who live by the charity of others should be careful not to upset their benefactors. ● Beggars can't be choosers. ♦ 其の樹を陰とする者は其の枝を折らず ♦ 珍客も三日目には居候

### 急がば回れ

[When in a hurry, take a detour.] ● Doing something in haste is often the surest road to failure; at such times it is better to pause and carefully consider the best way to proceed. ● The long way around is the shortest way home. ● Make haste slowly. ♦ 焦ると損する ♦ 慌てる蟹は穴へ入れぬ ♦ 急いた蟹は穴を失う ♦ 急いては事を仕損じる ♦ 短気は損気

### 痛い上の針

[Pins on top of pains.] ● Used when hardship is inflicted on those who are already suffering. ● To add insult to injury. = 重き馬に上荷打つ ♦ 弱り目に祟り目 ♦ 雨が降れば土砂降り ♦ 泣き面に蜂が刺す ♦ 二度ある事は三度ある ♦ 不幸は重なるもの ♦ ❷ 目の寄る所へ玉が寄る

### 板子一枚下は地獄

[One thickness of plank and hell below.] ● Used to convey the perilous nature of seafaring, where the survival of a ship's crew depends on the sturdiness of their vessel. ● One plank between peace and perdition. ● Those who go to sea are only four inches from death.

### 鼬 無き間の貂誇り

[The boasting of the marten when the weasels are away.] ● In the absence of those who are strong and superior, the weak and inferior have room for pride. ● Where there are no dogs the fox is king. = 鳥なき里の蝙蝠

### 一押し二金三 姿 四程五芸

[First audacity, second money, third appearance, fourth status, fifth accomplishments.] ● To win the heart of a beautiful woman it is necessary that one has the audacity to woo her, the money to

19

keep her, the looks to please her, the status to be worthy of her, and the accomplishments to entertain her, in that order.

## 一条の矢は折るべし十条の矢は折り難し

[One arrow will break; ten arrows will not.] ● Where one person would fail the concerted effort of many may succeed. • Union is strength. = 地の利は人の和に如かず

## 一難去って又一難

[One trouble departed, again trouble.] ● No sooner do we think that we are out of trouble or we are again enmeshed in more. • Out of the frying pan into the fire. = 火を避けて水に陥る

## 一日の計は朝に在り

[The measure of a day is found in the morning.] ● One should make careful preparations before setting out to do anything. Equally, one should begin every new day with a clear idea of what one wants to achieve. = 一年の計は元旦に在り ♦ 一生の計は幼きにあり ♦ 始めが大事

## 一念岩をも徹す

[Determination will pierce even a rock.] ☞ This proverb derives from an old folk tale in which a hunter releases his arrow in the assumption he has sighted a tiger. The tiger turn out to be a stone, yet the arrow, released with the intention to pierce, pierces even the stone. ● When done with determination and total dedication, even that which seems unachievable can be done. • Faith will move mountains. • Where there's a will, there's a way. = 石に立つ矢 = 一念天に通ず = 精神一到何事かならざらん = 為せば成る ♦ 石の上にも三年 ♦ 泥棒も十年

## 一念天に通ず

[Determination will pierce the heavens.] ● When done with determination and total dedication, even that which seems unattainable can be accomplished. • Faith will move mountains. • Where there's a will, there's a way. = 石に立つ矢 = 一念岩をも徹す = 精神一到何事かならざらん = 為せば成る ♦ 石の上にも三年 ♦ 泥棒も十年

い

### 一年の快楽、百年の後悔を残す

[One year of pleasure leaves a hundred years of repentance.]
● Giving way to the temptations of the moment may lead to life-long regrets. ● For one pleasure a thousand woes. ＝ 楽は一日苦は一年 ◆ 一寸嘗めたが身の詰まり

### 一年の計は元旦に在り

[The measure of a year is found in New Year's Day.] ● One should make careful preparations before setting out to do anything. Equally, one should begin every new day with a clear idea of what one wants to achieve. ● New Year's Day is the key to a successful year. ＝ 一日の計は朝に在り ◆ 一生の計は幼きにあり ◆ 始めが大事

### 一念は継ぐとも二念は継ぐな

[One fervent wish may be accomplished; two fervent wishes may not.] ● If one sets one's sights on a specific goal one may achieve it through single-minded devotion; to set one's sights on two goals at the same time will only lead to failure. ● He who runs after two hares will catch neither. ● Grasp all, lose all. ＝ 虻蜂取らず ＝ 二足の草蛙は履けぬ ＝ 二兎を追う者は一兎をも得ず ◆ 一念岩をも徹す ◆ 一念天に通ず ◆ 石の上にも三年 ◆ 泥棒も十年 ≠ 一挙両得 ≠ 一石二鳥

### 一目の網は以て鳥を得べからず

[One cannot catch a bird with a single meshed net.] ● One cannot achieve one's purpose without using the proper means and methods, nor can one expect to accomplish one's objective without careful preparation and the cooperation of others. ● 網無くて淵をのぞくな ◆ 差し金無くては雪隠も建たぬ ◆ 種の無い手品は使われぬ

### 逸物の鷹も放さねば捕らず

[Even a superior falcon will not catch (any prey) unless it is let loose.] ● No matter how much skill one has, it will be of no use without the opportunity to utilize it. ● A hooded falcon cannot strike the quarry. ＝ ❶ 千両の鷹も放さねば知れぬ ＝ 百貫の鷹も放さねば捕らず ◆ 才有れども用いざれば愚人の如し ◆ 猿を檻に置けば豚と同じ ◆ 蒔かぬ種は生えぬ ◆ 物は試し

## 逸物の猫は爪を隠す

[A superior cat will hide its claws.] ● Shrewd people do not make a display of their talents, so that (when those around them have become complacent) they may use them to greater advantage. • Cats hide their claws. • Who knows most says least. • Still waters run deep. = 獅子人を噛むに牙を露わさず = 泣かぬ猫は鼠を取る = 鼠を取る猫は爪を隠す = 能ある鷹は爪を隠す = 猟ある猫は爪を隠す ♦ 浅瀬に仇波 ♦ 言葉多き者は品少なし ♦ 静かに流れる川は深い

## 一文惜しみの百知らず

[The ignorance of the hundred of those who begrudge one *mon*.] ✍ The *mon* (文) was a currency unit that derived from the Chinese *wen*, and introduced to Japan during the Muromachi period (1333–1568). It was used up until 1870, when it was replaced with the *yen* (円). ● Those who are too thrifty to risk a small investment will suffer a major loss in the end. • That penny is well spent that saves a groat. ♦ 小利を見れば則ち大事成らず ♦ 爪で拾って箕で零す ♦ 安物買いの銭失い ≠ 一銭を笑う者は一銭に泣く ≠ 大遣いより小遣い

## 一文は無文の師

[One character is the teacher of no character.] ✍ *Mon* (文), here, denotes a (Chinese) character. ● Those who know how to read or write even a single Chinese character will know more than the illiterate and will thus be looked up to as a teacher. Similarly, among the ignorant, those who possess even a little knowledge will be looked up to for guidance. • In the land of the blind, the one-eyed man is king. ♦ 鶏群の一鶴 ♦ 掃き溜めに鶴

## 一葉落ちて天下の秋を知る

[One may know autumn by the falling of one leaf.] ❶ An apparently insignificant event may be the precursor to a far more important one. • A straw shows which way the wind blows. ❷ A wise person is able to infer the whole by knowing only one aspect. • One word is enough to a wise man. • Few words to the wise suffice. = 一を聞いて十を知る = 一班を見て全豹を卜す = 瓶中の氷を見て天下の寒さを知る ≠ 一を知って二を知らず ≠ 其の一を知りて其の二を知らず

## 一を聞いて十を知る

[Know ten by knowing one.] ● A wise person is able to infer the whole by knowing only one aspect. • One word is enough to a wise man. • Few words to the wise suffice. = 一班を見て全豹を卜す ▶❷ 一葉落ちて天下の秋を知る = 瓶中の氷を見て天下の寒さを知る ≠ 一を知って二を知らず ≠ 其の一を知りて其の二を知らず

## 一を知って二を知らず

[Know one but not know two.] ● Used to describe those who know one fact yet are unable to deduce a second that logically follows. • To look on only one side of the shield. = 其の一を知りて其の二を知らず ▶ 遠きを知りて近きを知らず ▶ 人を知る者は知なり、自ら知る者は明なり ≠ ❷ 一葉落ちて天下の秋を知る ≠ 一を聞いて十を知る ≠ 瓶中の氷を見て天下の寒さを知る

## 一果腐りて万果損ず

[When one fruit rots, ten thousand are spoiled.] ● A corrupt person free to mingle with others will, before long, corrupt them as well. • One rotten apple will spoil a barrel. • The rotten apple injures its neighbors. = 一桃腐りて百桃損ず

## 一挙両得

[One action, two gains.] ● Two objectives can be achieved by means of a single action. • Kill two birds with one stone. = 一石二鳥 ≠ 二兎を追う者は一兎をも得ず

## 一犬虚を吠ゆれば万犬実を伝う

[When one dog barks in error, a thousand bark in earnest.] ● When one person starts a false rumor, before long, everyone will spread it and accept it as truth. • One barking dog sets all the street to barking. ▶ 世間の口に戸は立てられぬ ▶ 人の口に戸は立てられぬ ▶ 流言は知者に止まる ≠ 人の噂も七十五日 ≠ 世の取り沙汰も七十五日

## 一州も誅八州も誅

[The death penalty for one state, the death penalty for eight states.] ☞ This proverb is attributed to the 10th century warlord

Taira Masakado, who, aware that the court in Kyoto would hang him for taking just one province, went on to conquer eight of Japan's northern provinces. ● If one contemplates committing a crime, one might as well commit a crime serious enough to yield commensurate profits, since, if caught, one will be punished anyway. ● As well be hanged for a sheep as for a lamb. ● Over shoes, over boots. ● In for a penny, in for a pound. = 毒を食らわば皿まで ▶ 鍵を盗む者は誅せられ、国を盗む者は諸侯となる ▶ 金を奪う者は殺され、国を奪う者は王となる ▶ 財を盗む者は盗人なり、国を盗む者は諸侯

## 一生の計は幼きにあり

[The measure of a life is found in youth.] ● In order to avoid regrets in old age it is crucial to carefully consider in youth what one wants to do with one's life. ● Reckless youth makes rueful age. ● Lazy youth, lousy age. ▶ 一日の計は朝に在り ▶ 一年の計は元旦に在り ▶ 始めが大事

## 一生は尽くれども希望は尽きず

[Lives run out but wishes do not.] ● While there are limits to the time one is given on earth, there are no limits to the hopes and desires one may entertain while alive. ● Hope springs eternal. ● Much would have more. ▶ 有るが上にも欲しがるのが人情 ▶ 有るは嫌なり、思うは成らず ▶ 昨日に優る今日の花 ▶ 千石を得て万石を恨む ▶ 成るは嫌なり、思うは成らず ▶ 隴を得て蜀を望む

## 一心に味方無し

[No allies in wholeheartedness.] ❶ One who sets about to do something wholeheartedly will not require the help of others. ▶ 杖に縋るとも人に縋るな ❷ In this life, all of us ultimately have to fend for ourselves and there is no one on whom we can fully rely. ▶ 明日は雨人は泥棒 ▶ 石橋を叩いて渡る ▶ 人を見たら泥棒と思え ▶ 火を見れば火事と思え

## 一寸先は闇

[One *sun* ahead there is darkness.] ✎ The Japanese *sun* (寸) is a traditional unit of measurement still used by Japanese craftsmen. One *sun* is roughly three centimeters. ● The road of life is known to none and there is no looking ahead to see what the future may bring. ● A man's destiny is always dark. ＝ 知者も面前に三尺の闇あり ♦ 明日の事を言えば鬼が笑う ♦ 三年先の事を言えば鬼が笑う ♦ 人の行方と水の流れ ♦ 水の流れと人の末 ♦ 三日先の事を言えば鬼が笑う ♦ 来年の事を言えば鬼が笑う

### 一寸の光陰軽んず可からず

[One should not ignore of one *sun* of time.] ✍ The Japanese *sun* (寸) is a traditional unit of measurement still used by Japanese craftsmen. One *sun* is roughly three centimeters. ● One should make good use of every minute. ● Make hay while the sun shines. ♦ 一寸の光陰は沙裏の金 ♦ 逢うた時に笠を脱げ ♦ 好機逸す可からず ♦ 善は急げ

### 一寸の光陰は沙裏の金

[One *sun* of time is like a golden coin in the sand.] ✍ The Japanese *sun* (寸) is a traditional unit of measurement still used by Japanese craftsmen. One *sun* is roughly three centimeters. ● Time is the most precious thing in life and even the shortest moment should be cherished. ● Time past cannot be recalled. ♦ 一寸の光陰軽んず可からず ♦ 好機逸す可からず ♦ 善は急げ ♦ 時は得難くして失い易し

### 一寸の舌に五尺の身を損ず

[One *sun* of tongue may destroy five *shaku* of body.] ✍ The Japanese *sun* (寸) is a traditional unit of measurement still used by Japanese craftsmen. One *sun* is roughly three centimeters; a *sun* is ten *bu* (分) and a tenth of a *shaku* (尺). ● A thoughtless remark made in an unguarded moment may well lead to someone's undoing. ● Tongue talks at the head's cost. ＝ 口は災いの元 ＝ 三寸の舌に五尺の身を亡ぼす ＝ 舌は禍の根 ＝ 禍は口から ♦ 言わぬが花 ♦ 口数の多い者は襤褸を出す ♦ 言葉多ければ恥多し ♦ 沈黙は金、雄弁は銀

### 一寸の虫にも五分の魂

[Even in an insect of one *sun* houses a soul of five *bu*.] ✍ The Japanese *sun* (寸) is a traditional unit of measurement still used by Japanese craftsmen. One *sun* is roughly three centimeters; a *sun* is ten *bu* (分) and a tenth of a *shaku* (尺). ● The humblest person has a soul equal to that of the greatest, and thus everyone should be treated with the same respect. ● A little body often harbors a great soul. = 蛞蝓にも角 = 痩せ腕にも骨 ♦ 窮鼠猫を噛む ♦ ❶ 時に遭えば鼠も虎となる ♦ 鼠窮して猫を噛み、人貧しゅして盗みす ♦ 貧の盗みに恋の歌 ♦ ❶ 用いる時は鼠も虎となる

## 一世の富貴死後までの文章

[One generation of wealth and rank, (but) writings that (last) until after one's death.] ● No matter how much wealth and honors one accumulates during one's life, all are lost when one passes away. A superior composition, however, will endure even after its author has passed away. ● The written letter remains, as the empty word perishes. ♦ 知恵は万代の宝 ♦ 富は一生の財、知は万代の財

## 一石二鳥

[One stone, two birds.] ● Two objectives can be achieved by means of a single action. ● Kill two birds with one stone. = 一挙両得 ≠ 二兎を追う者は一兎をも得ず

## 一銭を笑う者は一銭に泣く

[Those who laugh at one *sen* will cry over one *sen*.] ✍ The *sen* (銭) was a currency unit that derived from the Chinese *qian*, and introduced to Japan during the Muromachi period (1333-1568). Following the introduction of the *yen* (円) in 1870, it came to denote a hundredth of a *yen*. As such, it is still used in the Japanese stock exchange. ● Those who think light of making small expenditures will in the end waste their entire fortune. ● Take care of the penny and the pounds will take care of themselves. ♦ 一文惜しみの百知らず ♦ 大遣いより小遣い ≠ 小利を見れば則ち大事成らず

## 一朝一夕の故に非ず

[A capital is not (founded on) the intention of one night.] ● One cannot expect to achieve something in life overnight, but only through long and dedicated effort. ● Rome wasn't built in a day. ♦ 馬に乗るまで牛に乗れ ♦ 沙弥から長老にはなれぬ ♦ ❷ 将を射んと

欲すれば先ず馬を射よ ▶ 千里の道も一歩より始まる ▶ 高きに登るは低きよりす ▶ 始めから長老にはなれぬ ▶ 始めの一歩、末の千里 ▶ ❷ 人を射んとせば先ず馬を射よ

## 一桃腐りて百桃損ず

[When one peach rots, a hundred are spoiled.] ● A corrupt person free to mingle with others will, before long, corrupt them as well. • One rotten apple will spoil a barrel. • The rotten apple injures its neighbors. = 一果腐りて万果損ず

## 一杯は人酒を飲み、二杯は酒酒を飲み、三杯は酒人を飲む

[One cup, and a person drinks *sake*; two cups, and *sake* drinks *sake*; three cups, and *sake* drinks the person.] ● The more one indulges in alcohol, the more one loses the capacity to control one's drinking. • First glass for the thirst, the second for nourishment, the third for pleasure, and the fourth for madness. • Wine is a turncoat; first a friend, then an enemy. = 人酒を飲み、酒酒を飲み、酒人を飲む

## 一派僅かに動いて万波随う

[If one wave is stirred into motion, ten thousand will follow.] ● The actions of one individual can determine that of a group; if one panics, others will, too. • When one sheep is over the dam, the rest will follow. • One coward makes ten. = 一匹の馬狂えば千匹の馬も又狂う = 狂人走れば不狂人も走る

## 一班を見て全豹を卜す

[See one spot and know the whole leopard.] ● A wise person is able to infer the whole by knowing only one aspect. • One word is enough to a wise man. • Few words to the wise suffice. = ❷ 一葉落ちて天下の秋を知る = 一を聞いて十を知る = 瓶中の氷を見て天下の寒さを知る ≠ 一を知って二を知らず ≠ 其の一を知りて其の二を知らず

## 一匹の馬狂えば千匹の馬も又狂う

[If one horse runs wild, a thousand horses will run wild too.] ● The actions of one individual can determine that of a group; if one panics, others will, too. • When one sheep is over the dam, the rest

will follow. ● One coward makes ten. = 一派僅かに動いて万波随う
= 狂人走れば不狂人も走る

### 一夫両心なれば刺を抜くこと深からず

[Someone of two minds can only partially extract a splinter.] ● If one is undecided or unfocused one cannot even accomplish the most trivial task.

### 鷸蚌の争いは漁夫の利

[The contest between a kingfisher and a clam is to the fisherman's gain.] ● When two persons vie for something, it is often a third party that gets it. ● When two dogs fight for a bone, a third one runs off with it. ♦ 犬骨折って鷹に取られる

### 居て食らえば山も空し

[If one (merely) lives and eats, even mountains will come to naught.] ● No matter how much money one possesses, if one idles one's life away it will inevitably run out. = 座して食らえば山も空しい

### 住に跡へ行くとも、死に跡へ行くな

[Go where the wife has left, but do not go where the wife has died.] ● When a man has been left by his wife, he is likely to love his new wife; when he has lost his wife, he is likely to continue to mourn her memory. Hence, a woman who seeks a husband who has been married before should marry a divorcee, but not a widower. = 去る跡へ行くとも、死に跡へ行くな

### 犬猫も三年飼えば恩を忘れず

[Both dogs and cats, when kept for three years, will not forget (their owner's) kindness.] ● If animals are able to remember people's kindness, how much more should humans remember their obligations toward each other. ♦ 犬は三日飼えば三年恩を忘れぬ ≠ 猫は三年の恩を三日で忘れる

### 犬は三日飼えば三年恩を忘れぬ

[Dogs, when kept for three days, will be grateful for three years.]

● Used to express the faithful nature of dogs. ◆ 犬猫も三年飼えば恩を忘れず ≠ 猫は三年の恩を三日で忘れる

## 犬骨折って鷹に取られる

[The dog having labored, the hawk gets the prey.] ☞ In falconry, a sport practiced by Asian noblemen since time immemorial, the prey is driven by dogs after which it is caught by the falcon. ● Used in instances where the credit or rewards for one's hard labor go to someone else. • Fools build houses and wise men live in them. • Asses carry the oats and horses eat them. ◆ 鷸蚌の争いは漁夫の利

## 犬も歩けば棒に当たる

[When a dog is on the prowl it will eventually find a bone.] ❶ As long as one ventures out and tries, even without much talent or fortune, one may eventually strike lucky. • Nothing ventured nothing gained. • A flying crow always catches something. ◆ 三度目には芽が出る ◆ 盲のまぐれ当たり ❷ When one sets out on an enterprise one is bound to run into difficulties sooner or later. • A tall tree catches much wind. ◆ 今日は人の身、明日は我が身

## 命有っての物種

[Where there is life there is recourse.] ● As long as there is life there is opportunity; with death, all opportunity is lost. • While there is life there is hope. = 命有っての物種、畑有って芋種 ◆ 身有りて奉公

## 命有っての物種、畑有って芋種

[Where there is life there is recourse; where there is a field there are seed potatoes.] ● As long as there is life there is opportunity; with death, all opportunity is lost. • While there is life there is hope. = 命有っての物種 ◆ 身有りて奉公

## 命有れば海月も骨に会う

[If there is life, even the jellyfish may encounter bones (and thereby become whole).] ● While one is alive one should make the most of all opportunities. • They who live longest will see most. • The longer we live the more wonders we see. ＝ 命有れば蓬莱山にも会う ＝ 命長ければ蓬莱山に会う ≠ 命が辛き老後の恥 ≠ 命長ければ恥多し

## 命有れば蓬莱山にも会う

[If there is life one may encounter Mount Hōrai.] ☞ In Chinese mythology, Mount Hōrai is a sacred mountain situated in the East China Sea and said to be a place where one does not age nor die. ● While alive one has many opportunities to enjoy the pleasures life brings and so must make an effort not to miss them. ● They who live longest will see most. The longer we live the more wonders we see. ＝ 命有れば海月も骨に会う ＝ 命長ければ蓬莱山に会う ≠ 命が辛き老後の恥 ≠ 命長ければ恥多し

## 命が辛き老後の恥

[Life has hardships; old age has shame.] ● The longer one lives, the more one becomes aware of the miseries of life and the shame they bring. ● Long life has many miseries. ● He that lives long suffers much. ● The life of man is a winter way. ♦ 命長ければ恥多し ≠ 命有れば海月も骨に会う ≠ 命有れば蓬莱山にも会う

## 命長ければ恥多し

[The longer you live, the more shame you suffer.] ● The longer one lives, the more opportunities one has to suffer life's indignities. ● Long life has many miseries. He that lives long suffers much. ● The life of man is a winter way. ＝ 長生きすれば恥じ多し ♦ 命が辛き老後の恥

## 命長ければ蓬莱山に会う

[If life is long one may encounter (Mount) Hōrai.] ☞ In Chinese mythology, Mount Hōrai is a sacred mountain situated in the East China Sea and said to be a place where one does not age nor die. ● While alive one has many opportunities to enjoy the pleasures life brings and so must make an effort not to miss them. ● They who live longest will see most. ● The longer we live the more wonders we see. ＝ 命有れば海月も骨に会う ＝ 命有れば蓬莱山にも会う ≠ 命が辛き老後の恥 ≠ 命長ければ恥多し

## 井の中の蛙大海を知らず

[The frog in the well does not know the ocean.] ● Those who prefer the comfort of home and never travel do not know what the world has to offer, and thus will miss opportunities to live fuller lives. Similarly, those who fail to inquire into other people's thinking will become the self-complacent prisoners of their own limited knowledge and narrowmindedness. ● Home-keeping youth have ever homely wits. = 燕雀は天地の高きを知らず = 大海知らぬ井の蛙 ♦ 井蛙は以って海を語るべからず = 井魚は共に大を語るべからず ♦ 夏の虫氷を笑う

## 今の一針、後の十針

[Today's one stitch, tomorrow's ten stitches.] ● It is better to do simple repairs when needed than to postpone them and be faced with major repairs. Similarly, if one fails to do today's share of work one will have to do two days worth of work tomorrow. ● A stitch in time saves nine. = 今の一字は明日の二字 = 今日の一針は明日の十針

## 入り船あれば出船あり

[If ships come in, so do ships go out.] ● Like ships that enter and leave a harbor, so in life events will come and go and nothing will remain the same forever. ● Good and ill luck are next-door neighbors. = 有為転変は世の習い ♦ 禍福は糾える縄の如し ♦ 殺す神あれば助ける神あり ♦ 沈む瀬あれば浮かぶ瀬あり ♦ 捨てる神はあれば助ける神あり ♦ 損をする者あれば得をする者がある

## 入り船に良い風は出船に悪い

[If the wind is fair to come into port, it will not be good to leave port.] ● Conditions that are favorable for doing one thing may be unfavorable for another. Similarly, every thing and situation will have its advantages and drawbacks. ● The sun does not shine on both sides of the hedge at once. = 出船に良い風は入り船に悪い ♦ 尺も短き所あり、寸も長き所あり ≠ 此処ばかりに日は照らぬ

## 入るを量りて出ずるを為す

[Incur expenditures after calculating income.] ● To avoid financial troubles one should not to spend more than one earns. • Cut your coat according to your cloth. ▶ 蟹は甲羅に似せて穴を掘る ▶ 鳥は翼に従って巣を作る

## 色好まぬ男は玉の 杯 底無きが如し

[An unamorous man is like a treasured *sake* cup without a bottom.] 📖 This proverb is taken from the *Tsurezuregusa*, a 13th century Japanese collection of essays. ● Men who are accomplished in many fields yet have no interest for the other sex are incomplete human beings. ▶ 英雄色を好む

## 色の白いは七難隠す

[The color of white hides seven troubles.] ✍ 色の白い refers to the white powder with which Japanese women traditionally used to make themselves up. ● Make-up on women will make them look attractive, even if their beauty is less than perfect. • A fair complexion hides many faults. • An honest look covereth many faults. = 髪の長いは七難隠す

## 色気より食い気

[Hunger rather than amorousness.] ● In life, food on the table counts more that good looks. • Without bread and wine even love will pine. = 花より団子 ▶ 金の切れ目が縁の切れ目 ▶ 愛は多能で有り、金は万能で有る

## 色は思案の外

[Love affairs are beyond reflection.] ● Those deeply in love will not listen to reason. • Love and reason do not go together. • One cannot love and be wise. • Love is without reason. = 恋は思案の外 ▶ 愛屋烏に及ぶ ▶ 止めて止まらぬ恋の道 ▶ 惚れた病に薬無し ▶ 惚れ病と馬鹿の治る薬は無い

## 鰯の頭(をせん)より鯛の尾(に付け)

[Rather be the tail of a sea bream than the head of a sardine.] ● It is easier and safer to follow along as an unimportant member of a large and powerful group that to be a leader of a small and weak group. ● Rather the tail of a lion than the head of a fox. ≠ 鶏口（けいこう）となるも牛後（ぎゅうご）となる勿れ（なか）（たい）（お）≠ 鯛の尾（いわし）より鰯の頭（かしら）≠ 大鳥（おおとり）の尾（お）より小鳥（ことり）の頭（かしら）

## 言（い）わぬが花（はな）

[Not to speak is the flower of wisdom.] ● Those who know when not to speak are the wisest. ● No wisdom like silence. ● Silence is golden. ● Wise men have their mouth in their heart, fools have their heart in their mouth. = 沈黙（ちんもく）は金（きん）、雄弁（ゆうべん）は銀（ぎん）♦ 一寸（いっすん）の舌（した）に五尺（ごしゃく）の身（み）を損（そん）ず♦ 口数（くちかず）の多（おお）い者（もの）は襤褸（ぼろ）を出す♦ 口（くち）は災（わざわ）いの元（もと）♦ 君子（くんし）は九度（たびおも）思（ひとたびい）いて一度言う♦ 言葉（ことば）多（おお）ければ恥（はじ）多（おお）し♦ 三寸（さんずん）の舌（した）に五尺（ごしゃく）の身（み）を亡（ほろ）ぼす♦ 舌（した）は禍（わざわい）の根（ね）♦ 禍（わざわい）は口（くち）から

## 蔭徳（いんとく）有（あ）れば陽報（ようほう）有（あ）り

[Where there is hidden virtue the will be open rewards.] 📖 This proverb is taken from the *Huainanzi*, a 2nd-century BCE Chinese philosophical classic. ● Those who do good in secret will be rewarded in public. ● What is done by night appears by day. = 蔭徳（いんとく）は果報（かほう）の来（く）る門口（かどぐち）♦ 悪事（あくじ）千里（せんり）を走（はし）る ≠ 好事（こうじ）門（もん）を出（い）でず

## 蔭徳（いんとく）は果報（かほう）の来（く）る門口（かどぐち）

[Hidden virtue is a doorway visited by fortune.] ● Those who do good in secret will sooner or later be rewarded. ● What is done by night appears by day. = 蔭徳（いんとく）有（あ）れば陽報（ようほう）有（あ）り♦ 悪事（あくじ）千里（せんり）を走（はし）る ≠ 好事（こうじ）門（もん）を出（い）でず

# ウ

## 有為転変（ういてんぺん）は世（よ）の習（なら）い

[Shifts and changes are the way of life.] 📖 This proverb is taken from the *Taiheiki*, a 14th-century Japanese historical epic. ● In life, nothing is constant and everything is subject to change. ● Good and ill luck are next-door neighbors. = 入（い）り船（ふね）あれば出船（でふね）あり♦ 禍福（かふく）は糾（あざな）える縄（なわ）の如（ごと）し♦ 殺（ころ）す神（かみ）あれば助（たす）ける神（かみ）あり♦ 沈（しず）む瀬（せ）あれば浮（う）かぶ瀬（せ）あり♦ 捨（す）てる神（かみ）はあれば助（たす）ける神（かみ）あり♦ 損（そん）をする者（もの）あれば得（とく）をする者（もの）がある

う

## 飢えたる犬は棒を恐れず

[The hungry dog does not fear the stick.] ● Those who are in dire straits do not fear the negative consequences of desperate actions. ● Hunger will break through stone walls. ◆ 飢えては食を択ばず

## 飢えては食を択ばず

[Those who are hungry are not choosy about their food.] ● Those who are in dire straits are willing to try any means to help improve their situation. ● Hunger is not dainty. ● Hunger is the best sauce. = 空き腹にまずい物無し ◆ 飢えたる犬は棒を恐れず

## 魚心有れば水心

[If the fish has a mind (to take to the water), so the water will have a mind (to take to the fish).] ● One who approaches fellow human beings with respect and kindness, can expect to receive respect and kindness in return. ● He may freely receive courtesy that knows how to requite them. = 問い声良ければいらえ声良い = 仇も情けも我が身より出る ◆ 愛出ずる者は愛返り、福往く者は福来る ◆ 愛は愛を生む ◆ 君心有れば民心有り ◆ 旅は道連れ世は情け ◆ 情けは人の為ならず ◆ 人は情けの下に立つ

## 魚の目に水目えず、人の目に空目えず

[In the eyes of a fish, water cannot be seen; in the eyes of a human, the sky cannot be seen.] ● Those who experience something at close quarters or on a regular basis are often unable to give an objective account of it or have become so used to it that they fail to notice. ◆ 堤灯持ちの足元暗し ◆ 灯台下暗し ◆❷ 遠きを知りて近きを知らず ◆ 人の頭の蠅を追うより我が頭の蠅を追え ◆ 目脂が鼻垢を笑う ◆ 我が頭の蠅を追え ◆ 我が身の上は見えぬ

## 魚を得て筌を忘る

[Forgetting the fish trap, having caught the fish.] ● Even something that has proven to be of great use is often discarded when there is no longer any need for it. = 兎を得て蹄を忘る = 狡兎死して走狗亨らる = 飛鳥尽きて良弓蔵る ◆ 暑さ忘れて蔭忘る ◆ 雨晴れて笠を忘る ◆ 病治りて薬師忘る

う

## 浮き世に鬼は無い

[In this floating world there is no devil.] ● On the journey of life one is sure to encounter humane and compassionate people. ● The devil is not so black as he is painted. = 地獄にも鬼ばかりではない = 人に鬼は無い = 渡る世間に鬼は無い ≠ 人を見たら泥棒と思え

## 浮き世に苦労の無い者は無い

[In this fleeting world there is no one without suffering.] ● Suffering is part of life and everyone is subject to it to some degree at some stage in their life. = 苦は色変わる松の風

## 兎を得て蹄を忘る

[Forget the snare, having caught the rabbit.] ● Once a goal has been achieved one tends to forget the means by which it was accomplished. = 魚を得て筌を忘る = 飛鳥尽きて良弓蔵る ♦ 暑さ忘れて蔭忘る ♦ 雨晴れて笠を忘る ♦ 狡兎死して走狗烹らる ♦ 病治りて薬師忘る

## 氏素性は争えないもの

[Family background is incontestable.] ● No matter how much one may try to hide one's own ancestry or to assume the name of another, the personal traits and characteristics that run in a family will eventually tell. ● Blood will tell. = 血筋は争えないもの ♦ 隠すことは現わる ♦ 天知る地知る我知る人知る

## 牛は牛連れ

[Cows are led by cows.] ● People in similar circumstances or people with the same kind of personality tend to be drawn together. ● Birds of a feather flock together. ● Like attracts like. = 馬は馬連れ = 鬼の女房に鬼神 = 同気相求む = 友は類をもって集まる = ❶ 目の寄る所へ玉が寄る = 類は友を呼ぶ ♦ 同病相憐れむ ♦ 不幸の際の伴侶は不幸を軽減す

## 牛は水を飲んで乳とし、蛇は水を飲んで毒とし

[A cow drinks water and turns it to milk; a snake drinks water and turns it to poison.] ● Depending upon whose hands they are put into, the same materials and resources may be turned to good or evil purposes. • One man's meat is another man's poison. ◆ 木に付く虫は木を齧り、萱に付く虫は萱を啄む

## 氏より育ち

[Education rather than lineage.] ● Education counts more than high birth in the building of character and laying the foundations of a successful career. • Nurture is above nature. • Birth is much but breeding is more. ◆ 瑠璃も玻璃も照らせば光る

## 嘘から出た実

[Truth that comes out of a lie.] ● A falsehood may be turned into truth by an unexpected turn of events. • Tell a lie and find the truth. • Crooked logs make straight fires. ◆ 瓢箪から駒

## 嘘吐きは泥棒の始まり

[Lying is the beginning of stealing.] ● One capable of deceiving others by lying will progress to taking the possessions of others without scruple. • He that will lie will steal. • Show me a liar and I will show you a thief. = 嘘は盗みのもと ◆ 盗人の始まりは嘘から、嘘の始まりは身持ちから

## 嘘は後から剥げる

[A lie fades in the end.] ● A falsehood will sooner or later be exposed as such. • Lies have short legs. = 嘘は門口まで

## 嘘は門口まで

[A lie lasts only as far as up to the gate.] ● Once a falsehood is brought into the world, it will sooner or later inevitably be exposed as such. • Lies have short legs. ◆ 嘘は後から剥げる

## 嘘は盗みのもと

[Lying is the origin of theft.] ● One capable of deceiving others by lying will progress to taking the possessions of others without scruple. • A liar is worse than a thief. • Show me a liar and I will show you a thief. = 嘘吐きは泥棒の始まり ◆ 盗人の始まりは嘘から、嘘の始まりは身持ちから

う

### 嘘は誠の皮、誠は嘘の骨

[A lie is the skin of truth; truth is the bones of a lie.] ● Falsehoods are intended to conceal the truth; and a kernel of truth is needed to construct a falsehood. • Half the truth is often a great lie. ♦ 嘘らしい誠は言うども、誠らしい嘘を言うな

### 嘘も方便

[A lie, too, is a pious fraud.] ✍ The pious fraud (方便), or *upaya* in sanskrit, is a rhetorical device used in Buddhist teaching with the ultimate aim to teach truths to the masses. ● A lie, at times, may prove to be necessary. • Tell a lie and find the truth. • A white lie doesn't hurt. • A necessary lie is harmless. = 仏に方便聖人に権道 ♦ 方便の愚は正、無方便の智は邪

### 嘘らしい誠は言うども、誠らしい嘘を言うな

[One may tell a truth that sounds like a lie, but one must not tell a lie that sounds like the truth.] ● One should always tell the truth, no matter how unbelievable it may sound. One should, however, never tell a lie, no matter how believable it may sound. • Half the truth is often a great lie. • A thousand probabilities do not make one truth. ♦ 嘘は誠の皮、誠は嘘の骨

### 家に居ちゃ蛤貝、外へ出ちゃ蜆貝

[When at home a clam; when abroad a corbicula.] ✍ The corbicula is a variety of the clam but much smaller. ● Those who are dominant within the safety of home often grow timid as soon as they leave the front door. • A lion at home, a mouse abroad. ♦ 我が門にて吠えぬ犬無し ♦ 我が家に鳴かぬ犬無し

### 馬方船頭お乳の人

[Packhorse drivers, skippers, and wetnurses.] ✍ An *umakata* (馬方) is a packhorse driver. *O-chi* (お乳) is an old word for wetnurse. ☞ This proverb hails back to a time when skippers, packhorse drivers, and wetnurses were hard to come by. That demand, in combination with the power they exercised over the passengers, cargo, and siblings in their care, apparently gave them the confidence to pester their customers and employers for money or favors. ❶ Used to describe the demanding and bullying nature of those who have a little authority over others. ❷ Used to describe those who use abusive language to get what they want. = 船頭馬方お乳の人

## 馬に乗るまで牛に乗れ

[Before one rides a horse, first ride a cow.] ● Those who want to achieve greatness in life should lay the foundation for success by honing their skills on less ambitious goals. • He that would the daughter win, must with the mother first begin. = ❷ 将を射んと欲すれば先ず馬を射よ = 高きに登るは低きよりす = ❷ 人を射んとせば先ず馬を射よ ♦ 一朝一夕の故に非ず ♦ 沙弥から長老にはなれぬ ♦ 千里の道も一歩より始まる ♦ 始めから長老にはなれぬ ♦ 始めの一歩、末の千里

## 馬には乗ってみよ、人には添ってみよ

[As for horses, try to ride them; as for a people, try to live with them.] ● The only way to know the quality of a horse is to ride it; the only way to know someone really well is to be in their company over a protracted period of time. By extension, one can only really learn through personal experience. • Experience is the mother of wisdom. = 人には添ってみよ、馬には乗ってみよ

## 馬の耳に念仏

[A *nenbutsu* in the ear of a horse.] ✍ A *nenbutsu* (念仏) is a prayer to Amida Buddha. ● Describes counsel or criticism totally lost on the listener. • Sing psalms to a dead horse. • Preaching to the wind [deaf ears]. • In one ear and out the other. = 蛙の面に水 = 空吹く風と聞き流す = 馬耳東風 ♦ 糠に釘 ♦ 猫に小判 ♦ 豚に真珠

## 馬は馬連れ

[Horses are led by horses.] ● People in similar circumstances or people with the same kind of personality tend to be drawn together. • Birds of a feather flock together. • Like attracts like. = 牛は牛連れ = 鬼の女房に鬼神 = 同気相求む = 友は類をもって集まる = ❶ 目の寄る所へ玉が寄る = 類は友を呼ぶ ♦ 同病相憐れむ ♦ 不幸の際の伴侶は不幸を軽減す

## 生みの親より育ての親

[The parent who raises rather than the parent who gives birth.] ● A child is more indebted to the foster parents than to the real parents. ● A foster parent is dearer than a real parent. = 生みの恩より育ての恩

## 生みの恩より育ての恩

[The obligation for raising rather than for giving birth.] ● A child is more indebted to the foster parents than to the real parents. ● A foster parent is dearer than a real parent. = 生みの親より育ての親

## 海の事は漁父に問え

[About sea matters, ask a fisherman.] ● In all arts, crafts, and trades there are professionals on whose expertise it is best to rely. ● Every man to his trade. = 酒は酒屋に茶は茶屋に = 田作る道は農に問え = 餅は餅屋 ▶ 海老踊れども川を出でず ▶ 鴉が鵜の真似 ▶ 芸は道に依りて賢し ▶ 鹿つきの山は猟師知り、魚つきの浦は網人知る

## 海の物とも山の物ともつかぬ

[It belongs neither to the sea nor to the mountains.] ● Said of something the nature of which is yet undetermined. Similarly, said of those who have not yet made a name for themselves and are still unknown entities. ● Neither fish nor fowl, nor good red herring.

## 裏には裏が有る

[There is a reverse side to the reverse side.] ● Nothing in life is black and white; there are always hidden aspects that only reveal themselves on closer scrutiny. ● The reverse side of the shield. ● There are wheels within wheels.

## 瓜の蔓に茄子はならぬ

[Eggplants do not grow on melon vines.] ● People of humble birth cannot expect to rise to high positions. Similarly, parents with mediocre talents cannot expect to raise children with exceptional talents. ● The onion will not produce a rose. = 鳶の子鷹にならず ▶ 蛙の子は蛙 ▶ 鵙が鷹を生む ≠ 鳶が鷹を生む

## 噂を言わば目代

[If one is to gossip put out a guard.] ● It often happens that a person being talked about will appear by chance, so one who gossips should be on guard. ● Talk of the devil and he is sure to appear. ● To mention the wolf's name is to see the same. ● Talk of angels and you will hear their wings. = 噂をすれば影が差す

## 噂をすれば影が差す

[Gossip (about someone) and (their) shadow will appear.] ● It often happens that a person being talked about will appear by chance. ● Talk of the devil and he is sure to appear. ● To mention the wolf's name is to see the same. ● Talk of angels and you will hear their wings. = 噂を言わば目代

## 運の神は屋根の上に住む

[The god of fortune lives on the roof.] ● Though we might not be aware of it, we all have a destiny from which there is no escaping. ● No flying from fate. ♦ 運は天にあり

## 運は天にあり

[Fate is (decided by) heaven.] 📖 This proverb is from the *Taiheiki*, a 14th-century Japanese historical epic. ● Though one may try hard, ultimately, one cannot escape one's destiny. ● No flying from fate. = 富貴は天にあり ♦ 運の神は屋根の上に住む

## 運は天にあり、牡丹餅は棚にあり

[Fate resides in heaven, the *botamochi* on the shelf.] ✍ *Botamochi* (牡丹餅) are rice cake dumplings covered with bean jam. ☞ This proverb derives from the Japanese idiom 棚から牡丹餅, or "a bota-mochi from the shelf," which stands for a windfall or a godsend. Rice cakes, or *mochi* (餅) are made by pounding steamed rice into cakes with a large and heavy wooden hammer, a time-consuming and and tiring process. ● Good fortune and windfalls are not bestowed by men. All we can do is try our best and leave the outcome in the hands of the gods. ♦ 果報は寝て待て ♦ 堪忍は無事長久の基 ♦ 辛抱する木に金がなる ♦ 待てば海路の日和あり

運は天にあり、鎧は胸にあり

[Fate resides in heaven, one's armor on one's chest.] ● Though we may do what we can to protect ourselves in battle, ultimately our lives are in the hands of the gods. Hence, where we can influence things, we should plan as well as possible, but ultimately the outcome is in the hands of the gods. ● Man proposes, God disposes. ＝ 人事を尽くして天命を待つ

# エ

英雄色を好む

[Heroes are amorous.] ● The energy and vigor manifest in the actions of great people are also manifest in their love lives. ● All great men are also great lovers. ◆ 色好まぬ男は玉の杯底無きが如し

英雄並び立たず

[Heroes cannot stand in line.] ● Two great individuals with strong personalities find it hard to tolerate each other. Sooner or later they will vie for supremacy and only one will remain standing. ● Two cooks in one yard do not agree. ● Friends may meet, but mountains never greet. ● Diamond cuts diamond. ＝ 両雄並び立たず ◆ 英雄人を忌む ◆ 両虎相闘えば勢い倶に生きず

英雄人を欺く

[Heroes deceive people.] ● Great people are often endowed with great intelligence and may resort to ruses that bewilder ordinary people. ● Great men's favors are uncertain. ● Great men have great faults. ◆ 燕雀安んぞ鴻鵠の志を知らんや ◆ 大功を成す者は衆に謀らず ◆ 名将は名将を知る

英雄人を忌む

[Heroes loathe people.] ● Great people cannot stand people who are of even greater stature than themselves. ● A great man and a great river are often ill neighbors. ◆ 英雄並び立たず ◆ 両雄並び立たず ◆ 両虎相闘えば勢い倶に生きず

**え**

### 得食に毒無し

[There is no poison in food one likes to eat.] ● There is no harm in eating food one enjoys. ● Content works all ambrosia. = 好物に祟りなし

### 枝を矯めて花を散らす

[Scatter the flowers by trying to straighten the branches.] ● Attempting to correct minor flaws in an area of little importance may cause irreparable damage in an area of great importance. ● To burn the house to frighten away the mouse. ● Throw out the baby with the bath water. = 枝を矯めんとして幹を枯らす = 角を矯めて牛を殺す = 仏を直すとて鼻を欠く ♦ 流れを汲みて源を濁す

### 枝を矯めんとして幹を枯らす

[Blight the trunk by trying to straighten the branches.] ● Attempting to correct minor flaws in an area of little importance may cause irreparable damage in an area of great importance. ● To burn the house to frighten away the mouse. ● Throw out the baby with the bath water. = 枝を矯めて花を散らす = 角を矯めて牛を殺す = 仏を直すとて鼻を欠く ♦ 流れを汲みて源を濁す

### 越鳥南枝に巣をかけ、胡馬北風に嘶く

[A bird from Yue builds its nest on a southern branch; a Mongol horse will neigh with a northern wind.] ✍ Yue was a southern province in ancient China. ● Those who are far from their family and friends will grow homesick with the faintest reminder of home. ● Home is where the heart is. ● East or west, home is best. = 代馬北風に依る ♦ 故郷忘じ難し ♦ 住めば都

### 江戸中の白壁は皆旦那

[All the white walls in Edo belong to masters.] ☞ In old Japan storehouses were built with thick walls of white mortar to keep their contents cool in summer. The presence of a storehouse on the premise of an estate meant that its owner was a wealthy merchant. ● One's present employer is one among many. Used by those (apprentices) who are dissatisfied with their current position.

## 江戸の敵を長崎で討つ

[To slay Edo's enemies at Nagasaki.] ☞ An Edo period (1600-1867) tale relates how the proprietor of a curiosity shop in Osaka managed to outdo his competition in Edo, but was eventually forced out of business by the artifacts of a Nagasaki craftsman. ● Describes those who choose an unexpected place or pretext to avenge the wrongs they have suffered.

## 海老踊れども川を出でず

[Though lobsters may dance they will not leave the river.] ● Though one may explore the limits of one's vocation, it is not wise to leave it. ● Let the cobbler stick to his last. ♦ 海の事は漁父に問え ♦ 鴉が鵜の真似 ♦ 芸は道に依りて賢し ♦ 酒は酒屋に茶は茶屋に ♦ 鹿つきの山は猟師知り、魚つきの浦は網人知る ♦ 田作る道は農に問え ♦ 餅は餅屋

## 海老で鯛を釣る

[One catches a sea bream with a prawn.] ● It is possible to accomplish great feats with only modest means. Likewise, huge profits can be made with only small investments. ● Throw out a lobster and pull in a whale. ● Throw a sprat to catch a herring. ● Give an egg to gain an ox. = 雁は八百、矢は三文

## 燕雀安んぞ鴻鵠の志を知らんや

[How can the small bird know the aspirations of a large bird?] ✍ The word enjaku (燕雀) is composed of the character for swallow, or tsubame (燕), and sparrow, or suzume (雀), together connoting small birds and, by extension, insignificant or narrow-minded people. The word kōkoku (鴻鵠), by contrast, is composed of the characters for bean goose, or hishikui (鴻), and swan, kugui (鵠), together connoting large birds and, by extension, important and broad-minded people. ● Insignificant people cannot fathom the thoughts and ambitions of great people. ● A man must be a hero to understand a hero. ● It takes a great man to understand one. = 名将は名将を知る ♦ 英雄人を欺く ♦ 大功を成す者は衆に謀らず

**お**

## 燕雀は天地の高きを知らず

[Small birds do not know the height of heaven and earth.] ✍ The word *enjaku* (燕雀) is composed of the character for swallow, or *tsubame* (燕), and sparrow, or *suzume* (雀), together connoting small birds and, by extension, insignificant or narrow-minded people. ● People who fail to inquire into the world beyond their immediate purview, cannot know what the world has to offer, and will miss the opportunity to widen their scope and live fuller lives. ● A man must be a hero to understand a hero. ● It takes a great man to understand one. = 井の中の蛙大海を知らず = 大海知らぬ井の蛙 ♦ 井蛙は以って海を語るべからず ♦ 井魚は共に大を語るべからず ♦ 夏の虫氷を笑う

## 縁と浮世は末を待て

[Wait till the end for the right moment in life and marriage.] ● When it comes to marriage or to an auspicious moment to do something, it is better to wait than to hurry. ● Marry in haste, repent at leisure. = 縁と月日の末を待て ♦ 好き連れは泣き連れ

## 縁と月日の末を待て

[Wait till the end for the (right) month and day and marriage.] ● When it comes to marriage or to an auspicious moment, it is better to wait than to hurry. ● Marry in haste, repent at leisure. = 縁と浮世は末を待て ♦ 好き連れは泣き連れ

# オ

## 老いたる馬は路を忘れず

[An old horse does not forget the way.] ● What is learned early in life is retained in old age. ● An old ox makes a straight furrow. = 雀百まで踊り忘れず ♦ 亀の甲より年の劫

## 老いて死するは兵の恨み

[To die of old age is the soldier's grudge.] ● Rather than die of old age, the ancient Japanese warrior preferred a glorious death on the battlefield. ● A fair death honors the whole life.

お

## 老いては麒麟も駑馬に劣る

[In old age, even a *kirin* is reduced to a hack.] ✍ The *kirin* (麒麟), or *qilin* in Chinese, is a mythical animal with the body of a deer, the hooves of a horse, and a single horn on its head. It is also used to denote a horse that can run a thousand *ri* (里) in one day. ● When a person with great gifts grows old their talents eventually become worse than mediocre. = 麒麟も老ゆれば駑馬に劣る ≠ 腐っても鯛

## 老いては子に従え

[When in old age, obey your children.] ● When one grows old and dependent it is best to rely on one's children for support and guidance. ● Be guided by your children when you are old.

## 逢うた時に笠を脱げ

[When meeting, take off your hat.] ● At the right opportunity one should do the right thing. ● Make hay while the sun shines. = 一寸の光陰軽んず可からず ♦ 好機逸す可からず ♦ 善は急げ

## 王良も時として馬車を覆す

[Even a good horse handler may at times upset the cart.] ● Even those who seem complete masters of their craft may sometimes get it wrong. ● Homer sometimes nods. ● A good marksman may miss. = 河童の川流れ = 賢者も千慮の一失 = 弘法にも筆の誤り = 猿も木から落ちる = 知者にも千慮の一失 = 上手の手から水が漏れる = 竜馬の躓き

## 大網に盗人を乗せても物言い乗すな

[When fishing with a large net take on board a thief but never a critic.] ● When embarking on a venture that requires cooperation, it is better to have someone who might quietly pinch some of the profit than someone whose constant bickering might cause division and put the venture in jeopardy. ● The greatest talkers are always the least doers.

## 大風吹けば古家の祟り

[Raging storms are the curse of an old house.] ● It is only during

**お**

great storms that old houses will reveal their many weak points. By extension, it is only during trying times that the weaknesses in people or systems are exposed. ◆盤根錯節に遭いて利器を知る ◆雪圧して松の操を知る

### 大きい家に大きい風が吹く

[Great houses are exposed to great winds.] ❶ The misfortune that befalls illustrious families is often commensurate with their status. ● Tall trees catch much wind. ● Great winds blow upon high hills. ◆高山の巓には美木無し ◆高木風に憎まる ◆高木風に妬まる ◆高木は風に折らる ◆大木は風に折らる ◆大名の下には久しく居るべからず ◆❷ 出る杭は打たれる ◆誉れは謗りの基 ❷ The greater the scale of a venture, the greater the risk of failure, and the greater the disappointment when things do go wrong. ● The higher the fool, the greater the fall. ● The highest tree has the greatest fall. ◆棒ほど願って針ほど叶う

### 大きい大根は辛く無い

[Large radishes are mild in taste.] ● Things that at first glance appear ominous may, on closer scrutiny, be quite harmless. ● The Devil is not so black as he is painted. ◆幽霊の正体見たり枯れ尾花

### 大遣いより小遣い

[Small expenses, rather than big expenses.] ● One should pay close attention to small expenses, since it is often through the accumulation of those that larger sums are lost. ● Take care of the pence and the pounds will take care of themselves. ◆一銭を笑う者は一銭に泣く ◆爪で拾って箕で零す ≠ 一文惜しみの百知らず ≠ 小利を見れば則ち大事成らず

### 大鳥の尾より小鳥の頭

[Rather the head of a small bird than the tail of a large bird.] ● Rather than play a secondary role in a major event, it is better to play a leading role in a minor event. Similarly, rather than be a mere member of a large and powerful group, it is better to be a leader of a small though less powerful group. ● Better be a chick-

お

en's head than an ox's rump. • Better be first in a village than second in Rome. = 鶏口となるも牛後となる勿れ = 鯛の尾より鰯の頭 ≠ 鰯の頭より鯛の尾

## 大取りより小取り

[Small profits, rather than big profits.] ● It is better to try and accumulate one's fortune in small steps, rather than trying to make it all at once. • Little and often fills the purse. ◆ 明日の百より今日の五十 ◆ あの世千日この世の一日 ◆ 聞いた百文より見た一文 ◆ 末始終より今の三十 ◆ 後の千金より今の百文 ◆ 来年の百両より今年の一両 ≠ 小節を規る者は栄名を成す能わず ≠ 小利を見れば則ち大事成らず

## 起きて三尺寝て六尺

[Awake three *shaku*, asleep five *shaku*.] ✍ The Japanese *shaku* (尺) is an old unit of measurement still used by Japanese craftsmen. One *shaku* (尺) corresponds to roughly thirty centimeters. ● In life one only needs three *shaku* of space for sitting and five *shaku* of space for sleeping, so rather than covet wealth and land one should learn the art of being content with little. • Content is more than a kingdom. • Content is happiness. = 起きて半畳寝て一畳 ◆ 千石万石も飯一杯 ◆ 千畳敷で寝ても畳一枚

## 起きて半畳寝て一畳

[Awake half a *tatami*, asleep one *tatami*.] ✍ The *tatami* (畳) is a thick mat of woven straw of roughly one hundred and eighty by ninety centimeters. ● In life one only needs half a length of *tatami* for sitting and one length of *tatami* for sleeping, so rather than covet wealth and land one should learn the art of being content with little. • Content is more than a kingdom. • Content is happiness. = 起きて三尺寝て六尺 ◆ 千石万石も飯一杯 ◆ 千畳敷で寝ても畳一枚

## 驕る平家久しからず

[The haughty Heike do not last.] ☞ The Heike, or Taira, were a powerful military clan that ruled Japan during the 12th century, and whose decline is generally believed to have been brought about by their own decadence. ● Those who are conceited and have no regard

for others will sooner or later fall victim to the revenge of others.
• Pride goes before a fall. ♦ 亢竜悔い有り ♦ 平家を滅ぼす者は平家

## 驕る者は心常に貧し

[The extravagant are usually poor of heart.] ● Those who live in luxury usually do so to compensate for their spiritual poverty.

## お釈迦様に経を聞かせる

[Telling Buddha about Buddhist scriptures.] ● Describes someone trying to teach a lesson to an expert. • A sow teaching Minerva. • Teach your grandmother to suck eggs. = 孔子に論語 = 釈迦に説法

## 落ち武者は薄の穂に怖づ

[A fugitive warrior will tremble with fear in the face of the spike of a pampas grass.] ● A warrior who is on the run having lost in battle will live in constant fear of being caught and be terrified by the smallest threat. Conversely, those who let in fear will eventually be reduced to terror by the smallest threat. • All the weapons of war will not arm fear.

## 男の年は気、女の年は顔

[A man's age is (his) spirit, a woman's age is (her) face.] ● A man's age is determined by how he behaves, a woman's age is determined by how she looks. • A man is as old as he feels; a woman is as old as she looks.

## 男は知恵、女は情け

[Wisdom to man, compassion to woman.] ☞ In Japan, as in most other countries, there is a traditional allocation of virtues between the sexes. ● Men should act wisely, women with compassion. • In the husband wisdom, in the wife gentleness. ♦ 男は度胸、女は愛嬌

## 男は度胸、女は愛嬌

[Courage to man, attractiveness to woman.] ☞ In Japan, as in most other countries, there is a traditional allocation of virtues between the sexes. ● Men should be courageous, women should be attrac-

お

tive. ● In the husband wisdom, in the wife gentleness. ♦ 男<ruby>おとこ</ruby>は知恵<ruby>ちえ</ruby>、女<ruby>おんな</ruby>は情<ruby>なさ</ruby>け

## 音<ruby>おと</ruby>無<ruby>な</ruby>き川<ruby>かわ</ruby>は水<ruby>みず</ruby>深<ruby>ふか</ruby>し

[Quiet rivers run deep.] ● People who are quiet and composed in manner often have great depth of character. ● Still waters run deep. ● Who knows most says least. = 静<ruby>しず</ruby>かに流<ruby>なが</ruby>れる川<ruby>かわ</ruby>は深<ruby>ふか</ruby>い ♦ 浅瀬<ruby>あさせ</ruby>に仇波<ruby>あだなみ</ruby> ♦ 言葉<ruby>ことば</ruby>多<ruby>おお</ruby>き者<ruby>もの</ruby>は品少<ruby>しなすく</ruby>なし ♦ 能<ruby>のう</ruby>ある鷹<ruby>たか</ruby>は爪<ruby>つめ</ruby>を隠<ruby>かく</ruby>す

## 踊<ruby>おど</ruby>る阿呆<ruby>あほう</ruby>に見<ruby>み</ruby>る阿呆<ruby>あほう</ruby>

[Where fools are dancing, fools will be looking on.] ● Those who bother to give any attention to people acting foolishly are fools as well. ♦ 馬鹿さしじがれば二がえ馬鹿

## 鬼<ruby>おに</ruby>の女房<ruby>にょうぼう</ruby>に鬼神<ruby>きじん</ruby>

[In the wife of an ogre a destructive deity.] ● A man and a woman with similar personalities tend to be drawn together. ● Birds of a feather flock together. ● Like attracts like. ♦ 牛<ruby>うし</ruby>は牛<ruby>うし</ruby>連<ruby>づ</ruby>れ ♦ 馬<ruby>うま</ruby>は馬<ruby>うま</ruby>連<ruby>づ</ruby>れ ♦ 友<ruby>とも</ruby>は類<ruby>るい</ruby>をもって集<ruby>あつ</ruby>まる ♦ 同気相求<ruby>どうきあいもと</ruby>む ♦ 類<ruby>るい</ruby>は友<ruby>とも</ruby>を呼<ruby>よ</ruby>ぶ ♦ 同病相憐<ruby>どうびょうあいあわ</ruby>れむ ♦ 不幸<ruby>ふこう</ruby>の際<ruby>さい</ruby>の伴侶<ruby>はんりょ</ruby>は不幸<ruby>ふこう</ruby>を軽減<ruby>けいげん</ruby>す = ❶ 目<ruby>め</ruby>の寄<ruby>よ</ruby>る所<ruby>ところ</ruby>へ玉<ruby>たま</ruby>が寄<ruby>よ</ruby>る

## 鬼<ruby>おに</ruby>の目<ruby>め</ruby>にも涙<ruby>なみだ</ruby>

[Even in the eyes of an ogre there may be tears.] ● Even the most cruel and hardened of people may at times be overcome with pity. ● Even the hardest heart will sometimes feel pity.

## 鬼<ruby>おに</ruby>の目<ruby>め</ruby>にも見残<ruby>みのこ</ruby>し

[Even in the eyes of an ogre things may go unnoticed.] ● Even people with the most discerning of eyes may at times overlook something. ● Homer sometimes nods. ● No man is wise at all times. = 王良<ruby>おうりょう</ruby>も時<ruby>とき</ruby>として馬車<ruby>ばしゃ</ruby>を覆<ruby>くつがえ</ruby>す = 河童<ruby>かっぱ</ruby>の川流<ruby>かわなが</ruby>れ = 賢者<ruby>けんじゃ</ruby>も千慮<ruby>せんりょ</ruby>の一失<ruby>いっしつ</ruby> = 弘法<ruby>こうぼう</ruby>にも筆<ruby>ふで</ruby>の誤<ruby>あやま</ruby>り = 猿<ruby>さる</ruby>も木<ruby>き</ruby>から落<ruby>お</ruby>ちる = 知者<ruby>ちしゃ</ruby>にも千慮<ruby>せんりょ</ruby>の一失<ruby>いっしつ</ruby> = 上手<ruby>じょうず</ruby>の手<ruby>て</ruby>から水<ruby>みず</ruby>が漏<ruby>も</ruby>れる = 竜馬<ruby>りゅうめ</ruby>の躓<ruby>つまず</ruby>き

## 鬼<ruby>おに</ruby>の留守<ruby>るす</ruby>に洗濯<ruby>せんたく</ruby>

[When the ogre is away, do the washing.] ✍ *Sentaku* in this context

49

has the connotation of cleansing one's heart (命の洗濯), i.e. forgetting one's troubles by enjoying oneself. ● When husbands, masters, etc. are not at home the rest of the household can relax and enjoy itself. ● When the cat's away, the mice will play.

## 鬼も十八、番茶も出花

[Like an ogress at eighteen, so coarse tea at first infusion.] ● Poor quality tea will taste best at first infusion. Similarly, a homely girl will look her best when she has reached a marriageable age. ● Everything is good in its season. ♦ 薊の花も一盛り

## 己が身を抓みて痛さを知れ

[Pinch oneself and know the pain (of others).] ● When one considers the suffering of others one should imagine how one would feel in similar circumstances. ● Do as one would be done by. ● He who lives in a glass house should not throw stones. = 我が身を抓って人の痛さを知れ

## 己れを責めて人を責むるな

[Find fault with yourself and not with others.] 📖 This proverb is taken from Tokugawa Ieyasu's *Teachings on the Conduct of Life*. ● As long as there are flaws in one's own character there is no moral justification in criticizing the flaws in others. = 人の頭の蠅を追うより我が頭の蠅を追え = 我が頭の蠅を追え ♦ 五十歩をもって百歩を笑う ♦ 猿の尻笑い ♦ 近くて見えぬは睫 ♦ 人の一寸我が一尺 ♦ 人の七難より我が十難 ♦ 目糞が鼻糞を笑う ♦ 目脂が鼻垢を笑う

## 斧を研いで針にする

[To sharpen an axe into a needle.] ● If one perseveres in something long enough one will eventually be successful. ● Constant dripping wears away the stone. = 雨垂れ石を穿つ = ❷ 塵も積もれば山と成る = 点滴石をも穿つ ♦ 石の上にも三年 ♦ ❶ 倒れる事は必ず傾く方に有り ♦ 泥棒も十年 ♦ 始めの一歩、末の千里

## 重き馬荷に上荷打つ

[To pile another load atop a heavily loaded horse.] ● To inflict hard-

ship on those already suffering. • To add insult to injury. = 痛い上の
針 ♦ 弱り目に祟り目 ♦ 雨が降れば土砂降り ♦ 泣き面に蜂が刺す ♦ 二
度ある事は三度ある ♦ 不幸は重なるもの ♦ ❷ 目の寄る所へ玉が寄る

## 親子の仲でも金銭は他人

[Even parents and children are strangers where money matters are
concerned.] ● Greed can drive even parents and children apart, and
thus they should draw a line between family and financial dealings.
• Tell money after your own kin.

## 親子は一世、夫婦は二世、主従は三世

[Parents and children last but one lifetime; man and wife last two
lifetimes; lord and liege last three lifetimes.] ☞ This view of the
order of society prevailed throughout Japan's feudal era and is still
a strong force in modern day Japan. ● The relation between lord
and vassal is most important; next comes the relation between man
and wife; and only then comes the relation between father and
son. ♦ この君にしてこの臣あり ♦ 父も父なら子も子だ

## 親の因果が子に報う

[The fate of the parents will recoil upon their children.] ● Sins committed by the parents damage the prospects in life of their children.
• The sins of the father will be visited on the son.

## 親の光は七光

[Parental luster is sevenfold.] ● Those born into illustrious families
start out in life with great advantages. • He is born in a good hour
who gets a good name. ♦ 金の光は七光

## 親は苦労する、子は楽をする、孫は乞食する

[The parents labor hard, their children live at ease, and their
grandchildren go begging.] ● The awareness that one must work
hard for a living tends to fade with each generation that is brought
up in luxury. • The father buys, the son builds, the grandchild sells,
and his son begs. = 爺はしんどする、子は楽をする、孫の代は乞食す
る ♦ 前人樹を植えて後人涼を得

**親は千里行くとも子を忘れず**

[Even if parents travel a thousand *ri*, they cannot forget their children.] ✍ The *ri* (里) is an ancient Chinese measurement of distance, the equivalent of 0.3 miles. With time, it came to denote the distance one could walk in an hour, and during the Edo period (1600–1867) it was officially defined as 36 *chō*, or about 2.44 miles. ● The love and concern of parents for their children does not fade with distance. ♦ 惚れて通えば千里も一里

**及ばざるは過ぎたるより勝れり**

[To fall short is to surpass those who exceed.] 📖 This proverb is the last sentence form Tokugawa Ieyasu's *Teachings on the Conduct of Life* and was inspired by Confucius' injunction that "to exceed is to fall short." ● In all things moderation is important; to do something in excess may be more ineffective as not having done it at all. ● Overdone is worse than undone. = 過ぎたる猶及ばざるが如し ♦ 薬も過ぎれば毒となる

**恩が仇**

[Kindness is a disservice.] ● Something done with the intention to assist someone may prove to have the opposite effect. ● A pitiful surgeon spoileth a sore. = 情けが仇 ♦ 始めの情け今の仇

**女 三人寄れば姦し**

[When three woman gather there will be a clamor.] ● Woman are prone to chattering, and when several women gather it will soon become a noisy affair. ● Three women make a market.

**女に廃りがない**

[There are no castaways among women.] ● No matter how slim her prospects for marriage, sooner or later every woman will find a partner. ● Every Jill has her Jack. ♦❷ 合わぬ蓋有れば合う蓋有り ♦ 割れ鍋に綴じ蓋

**女の言うことには富士の山も靡く**

[The words of a woman can sway even mount Fuji.] ● The persuasiveness of a woman can be impossible to resist. ● One hair of a woman draws more than a hundred yoke of oxen. ◆ 女の一念岩をも通す ◆ 女の髪の毛には大象も繋がる ◆ 大象も女の髪には繋がれる

### 女の一念岩をも通す

[The will of a woman can pierce a rock.] ● A woman who has set her mind on something can attain any goal. ● Women will have their wills. ● One hair of a woman draws more than a hundred yoke of oxen. ◆ 女の言うことには富士の山も靡く ◆ 女の髪の毛には大象も繋がる ◆ 大象も女の髪には繋がれる

### 女の髪の毛には大象も繋がる

[The hair of a woman will suffice to tie an elephant.] ● The sway a woman can hold over men bewitched by her charms can be extremely powerful. ● One hair of a woman draws more than a hundred yoke of oxen. = 大象も女の髪には繋がれる ◆ 女の言うことには富士の山も靡く ◆ 女の一念岩をも通す

### 女は氏無くて玉の輿に乗る

[Though not of noble birth, a woman may ride the palanquin of nobility.] ☞ Throughout Japanese history women not of high birth have borne out this proverb. In recent times, Emperor Akihito married a commoner, as did Crown Prince Naruhito. ● Even if a woman is not of noble birth, if she has beauty and grace she may marry into high rank. ● A woman of no birth may marry into the purple.

### 女は三界に家無し

[There is no house for a woman in the Three Worlds.] ☞ In Buddhist tradition the Three Worlds are those of the past, the present, and the future, as well as those of desire, form, and formlessness. ● A woman in traditional Japanese society had practically no independence; as a child she had to obey her parents, when she married she had to obey her husband, and in old age she had to obey her children.

### 女寡に花が咲く、男寡に蛆が湧く

[Widows bear flowers; widowers breed maggots.] ● When women

are widowed, they often take care of themselves and may even grow more attractive; when men are widowed they often neglect themselves and soon look scruffy and old.

# か

# カ

### 楷書書かねば手書きでない

[If one does not write in *kaisho*, one is not a skilled penman.] ☞ In Japanese calligraphy, there are three basic styles of writing Chinese characters: *kaisho* (楷書), the formal or square printed style; *gyōsho* (行書), the semicursive style; and *sōsho* (草書), the cursive or running (literally the "grass" hand) style. To be considered a good calligrapher one must first master the formal style of writing. ● If one cannot write in formal style, one cannot be considered to be a good calligrapher.

### 海賊が山賊の罪をあげる

[A pirate will point out the crimes of the mountain bandit.] 📖 This proverb is taken from the *Taiheiki*, a 14th-century Japanese historical epic. ❶ If people have no common interests, nothing in the world will unite them, even if they share some characteristics. ● There is no love lost between sailors and soldiers. One false knave accuses another. = 山賊の罪を海賊があげる ❷ Used when people point out the mistakes in others, while ignoring their own shortcomings. ● The pot calling the kettle black. ♦ 五十歩をもって百歩を笑う ♦ 猿の尻笑い ♦ 目糞が鼻糞を笑う ♦ 目脂が鼻垢を笑う

### 隗より始めよ

[Let's begin with Kai.] ☞ Kai, or Guo Wei, was a low official at the court of the northern Chinese province of Yan during the Chinese Warring States Period (475-221BC). When consulted by his lord on how best to enlist the counsel of wise men, Guo Wei replied that the best way to do so was to start by treating men like himself well. If word got around that even humble courtiers were treated well, superior men would soon flock to the court in great numbers. ● When one sets out on a major enterprise one should begin with the tasks close at hand. Similarly, those who formulate ideas about how to do things should be the first to put them into practice. • He who suggests something should be the first to do it. ◆ 死馬の骨を買う

## 蛙の子は蛙

[The offspring of frogs are frogs.] ● It is inevitable that children will take after their parents. • Like father, like son. • Like breeds like. = この君にしてこの臣あり = 父も父なら子も子だ ◆ 瓜の蔓に茄子はならぬ ◆ 子は生むも心は生まぬ

## 蛙の面に水

[Water on a frog's face.] ● Describes a situation in which good counsel or criticism is totally lost on someone. • Like water off a duck's back. = 馬の耳に念仏 = 空吹く風と聞き流す = 馬耳東風 ◆ 猫に小判 ◆ 豚に真珠

## 河海は細流を択ばず

[The oceans and great rivers do not single out small streams.] ● Great people are big-hearted and can get along with all sorts of people. = 大海は細流を択ばず ◆ 大人は小目を遣わず ≠ 象は兎の小道に遊ばず ≠ 大魚は小池に棲まず ≠ 呑舟の魚は枝流に泳がず

## 鍵を盗む者は誅せられ、国を盗む者は諸侯となる

[Those who steal a key are put to death; those who steal a country become king.] 📖 This proverb is attributed to the Chinese philosopher Zhuangzi. ● Those who commit ordinary crimes are usually brought to justice, but those who commit huge crimes often get away with them. • Little thieves are hanged, but great ones escape. • One murder makes a criminal, a million a hero. = 金を奪う者は殺され、国を奪う者は王となる = 財を盗む者は盗人なり、国を盗む者は諸侯

## 学者の取った天下無し

[There are no scholars who have conquered a realm.] ● Though scholars may have a deep intellectual understanding of a country, its people, and its history, when it comes to ruling a country they are not suited to the task. • If philosophers were kings and kings philosophers there would be no wars.

## 隠すこと千里

[Hidden things (will travel) a thousand *ri*.] ✍ The *ri* (里) is an ancient Chinese measurement of distance, the equivalent of 0.3 miles. With time, it came to denote the distance one could walk in an hour, and during the Edo period (1600–1867) it was officially defined as 36 *chō*, or about 2.44 miles. • No matter how one tries to hide a secret, sooner or later it will out. • Murder will out. • The truth will out. = 隠すことは現わる ♦ 氏素性は争えないもの ♦ 天知る地知る我知る人知る ♦ 血筋は争えないもの

## 隠すことは現わる

[What is hidden will be revealed.] • No matter how one tries to hide a secret, sooner or later it will out. • Murder will out. • The truth will out. = 隠すこと千里 ♦ 氏素性は争えないもの ♦ 天知る地知る我知る人知る ♦ 血筋は争えないもの

## 学問に王道無し

[There is no royal road to learning.] • To acquire knowledge is a long and arduous road, as it is only acquired through experience and diligent study. • There is no royal road to learning. = 学問に近道無し ♦ 少年老い易く学成り難しく

## 学問に近道無し

[There is no short road to learning.] • To acquire knowledge is a long and arduous road, as it is only acquired through experience and diligent study. • There is no royal road to learning. = 学問に王道無し ♦ 少年老い易く学成り難しく

## 学問は置きどころによって善悪分かる、臍の下良し鼻の先悪し

[The good or bad nature of learning is revealed by where it resides: if below the navel it is good, if at the end of the nose it is bad.] ☞ The nose features in a number of Japanese idiomatic expressions relating to pride and arrogance. The expression 鼻に掛

けろ (to hang something on one's nose) means to "be proud" or to "take pride in," whilst 鼻が高い (have a high nose) means to "be puffed up with pride." The expression 鼻を折る (to break one's nose) conversely means "to humble someone." ● Good learning is done with modesty. = 実る稲田は頭垂る ◆ 大賢は愚なるが如し ◆ 大功は拙なるが如し ◆ 大知は愚の如し

か

## 駕籠昇き駕籠に乗らず

[Palanquin bearers do not ride.] ● Those who make their living serving others usually do not have the means to enjoy the comforts they provide. ● The shoemaker's children go barefoot. ● The tailor's wife is worst clad. = 紺屋の白袴 = 大工の掘っ立て = 耕す者は食わず、織る者は着ず ◆ 医者の不養生

## 籠で水を汲む

[The wind is not caught in the meshes of a net.] ● Describes a futile action. = 網の目に風たまらす = 糠に釘 ◆ 株を守りて兎を待つ ◆ 馬の耳に念仏 ◆ 蛙の面に水 ◆ 株を守りて兎を待つ ◆ 空吹く風と聞き流す ◆ 猫に小判 ◆ 馬耳東風 ◆ 豚に真珠

## 過言一度出ずれば駟も舌に及ばず

[Once a slip of the tongue has been made, even a four-horse chariot cannot keep up with it.] ● A *faux pas*, once committed, cannot be recalled. ● A word and a stone let go cannot be called back. = 駟も舌に及ばず

## 貸した物は忘れず、借りた物は忘れる

[What one lends one does not forget; what one borrows one forgets.] ● It is easy to forget to return something that one has borrowed, but few people forget what they have lent to others. Similarly, a favor bestowed is keenly remembered, while a favor received is easily forgotten. ● Creditors have better memories than debtors. ● When I lent I was a friend; when I asked I was unkind. ◆ 借りる時の地蔵顔、返す時の閻魔顔 ◆ 済す時の閻魔顔、借る時の地蔵顔 ◆ 用有る時の地蔵顔、◆ 用無き時の閻魔顔

## 風起こらざれば木動かず
### かぜお　きうご

[If there is no wind the trees will not move.] ● Nothing happens without a clear cause. • Where there's smoke there's fire. • No smoke without fire. ♦ 火の無い所に煙は立たない

## 稼ぐに追い付く貧乏無し
### かせ　お　つ　びんぼう な

[There is no poverty that overtakes toil.] ● Those who work hard will always have some money to spend. • Poverty is a stranger to industry. • Where bees are there is honey. ♦ 朝謡は貧乏の相 ♦ 勤勉は福の神 ♦ 酒と朝寝は貧乏の近道 ♦ 好きの道には薦被る

## 勝つ事ばかり知りて負くる事を知らざれば害其の身に至る
### か　こと　し　ま　こと　し　がいそ　み　いた

[Harm comes to those who know only victory and do not know defeat.] 📖 This proverb is taken from Tokugawa Ieyasu's *Teachings on the Conduct of Life*. ● When one is used to having only success and has never experienced failure one may be destroyed either by self-indulgence or by an incapacity to cope with inevitable setbacks. • Failure teaches success. ♦ 勝って兜の緒を締めよ

## 勝って兜の緒を締めよ
### か　かぶと　お　し

[When victorious, tighten the thongs of your helmet.] 📖 This proverb is taken from the *Mikawa monogatari*, a 17th century book on the way of the warrior and a chronicle of famous Japanese clans. ● Success should never be a reason for complacence. • Don't crow over your enemy. • In the time of mirth take heed. ♦ 勝つ事ばかり知りて負くる事を知らざれば害其の身に至る ♦ 好事魔多し

## 河童の川流れ
### かっぱ　かわなが

[A river monster swept away by the river's current.] ● Even complete masters of their craft may sometimes get it wrong. • Homer sometimes nods. • A good marksman may miss. = 王良も時として馬車を覆す = 賢者も千慮の一失 = 弘法にも筆の誤り = 猿も木から落ちる = 知者にも千慮の一失 = 上手の手から水が漏れる = 竜馬の躓き

## 勝てば官軍、負ければ賊軍
### か　かんぐん　ま　ぞくぐん

[When victorious, the Imperial forces; when defeated, a rebel army.] ● Success often gives sanction to an act with little moral foundation. • Losers are always in the wrong. • It is hard to argue with success. • Nothing succeeds like success. ♦ 鍵を盗む者は誅せられ、国を盗む者は諸侯となる ♦ 金を奪う者は殺され、国を奪う者は王となる ♦ 財を盗む者は盗人なり、国を盗む者は諸侯

## 糧を捨てて船を沈む

[Abandon one's rations, sink one's ships.] ☞ A proverb based on an episode in Chinese military history in which general Xiang Yu defeats superior Qín forces by destroying all avenues of retreat for his own men. ● Describes one who embarks upon a venture with the resolve to perish if it fails. • Cross the Rubicon. = 清水の舞台から飛び降りる = 背水の陣 ♦ 死を先んずる者は必ず生ず ♦ 身を捨ててこそ浮かぶ瀬も有れ

## 瓜田に靴を納れず

[Do not put on your shoes in a field of eggplants.] ● When one goes into a field of eggplants bare-footed, one should not stoop to put on one's shoes lest one be suspected of pinching an eggplant. By extension, when in a position subject to public scrutiny one should always act with integrity and circumspection so as to avoid the least suspicion. • Leave no room for scandal. = 李下に冠を正さず

## 門松は冥途の旅の一里塚

[Pine trees at the gate are but the milestones on one's journey to Hades.] ☞ The pine tree in Japanese culture stands for constancy and longevity. Traditionally, at New Year's time pine trees or branches were placed at each side of the gate or the entrance of a house to usher in the spirits of longevity in the hope that the occupants would lead long and fruitful lives. ● All occasions for celebration and remembrance are but transitory moments in a life that is fleeting. ♦ 会うは別れの始め ♦ 三日見ぬ間の桜

## 門脇の姥にさえ用あれば笑顔

[Even the old woman at the side of the gate will smile when she has business.] ● Even the most churlish of people will try to make a favorable impression when they have need of something. • When I lent I was a friend; when I asked I was unkind. ▶ 借りる時の地蔵顔、返す時の閻魔顔 ▶ 貸した物は忘れず、借りた物は忘れる ▶ 済す時の閻魔顔、借る時の地蔵顔 ▶ 用有る時の地蔵顔、用無き時の閻魔顔

## 門脇の姥にも用有り

[Even the old woman at the side of the gate has her use.] ● Even those whose presence seems of no consequence may have their part to play in the greater scheme of things. • For the want of a nail the shoe was lost, for the want of a shoe the horse was lost, for the want of a horse the battle was lost. ▶ 枯れ木も山の賑わい ▶ 愚者も千慮に一得あり ▶ 癖ある馬に乗りあり ▶ 蹴る馬も乗り手次第 ▶ 鵜目鷹なれど観ること鼠に若かず ▶ ❷ 時に遭えば鼠も虎となる ▶ 馬鹿と鋏は使い様 ▶ 馬鹿も一芸 ▶ 貧乏人も三年置けば用に立つ ▶ ❷ 用いる時は鼠も虎となる ▶ 野郎と鋏が使い様 ▶ 湯腹も一時、松の木柱も三年 ▶ 割れ鍋も三年置けば用に立つ

## 家内喧嘩は貧乏の種蒔き

[Domestic quarrels sow the seeds of poverty.] ● Fighting between husband and wife will ultimately lead to a family's ruin.

## 叶わぬ時の神叩き

[Praying to gods when dreams are unfulfilled.] ● When things do not go as desired, people turn to their gods for help; when things are going fine, people tend to forget their gods. • Vows made in storms are forgotten in calms. • Danger past and God forgotten. • The peril past, the saint mocked. ▶ 暑さ忘れて蔭忘る ▶ 雨晴れて笠を忘る ▶ 苦しい時の神頼み ▶ 狡兎死して走狗烹らる ▶ 恐い時の仏頼み ▶ 災害は忘れた頃にやって来る ▶ 喉元過ぎれば熱さを忘れる ▶ 病治りて薬師忘る

## 蟹は甲羅に似せて穴を掘る

[The crab digs a hole to fit its shell.] ● People should carve out their place in the world according to their talents and powers. Similarly, one should act in accordance with one's position in life. • Cut your coat according to your cloth. = 鳥は翼に従って巣を作る ▶ 入るを量りて出ずるを為す

## 金が有れば馬鹿も旦那

[With money, even a fool is master.] ● As long as they have money, even fools can enjoy influence and respect. ● Success makes a fool seem wise. ● He is wise that is rich. ● Money makes the man. ◆ 金の世の中 ◆ 人間万事金の世の中

## 金の切れ目が縁の切れ目

[The end of money, the end of the relationship.] ● When money runs out a relationship will come under great pressure, as it is impossible to live on love alone. ● The end of money is the end of love. ● Love lasts as long as money endures. ● When poverty comes in at the door, love flies out at the window. ◆ 愛は多能で有り、金は万能で有る ◆ 色気より食い気

## 金の光は阿弥陀ほど

[The luster of money is as great as that of the Buddha.] ☞ Images of Buddha are often gilded, so that this proverb can be taken quite literally. ● Material wealth vies with spirituality in its attractiveness. ● No penny, no paternoster. ◆ 阿弥陀の光も金次第 ◆ 地獄の沙汰も金次第 ◆ 釈迦も銭ほど光る ◆ 仏の光より金の光

## 金の光は七光

[Money's luster is sevenfold.] ● The rich enjoy not only material well-being but also the additional benefits money brings, such as influence and respect. ● Money recommends a man everywhere. ● Money makes the man. ◆ 親の光は七光

## 金の世の中

[A world of money.] ● In all human affairs money has its role to play, for better or for worse. ● All things are obedient to money. ● Money rules the world. ● All things are obedient to money. = 人間万事金の世の中 ◆ 金有れば馬鹿も旦那

## 金は世界の回り物

[Money is the world's turn-taker.] ● Money is no one's sole property, it changes hands continually, and those who possess large amounts of money today may lose it tomorrow, while those who have none today may become rich tomorrow. • Money will come and go. = 金は天下の回り持ち ▶ 悪銭身に付かず ▶ 地獄の沙汰も金次第

## 金は天下の回り持ち

[Money goes round in the world.] ● Money changes hands continually; those who possess large amounts today may lose it tomorrow, while those who have none today may become rich tomorrow. • Money will come and go. = 金は世界の回り物 ▶ 悪銭身に付かず ▶ 地獄の沙汰も金次第

## 金は山に棄て玉は淵に投ぐべし

[Discard money on the mountain and throw jewels into the abyss.] 📖 This proverb is attributed to the Chinese philosopher Zhuangzi. ● If one is to lead an honest life, it is better not to expose oneself to the temptations of wealth. • He is rich enough that wants nothing. = 金を泥に棄て玉を淵に沈む

## 金持ち苦労多し

[The rich have many hardships.] ● The more money one accumulates the more one will worry about how to secure it from the greed of others. • Much coin, much care. ▶ 金持ちと貧乏者はじっとしていられない ▶ 財少なければ悲しみ少ない

## 金持ちと貧乏者はじっとしていられない

[The rich and the poor cannot sit still.] ● Money is a perpetual source of worry: the rich worry about how to keep it, the poor about how to obtain it. • Every one is weary: the poor in seeking, the rich in keeping, the good in learning. ▶ 金持ち苦労多し ▶ 財少なければ悲しみ少ない

## 金持ちの貧乏人、貧乏人の金持ち

[The poor rich person, the rich poor person.] ● The rich cannot find contentment in what they have and are thus spiritually poor; the poor have learned to find contentment in the little they have and are thus spiritually rich. • He is not poor that hath little, but he that desireth much. • He is rich enough that wants nothing.

## 金を奪う者は殺され、国を奪う者は王となる

[Those who take money by force are put to death; those who take a country by force become king.] ● Those who commit ordinary crimes are usually brought to justice, but those who commit huge crimes often get away with them. • Little thieves are hanged, but great ones escape. • One murder makes a criminal, a million a hero. = 鍵を盗む者は誅せられ、国を盗む者は諸侯となる = 財を盗む者は盗人なり、国を盗む者は諸侯

## 金を貸せば友を失う

[When one lends money one loses friends.] ● To lend money is to make someone indebted to you, which will lead to mistrust and resentment. • Lend your money and lose your friends. • If you would make an enemy lend a man money, and ask it of him again. ◆ 貸した物は忘れず、借りた物は忘れる ◆ 借りる時の地蔵顔、返す時の閻魔顔 ◆ 済す時の閻魔顔、借る時の地蔵顔 ◆ 用有る時の地蔵顔、用無き時の閻魔顔

## 金を山に蔵し玉は淵に蔵す

[Store money in the mountains and jewels in the abyss.] 📖 This proverb is taken from the *Taiheiki*, a 14th-century Japanese historical epic. ● If one is to lead an honest life, it is better not to expose oneself to the temptations of wealth. • He is rich enough that wants nothing. = 金を泥に棄て玉を淵に沈む

## 禍福己に由る

[Fortune and misfortune are in the eye of the beholder.] ● Whether one feels fortunate or unfortunate is largely a matter of one's perception of the situation.

## 禍福は糾える縄の如し

[Fortune and misfortune are like a twisted rope.] ● Fortune and misfortune are like the two sides of a coin; one may change to the other

か

in a moment. ● Good and ill luck are next-door neighbors. = 殺す神あれば助ける神あり = 沈む瀬あれば浮かぶ瀬あり = 捨てる神はあれば助ける神あり = 人間万事塞翁が馬 ▶ 入り船あれば出船あり ▶ 有為転変は世の習い ▶ 損をする者あれば得をする者がある

## 株を守りて兎を待つ

[Keep watch at the stump, waiting for the rabbit.] ☞ This proverb is taken from a Chinese folk tale in which a farmer observes a rabbit that runs into a tree stump and breaks its neck. The farmer is so pleased with the easy way in which he has obtained food he abandons his farming to keep watch at the stump, expecting another rabbit to die in the same manner. ● Describes those who persevere in an exercise that will never yield any fruit. = 柳の下に何時も泥鰌は居らぬ ▶ 網の目に風たまらす ▶ 籠で水を汲む ▶ 糠に釘 ≠ 果報は寝て待て ≠ 辛抱する木に金がなる ≠ 待てば海路の日和あり

## 果報は寝て待て

[For good luck, sleep and wait.] ● Good fortune cannot be compelled to happen; all one can do is to bide one's time and wait for the right opportunity. ● Everything comes to him who waits. 運は天にあり、牡丹餅は棚にあり = 待てば海路の日和あり ▶ 堪忍は無事長久の基 ▶ 辛抱する木に金がなる ≠ 株を守りて兎を待つ

## 紙千年絹五百年

[Paper a thousand years, silk a hundred years.] ☞ Traditional Japanese paper, or *washi* (和紙), is among the strongest and most durable papers in the world. Is still used in traditional Japanese artifacts such as folding fans (扇子), scrolls (掛軸), and folding screens (屏風). ● Paper will last a thousand years, while silk will last only five hundred years.

## 髪の長いは七難隠す

[Long hair hides seven troubles.] ✍ 色の白い refers to the white powder with which Japanese women traditionally used to make themselves up. ● Long hair on women will make them look attractive, even if they are not particularly beautiful. ● A fair com-

plexion hides many faults. • An honest look covereth many faults. =
色の白いは七難隠す

## 亀の甲より年の劫

[Rather than the shell of a tortoise, the years of the old.] ✍ This proverb contains a pun on the homonyms of 甲 (the shell of a tortoise) and 劫 (long years). ☞ In ancient Japan tortoise shells were used in a ritual in which a diviner heated a shell over a fire and interpreted events according to cracks that appeared. Even today, fortune-telling, whether it be in the form of having one's palms read on a street corner by a palmist (手相見) or drawing a sacred lot (神籤) at a Shintō shrine, is popular in Japan. ● Rather than rely on a sign from the gods it is better to rely on the experience and wisdom of the old. • Years know more than books. ◆ 老いたる馬は路を忘れず

## 鴉が鵜の真似

[The crow imitates the cormorant.] ● Those who try to succeed in a field by pretending to possess the required knowledge will inevitably be exposed as frauds. • Let the cobbler stick to his last. ◆ 海の事は漁父に問え ◆ 海老踊れども川を出でず ◆ 芸は道に依りて賢し ◆ 酒は酒屋に茶は茶屋に ◆ 鹿つきの山は猟師知り、魚つきの浦は網人知る ◆ 田作る道は農に問え ◆ 餅は餅屋

## 狩人も罠に掛かる

[Hunters, too, are caught in snares.] ● Those who wish to cause harm to others will eventually come to harm themselves. • They hurt themselves who wrong others. • Curses, like chickens, come home to roost. = 天を仰ぎて唾す = 人を取る亀人に取られる = 人を呪わば穴二つ ◆ 策士策に溺れる

## 借りる時の地蔵顔、返す時の閻魔顔

[The face of Jizo when borrowing, the face of Emma when repaying.] ☞ Jizo is the guardian deity of children and has a round, benign face; Emma is the King of Hell and has a square, scowling face. ● Asking someone for money is easy, repaying it is painful.

• When I lent I was a friend; when I asked I was unkind. • If you would make an enemy lend a man money, and ask it of him again. ＝ 済す時の閻魔顔、借る時の地蔵顔 ＝ 用有る時の地蔵顔、用無き時の閻魔顔 ◆ 貸した物は忘れず、借りた物は忘れる

## 枯れ木も山の賑わい

[Withered trees, too, add to the mountain's prosperity.] ● Even those whose presence seems of no consequence have their part to play. • For the want of a nail the shoe was lost, for the want of a shoe the horse was lost, for the want of a horse the battle was lost. ◆ 門脇の姥にも用有り ◆ 愚者も千慮に一徳あり ◆ 癖ある馬に乗りあり ◆ 蹴る馬も乗り手次第 ◆ 鴎目大なれど観ること鼠に若かず ◆ ❷ 時に遭えば鼠も虎となる ◆ 馬鹿と鋏は使い様 ◆ 馬鹿も一芸 ◆ 貧乏人も三年置けば用に立つ ◆ ❷ 用いる時は鼠も虎となる ◆ 野郎と鋏が使い様 ◆ 湯腹も一時、松の木柱も三年 ◆ 割れ鍋も三年置けば用に立つ

## 彼を知り己を知れば百戦殆うからず

[When one knows the other and oneself, there will be no mistakes in a hundred battles.] 📖 This proverb is taken from *The Art of War* by the Chinese general Sun Tzu. ● To ensure victory one should go into battle with a thorough knowledge of both one's own and one's opponent's strengths and weaknesses.

## 可愛い子には旅をさせよ

[Send a pampered child on a journey.] ● Rather than keep children at home where they will become pampered and spoiled, one should send them out into the world so that they will experience at first hand the hardships of life and grow into mature adults. • Home-keeping youth have ever homely wits. • Spare the rod and spoil the child. ＝ 獅子の子落とし ◆ 祖母育ちは三百安い

## 可愛さ余って憎さ百倍

[Excessive tenderness becomes a hundredfold hatred.] ● When one loves someone to excess, one's hatred will be likewise excessive if jilted. • Who loves too much hates in like extreme. ◆ 愛は小出しにせよ ◆ 鼠壁を忘る、壁鼠を忘れず ≠ 坊主憎けりゃ袈裟まで憎い

## 瓦は磨いても玉にはならぬ

[No matter how polished, a tile will not become a jewel.]
● However polished one's manners and appearance may be, one will always remain the product of the social stratum into which one was born. ● One cannot make a silk purse out of a sow's ear. = 度場は伯楽に会わず = 鳶の子鷹にならず ◆ 玉磨かざれば光なし ◆ 瑠璃の光も磨きがら ≠ 瓦も磨けば玉となる

## 瓦も磨けば玉となる

[Even a tile, when polished, will become a jewel.] ● Even people of humble birth or limited talents may surpass others if they exert themselves. ◆ 玉磨かざれば光なし ◆ 瑠璃の光も磨きがら ≠ 瓦は磨いても玉にはならぬ ≠ 度場は伯楽に会わず ≠ 鳶の子鷹にならず

## 勧学院の雀は蒙求を囀る

[The sparrows of the Kangakuin can chirp its textbooks.] ☞ The Kangakuin (勧学院) was the academic dormitory (大学別曹) of the powerful Fujiwara clan during the Heian period (794-1185). ● When one is constantly exposed to a practice or doctrine, one will necessarily learn it with time. ● A saint's maid quotes Latin. = 門前の小僧習わぬ経を読む ◆ 朱に交われば赤くなる ◆ 習い性と成る ◆ 習うより慣れよ ◆ 下手な鉄砲も数打ちゃ当たる ◆ 下手な鍛冶屋も一度は名剣

## 甘言が愚人を喜ばしむ

[Sweet words delight fools.] ● Only fools fail to see through the flattery of sycophants. ● Fair words please fools. ● Fair words make fools fain. ◆ 口に蜜有り腹に剣有り ◆ 信言は美ならず、美言は信ならず ◆ 追従する者陰にて誹る ◆ 天子将軍の事でも陰では言う ◆ 天子将軍も障子の内 ◆ 耳の楽しむ時は慎むべし

## 諫言耳に逆らう

[Admonitions are harsh to the ear.] ● It is unpleasant to have one's shortcomings or mistakes pointed out. ● If the counsel be good, no matter who gave it. ● He that will not be counselled cannot be helped. = 忠言耳に逆らう ◆ 良薬口に苦し

## 艱難汝を玉にす

[Hardships (will) make a jewel out of one.] ● One's character and hidden potential will only be revealed and developed when put to the test under adverse conditions. • The school of adversity is the best school. • Adversity makes a man wise. = 若い時の苦労は買うてもよせ ◗ 盤根錯節に遭いて利器を知る ◗ 雪圧して松の操を知る ◗ 瑠璃も玻璃も照らせば光る

## 堪忍家督、短気は損気、辛抱は金

[In (running the) affairs of an estate with forbearance, a short temper is loss and patience is money.] ● In order to run a household successfully, patience and perseverance are indispensible virtues.

## 堪忍は無事長久の基

[Forbearance is the root of peace and prosperity.] 📖 This proverb is taken from Tokugawa Ieyasu's *Teachings on the Conduct of Life.* ● Those who are patient will be free from worries. As a result they will avoid making the wrong decisions in haste and acquire wealth and status by waiting for an auspicious time to act. • Everything comes to him who waits. • Patient men win the day. ◗ 運は天にあり、牡丹餅は棚にあり ◗ 果報は寝て待て ◗ 辛抱する木に金がなる ◗ 待てば海路の日和あり

## 雁は八百、矢は三文

[A wild goose is (worth) eight hundred *mon*, an arrow three *mon*.] ✍ The *mon* (文) was a currency unit that derived from the Chinese *wen*, and introduced to Japan during the Muromachi period (1333–1568). It was used up until 1870, when it was replaced with the *yen* (円). ● It is possible to accomplish great feats with only modest means. Likewise, large profits can be made with only small investment. • Throw out a lobster and pull in a whale. • Throw a sprat to catch a herring. • Give an egg to gain an ox. = 海老で鯛を釣る ◗ ❶ 蛍火をもって酒弥山を焼く

## 棺を蓋いて事定まる

[Affairs are settled when the coffin is closed.] ● Only after someone has been laid to rest can one draw up the balance of their life. ● Call no man great before he is dead. = 三枚うら冠らぬうちは人の運が分からぬ

# キ

### 聞いた百文より見た一文

[Rather than hearing of a hundred *mon*, seeing one *mon*.] ✍ The *mon* (文) was a currency unit that derived from the Chinese *wen*, and introduced to Japan during the Muromachi period (1333-1568). It was used up until 1870, when it was replaced with the *yen* (円). ● Rather than speculate about huge potential gains it is better to possess even the smallest amount of money. ● Seeing is believing. ▶ 明日の百より今日の五十 ▶ 大取りより小取り ▶ あの世千日この世の一日 ▶ 末始終より今の三十 ▶ ❶ 近火で手を焙れ ▶ 後の千金より今の百文 ▶ 来年の百両より今年の一両

### 聞いて極楽、見て地獄

[On hearing, it is (Buddhist) paradise; on seeing, it is Hades.] ● There is often a great difference between what one hears about something and what one finally observes first hand. ● Heaven by hearsay, hell at sight. = 聞いて千金、見て一文

### 聞いて千金、見て一文

[On hearing a fortune, on seeing one *mon*.] ✍ The *mon* (文) was a currency unit that derived from the Chinese *wen*, and introduced to Japan during the Muromachi period (1333-1568). It was used up until 1870, when it was replaced with the *yen* (円). ● There may be a great difference between what one hears by way of rumor and hearsay and that which one finally observes and experience at first hand. ● Heaven by hearsay, hell at sight. = 聞いて極楽、見て地獄

### 聞くは一時の恥、聞かぬは末代の恥

[To ask may be a moment's shame; not to ask may lead to lifelong disgrace.] ● Rather than remain ignorant, it is better to endure the temporary shame of owning up to one's ignorance by asking. ● He that nothing questioneth, nothing learneth. ● Be brave to ask so as to learn. ● Better ask than go astray. = 問うは一時の恥、問わぬは末代の恥 ◆ 知らざるを知らずとせよ

## 木強ければ折れ易し

[When trees are strong they break easily.] ● Those with rigid characters are more likely to be frustrated in their endeavors than those with flexible characters. ● Oaks may fall when reeds stand the storm. = 強き木はむず折れ = 柳に風折れなし = 柳の枝に雪折れ無し ◆ 柔能く剛を制する、弱能く強を制する ◆ 茶碗を投げば綿で抱えよ

## 木に付く虫は木を齧り、萱に付く虫は萱を啄む

[Insects that land on trees chew the trees; insects that land on cogon grass peck at (the insects on) cogon grass.] ✍ Cogon grass, native to East and Southeast Asia, is also known as Kunai grass, or Japanese blood grass. 📖 This proverb is taken from the *Genpei jōsuiki*, an extended account of the struggle for control of Japan at the end of the 12th century. ● There are relations that are mutually detrimental and those that are mutually beneficial. ◆ 牛は水を飲んで乳とし、蛇は水を飲んで毒とし

## 昨日に優る今日の花

[Today's flower surpasses yesterday's.] ● What appeared desirable yesterday may, due to our ever changing desires, appear unsatisfactory today. ● Avarice knows no bounds. ◆ 有るが上にも欲しがるのが人情 ◆ 有るは嫌なり、思うは成らず ◆ 千石を得て万石を恨む ◆ 成るは嫌なり、思うは成らず ◆ 隴を得て蜀を望む

## 昨日の綴れ、今日の錦

[Yesterday's rags, today's brocade.] ● Though one be in dire straits today, one may be wealthy tomorrow. ● A nobody today, a prince tomorrow. = 今日の綴れ、明日の錦 = 昨日の淵は今日の瀬 ◆ 入り船あれば出船あり ◆ 有為転変は世の習い ◆ 禍福は糾える縄の如し ◆ 殺す神あれば助ける神あり ◆ 沈む瀬あれば浮かぶ瀬あり ◆ 捨てる神はあれば助ける神あり ≠ 昨日の錦、今日の綴れ ≠ 昨日の花は今日の夢

## 昨日の敵は今日の味方

[Yesterday's foe may be today's ally.] ● People change; those who were enemies in the past may prove to be allies today. • A friend today may turn a foe tomorrow. ＝ 今日の敵は明日の味方 ▶ 入り船あれば出船あり ▶ 有為転変は世の習い ▶ 禍福は糾える縄の如し ▶ 殺す神あれば助ける神あり ▶ 沈む瀬あれば浮かぶ瀬あり ▶ 捨てる神はあれば助ける神あり ≠ 昨日の友は今日の仇 ≠ 昨日の情けは今日の仇 ≠ 今日の味方は明日の敵

## 昨日の友は今日の仇

[Yesterday's friend may be today's foe.] ● People change; those who were allies in the past may prove to be enemies today. • A friend today may turn a foe tomorrow. ＝ 昨日の情けは今日の仇 ＝ 今日の味方は明日の敵 ▶ 入り船あれば出船あり ▶ 有為転変は世の習い ▶ 禍福は糾える縄の如し ▶ 殺す神あれば助ける神あり ▶ 沈む瀬あれば浮かぶ瀬あり ▶ 捨てる神はあれば助ける神あり ≠ 昨日の敵は今日の味方 ≠ 今日の敵は明日の味方

## 昨日の情けは今日の仇

[Yesterday's (act of) kindness may be today's (act of) revenge.] ● People change; those who were kindly disposed toward one yesterday may prove to be a foe today. • A friend today may turn a foe tomorrow. ＝ 昨日の友は今日の仇 ＝ 今日の味方は明日の敵 ▶ 入り船あれば出船あり ▶ 有為転変は世の習い ▶ 禍福は糾える縄の如し ▶ 殺す神あれば助ける神あり ▶ 沈む瀬あれば浮かぶ瀬あり ▶ 捨てる神はあれば助ける神あり ≠ 昨日の敵は今日の味方 ≠ 今日の敵は明日の味方

## 昨日の錦、今日の綴れ

[Yesterday's brocade, today's rags.] ● Though one may wallow in wealth today, one may well go begging tomorrow. • Today a man, tomorrow none. • Who today was a haughty night, is tomorrow a penniless wight. ＝ 昨日の花は今日の夢 ▶ 入り船あれば出船あり ▶ 有為転変は世の習い ▶ 禍福は糾える縄の如し ▶ 殺す神あれば助ける神あり ▶ 沈む瀬あれば浮かぶ瀬あり ▶ 捨てる神はあれば助ける神あり ≠ 昨日の綴れ、今日の錦 ≠ 昨日の淵は今日の瀬 ≠ 今日の綴れ、明日の錦

き

## 昨日の花は今日の夢

[Yesterday's flower may be today's dream.] ● What seemed a promising prospect yesterday may be a dismal disappointment today.
● Today a man, tomorrow none. ● Who today was a haughty night, is tomorrow a penniless wight. ＝ 昨日の錦、今日の綴れ ♦ 入り船あれば出船あり ♦ 有為転変は世の習い ♦ 禍福は糾える縄の如し ♦ 殺す神あれば助ける神あり ♦ 沈む瀬あれば浮かぶ瀬あり ♦ 捨てる神はあれば助ける神あり ≠ 昨日の綴れ、今日の錦 ≠ 昨日の淵は今日の瀬 ≠ 今日の綴れ、明日の錦

## 昨日の淵は今日の瀬

[Yesterday's slough may be today's shoal.] ● What seemed an insurmountable obstacle may prove to be easier to deal with than supposed. ＝ 昨日の綴れ、今日の錦 ＝ 今日の綴れ、明日の錦 ♦ 入り船あれば出船あり ♦ 有為転変は世の習い ♦ 禍福は糾える縄の如し ♦ 殺す神あれば助ける神あり ♦ 沈む瀬あれば浮かぶ瀬あり ♦ 捨てる神はあれば助ける神あり ≠ 昨日の錦、今日の綴れ ≠ 昨日の花は今日の夢

## 木の長きを求むる者は必ず根本を固くす

[Those who desire a tall tree should strengthen its roots.] ● When one sets out on a major enterprise it is essential to begin by laying a solid foundation. ♦ 一朝一夕の故に非ず ♦ 馬に乗るまで牛に乗れ ♦ 沙弥から長老にはなれぬ ♦ ❷ 将を射んと欲すれば先ず馬を射よ ♦ 千里の道も一歩より始まる ♦ 大事の前の小事 ♦ 高きに登るは低きよりす ♦ 始めから長老にはなれぬ ♦ 始めの一歩、末の千里 ♦ ❷ 人を射んとせば先ず馬を射よ

## 木は規に依って直く人は人に依って賢し

[Trees are made straight by means of a ruler; people are made straight by means of people.] ● Whilst trees can be made to grow straight by pruning and cutting, the characters of people are developed by mixing with and learning from others. ♦ 前車の覆るは後車の戒め ♦ 人のふり見て我がふり直せ

## 木は縄に従って材なり、君は諫めに従って聖なり

[Trees may be cut into (straight) planks by means of a (carpenter's ink) line; a lord may become a sage by means of counsel.] ● Those who are in high positions do well to heed the advice of their advisers. ● He hath a good judgment that relieth not wholly on his own. ● He that is his own counsel has a fool for a client. = 君に争臣有れば、身不義に陥らず = 父に諫むる子有ればその家必ず繁栄す ♦ 諫言耳に逆らう ♦ 忠言耳に逆らう ♦ 良薬口に苦し

## 君君たらずとも臣臣たらざるべからず

[Even if the lord is unlordly, his retainers should be worthy.] 📖 This proverb is taken from the *Analects* of Confucius. ● Even when leaders fail to live up to the moral requirements of their positions, their advisers should act with integrity. ♦ 君君たり臣臣たり ♦ 主人なら下男も下男 ♦ 父も父なら子も子だ

## 君君たり臣臣たり

[As a lord must be a lord, so a vassal must be a vassal.] 📖 This proverb is taken from the *Analects* of Confucius. ● As leaders must strive to live up to the responsibilities of their positions, so should their followers strive to live up to the requirements of theirs. ● Like master, Like man. ● Like lord, like chaplain. = この君にしてこの臣あり ♦ 君君たらずとも臣臣たらざるべからず ♦ 主人なら下男も下男 ♦ 父も父なら子も子だ

## 君心有れば民心有り

[If a lord has heart, the people will have heart.] If leaders care for the people under their rule, the people will show respect to their leaders in return. ● The subject's love is the king's lifeguard. ● He that is hated of his subjects cannot be counted king. ♦ 魚心有れば水心

## 君、臣を選ぶのみに非ず、臣も亦君を選ぶ

[Not only may a lord choose his retainers; a retainer, too, may choose his lord.] ● Whilst masters have the freedom to select and employ those they deem suitable, so, too, servants have the freedom to work for whomever they deem worthy. ≠ 鳥は木を択べども木は鳥を択ばず

き

### 君と共にする一夜の話は十年の書を読むに優る

[The one-night talk with a wise man exceeds the reading of ten years.] ● Rather than try to acquire knowledge on one's own, one should seek the guidance of the wise, since only they know how to correctly interpret the teachings of the sages. ● In every art it is good to have a master. = 千日の勤学より一時の名匠 ◆ 師は針の如し、弟子は糸の如し

### 君に争臣有れば、身不義に陥らず

[If a lord has a retainer who remonstrates with him, he will not fall into immorality.] ● As long as leaders have the wisdom to employ and listen to those who have the courage to remonstrate with them, they will avoid doing immoral things. = 木は縄に従って材なり、君は諫めに従って聖なり = 父に諫むる子有ればその家必ず繁栄す ◆ 諫言耳に逆らう ◆ 忠言耳に逆らう ◆ 良薬口に苦し

### 君は臣を選びて官を授け、臣は己を量りて職を受く

[The lord bestows a post by choosing a retainer; the retainer accepts a post by measuring himself.] ● Just as masters have the responsibility to choose carefully those whom they deem suitable for each post, those chosen have the responsibility to consider carefully whether they have the qualifications the office requires.

### 君は舟臣は水

[The lord is the boat; the retainers are the water.] 📖 This proverb is attributed to the Chinese Confucianist Xunzi. ● The relationship between leaders and the people is like that of a boat on the water: Just as the supportive power of the water keeps the boat afloat, so the support of the people keeps the leader in power. Yet in the same way as a rough sea may topple the boat and cause the boat to sink, so the rising of discontent masses may topple their leader.

### 窮すれば通ず

[When in distress, one finds a way out.] ● Being pushed to one's limits forces one to find a new road by which to continue. ● Necessity is the mother of invention. ◆ 必要は発明の母

74

## 窮すれば鈍する

[When in distress one becomes dull-witted.] ● Those who are impoverished soon lose their airs and graces as they are forced to concentrate on day-to-day survival. ● Poverty dulls the wit. = 貧すれば鈍する

## 窮鼠猫を噛む

[A mouse in distress will bite a cat.] 📖 This proverb is taken from the *Taiheiki*, a 14th-century Japanese historical epic. ● Even the most timid will show a degree of courage when driven into a corner. ● Despair gives courage to the coward. ● Put a coward to his mettle and he'll fight the devil. ♦ 一寸の虫にも五分の魂 ♦❶ 時に遭えば鼠も虎となる ♦ 蛞蝓にも角 ♦ 鼠窮して猫を噛み、人貧しゅして盗みす ♦❶ 用いる時は鼠も虎となる

## 窮鳥 枝を選ばず

[A bird in distress does not choose the branch (on which to land).] ● In an emergency, one cannot be too particular about the means of relief. ● Any port in a storm. = 逃げる者は道を選ばず ♦ 恋と戦は手段を選ばず

## 窮鳥 懐 に入れば猟師も殺さず

[If a bird in distress seeks refuge at one's bosom even the hunter will not kill it.] ● When someone in distress appeals for help, it is only human to offer assistance, even to an adversary. ● Any port in a storm. = 飛ぶ鳥懐 に入る時は狩人も助くる ♦ 杖の下に回る犬は打てぬ ♦ 棒の下に回る犬は打てぬ

## 今日有って明日無い身

[Here today, gone tomorrow.] ● Life is fleeting and no one can predict the future or when their end will come. ● Here today, gone tomorrow. ● Today a man; tomorrow none. = 朝には紅顔有りて夕べには白骨となる

## 強将 の下に弱卒無し

[There are no weak soldiers under a strong general.] ● Talented leaders will make sure they have talented people at their disposal. Equally, courageous leaders will bring out the best in those under their command. ● A good general makes good men. ● A good officer will make good men. = 勇将の下に弱卒無し = 良将の下に弱卒無し ♦ 麻に連るる蓬 ♦ 朱に交われば赤くなる ♦ 大木の下に小木育つ

## 狂人 走れば不狂人も走る

[If the mad run wild, the sane will, too.] ● The action of an individual can influence that of a group; if one person panics, others will, too. ● When one sheep is over the dam, the rest will follow. = 一派僅かに動いて万波随う = 一匹の馬狂えば千匹の馬も又狂う

## 今日の哀れ、明日は我が身

[Today the misery (of others); tomorrow my own plight.] ● No matter how fortunate one may count oneself, no one is immune from hardships; tomorrow one may suffer the same setbacks that are today suffered by others. ● What chances to one man may happen to all. = 今日は人の身、明日は我が身

## 今日の一字は明日の二字

[Today's one character, tomorrow's two characters.] ☞ In order to master the written language, Japanese children must learn to read and write some two-and-a-half thousand Chinese ideographs. The full Chinese alphabet, however, consists of as many as twenty thousand characters. ● If one fails to master one character today, one must master two tomorrow. By extension, if one leaves today's work undone one will have to do two days worth of work tomorrow. ● A stitch in time saves nine. = 今の一針、後の十針 = 今日の一針は明日の十針

## 京の妹に隣代えず

[Do not exchange a neighbor for a younger sister in the capital.] ● Often a sympathetic neighbor is of more use than a distant relative. ● A near neighbor is better than a distant cousin. = 親しき隣は遠き兄弟に優る = 遠い親類より近くの他人 ♦ ❷ 近火で手を焙れ

### 今日の綴れ、明日の錦

[Today's rags, tomorrow's brocade.] ● In life, nothing is constant; though in dire straits today, one may be wealthy tomorrow. ● A nobody today, a prince tomorrow. ＝ 昨日の綴れ、今日の錦 ＝ 昨日の淵は今日の瀬 ♦ 入り船あれば出船あり ♦ 有為転変は世の習い ♦ 禍福は糾える縄の如し ♦ 殺す神あれば助ける神あり ♦ 沈む瀬あれば浮かぶ瀬あり ♦ 捨てる神はあれば助ける神あり ≠ 昨日の錦、今日の綴れ ≠ 昨日の花は今日の夢

### 今日の敵は明日の味方

[Today's foe may be tomorrow's ally.] ● People change; those who are enemies today may prove to be allies tomorrow. ● A friend today may turn a foe tomorrow. ＝ 昨日の敵は今日の味方 ♦ 入り船あれば出船あり ♦ 有為転変は世の習い ♦ 禍福は糾える縄の如し ♦ 殺す神あれば助ける神あり ♦ 沈む瀬あれば浮かぶ瀬あり ♦ 捨てる神はあれば助ける神あり ≠ 昨日の友は今日の仇 ≠ 昨日の情けは今日の仇 ≠ 今日の味方は明日の敵

### 今日の一針は明日の十針

[Today's one stitch, tomorrow's ten stitches.] ● It is better to do simple repairs at regular intervals than wait and be faced with major repairs. Similarly, if one leaves today's work undone one will have to do two days worth of work tomorrow. ● A stitch in time saves nine. ＝ 今の一針、後の十針 ＝ 今の一字は明日の二字

### 今日の味方は明日の敵

[Today's ally may be tomorrow's foe.] ● In life, nothing is constant and those who are friends today may prove to be enemies tomorrow. ● A friend today may turn a foe tomorrow. ＝ 昨日の友は今日の仇 ＝ 昨日の情けは今日の仇 ♦ 入り船あれば出船あり ♦ 禍福は糾える縄の如し ♦ 殺す神あれば助ける神あり ♦ 沈む瀬あれば浮かぶ瀬あり ♦ 捨てる神はあれば助ける神あり ≠ 昨日の友は今日の仇 ≠ 昨日の敵は今日の味方

### 今日は今日、明日は明日の風が吹く

[Today, today's wind blows; tomorrow, tomorrow's wind blows.]

● There is no knowing what tomorrow will bring, so there is no use in worrying about future problems. • Tomorrow will take care of itself. • Sufficient unto the day is the evil thereof. = 明日は明日の風が吹く = 明日の事は明日案じよ

### 今日は人の身、明日は我が身

[Today the plight of others; tomorrow my own plight.] ● No matter how fortunate one may count oneself, no one is immune from hardships; tomorrow one may suffer the same setbacks that are today suffered by others. • What chances to one man may happen to all. =今日の哀れ、明日は我が身

### 局に当たる者は惑う

[(It is) those who are in charge of affairs (who) are at a loss.] ● Those who are in power often have difficulty getting a balanced view of the situation and may need the advice of a disinterested observer to be able to make the right decisions. • Lookers-on see more than players. ◆ 近くて見えぬは睫 ◆ 我が身の上は見えぬ ◆ ❶ 堤灯持ちの足元暗し ◆ ❶ 灯台下暗し

### 清水の舞台から飛び降りる

[Jump from the platform of Kiyomizu temple.] ☞ The shrine of the Goddess of Mercy at Kiyomizu Temple in Kyoto is situated at the edge of a bluff. Consequently, to jump from the shrine's platform is to irrevocably risk one's life. ● Describes making a decision that will determine one's success or ruin. • Cross the Rubicon. = 糧を捨てて船を沈む = 背水の陣 ◆ 死を先んずる者は必ず生ず ◆ 身を捨ててこそ浮かぶ瀬も有れ

### 麒麟も老ゆれば駑馬に劣る

[A *kirin* grown old is inferior to a hack.] ✍ The *kirin* (麒麟), or *qilin* in Chinese, is a mythical animal with the body of a deer, the hoofs of a horse and horns. It is also used to denote a horse that can run a thousand *ri* (里) in one day. ● When a person with great gifts grows old, their talents eventually become worse than mediocre. = 老いては麒麟も駑馬に劣る ≠ 腐っても鯛

## 金牛を駆りて路を開く

[Open the road by driving a golden ox.] ☞ This proverb is based on a Chinese historical anecdote in which the lord of Qin sets out to conquer the neighboring province of Shu. The main obstacle in achieving his aim is the absence of any road from Qin to the capital of Shu. The lord thus has craftsmen make a large ox of stone, which he places on the border between the two provinces while spreading a rumor that the cow excretes gold. On hearing this, the covetous lord of Shu has a road built to reach the ox, so it can be transported to his capital. No sooner is the road completed than the forces of Qin march on the capital of Shu and conquer it. ● Used in cases where (some)one gains the upper hand by cleverly utilizing the opponent's greed.

## 金玉の宝も正直の宝に如かず

[Not even a treasure of gold is equal to the treasure of honesty.] ● The value of honesty supersedes that of all the riches in the world.
• Knavery may serve but for a turn, but honesty is best at long run.
♦ 正しき者は艱難多し ≠ 商人と屏風は曲がらねば世に立たぬ ≠ 商売と屏風は曲がらぬと立たぬ ≠ 屏風と商人は真直ぐにては立たぬもの

## 金玉は実の宝にあらず、善人を以て宝とす

[Golden riches are not a real treasure, but a good person is.] ● The deeds of the good are of greater value to their country than the greatest riches.

## 勤勉は福の神

[Diligence is the god of good fortune.] ● Those who are diligent are likely to lead a life of prosperity and fulfillment. • Care and diligence bring good luck. • Industry is fortune's right hand. • Diligence is the mother of good luck. ♦ 朝謡は貧乏の相 ♦ 稼ぐに追い付く貧乏無し ♦ 酒と朝寝は貧乏の近道 ♦ 好きの道には薦被る

## 金を泥に棄て玉を淵に沈む

[Discard money in the mud and let jewels sink into the abyss.] 📖 This proverb is taken from the *Taiheiki*, a 14th-century Japanese historical epic. ● If one is to lead an upright and honest life, it is better not to expose oneself to the temptations of wealth. ● He is rich enough that wants nothing. = 金を山に蔵し玉は淵に蔵す

# ク

## 苦有れば楽有り

[If there is suffering there is comfort.] ● True happiness is only found by living through hardships and overcoming them. Consequently, if there suffering today, there may be joy tomorrow. ● After pain comes pleasure. ● No pleasure without pain. = 喜び有れば憂い有り = 楽有れば苦有り ◆ 苦は楽の種 ◆ 苦を知らぬ者は楽を知らぬ ◆ 現在の甘露は未来の鉄丸なり ◆ 楽しみは憂いに生ず ◆ 楽しみは苦しみの種 ◆ 夏歌う者は冬泣く ◆ 楽は苦の種

## 腐っても鯛

[Though rotten, it is still a sea bream.] ● Though they may get old and appear obsolete, superior things always keep their value. ● An old eagle is better than a young crow. ● Once a winner, always a winner. ≠ 麒麟も老ゆれば駑馬に劣る

## 愚者の作る善は善ともに罪、知者の作る罪は罪ともに善

[The good of fools, though good, contains wrong; the wrongs of the wise, though wrong, contain good.] ● The actions of a fool, even though intended to achieve good, may be the cause of ill; the actions of a wise person, though they may be intended as a punishment, will be the source of good.

## 愚者の雄弁は沈黙なり

[A fool's eloquence is silence.] ● For fools it is better to say nothing rather than embarrass themselves. ● Little said is soon amended. = 沈黙は愚者の機知である ◆ 知る者は言わず言う者は知らず ◆ 雀の千声鶴の一声

## 愚者は書を得て賢に、賢者は書に因って利あり

[The ignorant may become wise by obtaining books; the wise may gain by writing books.] ● The ignorant may gain knowledge by acquiring the works of the wise; the wise may gain profit by writing books. ● Reading maketh a full man, conference a ready man, and writing an exact man. ● Learning makes a good man better and an ill man worse. = 愚は書を得て賢となり、賢は書に因って利あり ◆ 性相近し、習い相遠し ◆ 貧しき者は書に因って富み、富める者は書に因って貴し

## 愚者も千慮に一得あり

[Fools, too, may have their virtue.] ● Even less talented people will be good at at least one skill or task, and thus be able to play a useful role. ● A fool's bolt may sometimes hit the mark. ● Even a fool may at times give good counsel. = 馬鹿も一芸 ◆ 門脇の姥にも用有り ◆ 枯れ木も山の賑わい ◆ 癖ある馬に乗りあり ◆ 蹴る馬も乗り手次第 ◆ ❷ 時に遭えば鼠も虎となる ◆ 馬鹿と鋏は使い様 ◆ 貧乏人も三年置けば用に立つ ◆ ❷ 用いる時は鼠も虎となる ◆ 野郎と鋏が使い様 ◆ 湯腹も一時、松の木柱も三年 ◆ 割れ鍋も三年置けば用に立つ

## 薬も過ぎれば毒となる

[Medicine when taken in excess turns into poison.] ● Even things that are good for the body and soul may be harmful when taken in excess. ● Too much wax burns the church. ● Too much water drowns the miller. ◆ 酒は百毒の長 ◆ 酒は百薬の長 ◆ 及ばざるは過ぎたるより勝れり ◆ 過ぎたる猶及ばざるが如し

## 癖ある馬に乗りあり

[Even a vicious horse may be broken in]. ● Even difficult people may change their attitudes when approached in the right manner. = 蹴る馬も乗り手次第 ◆ 門脇の姥にも用有り ◆ 枯れ木も山の賑わい ◆ 愚者も千慮に一徳あり ◆ ❷ 時に遭えば鼠も虎となる ◆ 馬鹿と鋏は使い様 ◆ 馬鹿も一芸 ◆ 貧乏人も三年置けば用に立つ ◆ ❷ 用いる時は鼠も虎となる ◆ 野郎と鋏が使い様 ◆ 湯腹も一時、松の木柱も三年 ◆ 割れ鍋も三年置けば用に立つ

## 口数の多い者は襤褸を出す

[Those who talk much expose their faults.] ● The more one talks, the more one increases the risk of being caught stating inaccuracies.

• One who talks much errs much. ＝言葉多ければ恥多し ◆ 一寸の舌に五尺の身を損ず ◆ 言わぬが花 ◆ 口は災いの元 ◆ 君子は九度思いて一度言う ◆ 三寸の舌に五尺の身を亡ぼす ◆ 舌は禍の根 ◆ 沈黙は金、雄弁は銀 ◆ 禍は口から

## 口に甘き物かならずしも腹を養わず

[What is sweet in the mouth does not necessarily nourish the stomach.] ● Things desirable at first sight are not necessarily good in the long run. • That is not always good in the maw that is sweet. • Bitter pills may have wholesome effects. ◆ 良薬口に苦し

## 口に蜜有り腹に剣有り

[To have honey in one's mouth, and a sword in one's stomach.] ● Said of those who speak sweet words with an evil intent. • A honey tongue, a heart of gall. ＝追従する者陰にて誹る ◆ 甘言は愚人を喜ばしむ ◆ 信言は美ならず、美言は信ならず ◆ 天子将軍の事でも陰では言う ◆ 天子将軍も障子の内 ◆ 耳の楽しむ時は慎むべし

## 口は災いの元

[The mouth is the origin of disaster.] ● A remark made in an unguarded moment may be the cause of irreparable damage. • Little said is soon amended. ＝一寸の舌に五尺の身を損ず ＝三寸の舌に五尺の身を亡ぼす ＝舌は禍の根 ＝禍は口から ◆ 言わぬが花 ◆ 口数の多い者は襤褸を出す ◆ 君子は九度思いて一度言う ◆ 言葉多ければ恥多し ◆ 沈黙は金、雄弁は銀

## 国に入っては先ずその法を聞く

[When entering a country, first learn its laws.] 📖 This proverb is attributed to Mencius. ● To achieve one's goals one should obey the laws of the place one is in. • When in Rome, do as the Romans do. ＝境に入っては禁を問え ◆ 郷に入っては郷に従え ◆ 里に入りては里に従う ◆ 俗に入っては俗に従え ◆ 其の国に入れば其の俗に従う

## 国に盗人家に鼠

[Robbers in countries, mice in houses.] ● Each entity has its own particular parasites.

## 国乱れて忠臣現わる

[When a country is in turmoil loyal retainers (will) appear.] ● When a country is in danger and without strong leadership, capable people who love their country will rise to lead it. Similarly, people of quality tend to come to the fore in times of trouble. • The night bring out the stars. = 国家昏乱して忠臣あり ◆ 家貧しくして孝子顕わる

## 苦は色変わる松の風

[Among the pines the wind of a changed hardship.] ☞ This proverb derives from an old Japanese song that relates how a man renounces the world to go and live in the mountains so that his spirit may be soothed by the wind in the pine trees, only to find that even in exile he is beset by hardships though they may have changed in nature. ● Suffering is an inalienable part of life and all of us are subject to it at some point. = 浮き世に苦労の無い者は無い

## 愚は書を得て賢となり、賢は書に因って利あり

[The ignorant may become wise by obtaining books; the wise may gain by writing books.] ● The ignorant may gain in knowledge by acquiring the works of the wise; the wise may gain profit by writing books. • Reading maketh a full man, conference a ready man, and writing an exact man. • Learning makes a good man better and an ill man worse. = 愚者は書を得て賢に、賢者は書に因って利あり ◆ 性相近し、習い相遠し ◆ 貧しき者は書に因って富み、富める者は書に因って貴し

## 苦は楽の種

[Suffering is the seed of comfort.] ● True happiness is only found by living through hardships and overcoming them. Consequently, the suffering one undergoes at present may be the price one has to pay to enjoy a life of comfort in the future. • After pain comes pleasure. • No cross, no crown. • No pleasure without pain. = 苦を知らぬ者は楽を知らぬ = 楽しみは憂いに生ず ◆ 苦有れば楽有り ◆ 喜び有れば憂い有り ◆ 楽有れば苦有り ≠ 現在の甘露は未来の鉄丸なり ≠ 楽しみは苦しみの種 ≠ 夏歌う者は冬泣く ≠ 楽は苦の種

## 窪い所に水溜まる

[Water will gather in a hollow.] ❶ Where the right conditions are met, people and money will gather naturally. ❷ Where the coarse and common gather, crime will flourish naturally.

## 苦しい時の神頼み

[Invoking the gods in times of distress.] ● When times turn hard people turn to their gods; when times are good they forget them. • Vows made in storms are forgotten in calms. • Danger past and God forgotten. • The peril past, the saint mocked. = 恐い時の仏頼み ♦ 暑さ忘れて蔭忘る ♦ 雨晴れて笠を忘る ♦ 叶わぬ時の神叩き ♦ 狡兎死して走狗烹らる ♦ 災害は忘れた頃にやって来る ♦ 喉元過ぎれば熱さを忘れる ♦ 病治りて薬師忘る

## 苦労は出世の梯子

[Hardships are the ladder to advancement.] ● One cannot expect to make headway in life without trials and tribulations. • Who in time present from pleasure refrain shall in time to come the more pleasure obtain. ♦ 浮き世に苦労の無い者は無い ♦ 苦を知らぬ者は楽を知らぬ ♦ 失敗は成功の基

## 苦を知らぬ者は楽を知らぬ

[Those who know no hardships know no comfort.] ● If one has not experienced the pains of a life of hardships one will not be able to compare and thus appreciate the joys of a life of ease. • River deep, mountain high. • No pleasure without pain. • Rest comes from unrest. = 苦は楽の種 = 楽しみは憂いに生ず ♦ 苦有れば楽有り ♦ 喜び有れば憂い有り ♦ 楽有れば苦有り ≠ 現在の甘露は未来の鉄丸なり ≠ 楽しみは苦しみの種 ≠ 夏歌う者は冬泣く ≠ 楽は苦の種

## 君子の過ちは日月の食の如し

[The erring of a man of virtue is like the eclipse of the sun and moon.] 📖 This proverb is taken from the works of Mencius. ● When good people stray from the proper path, their error will be obvious to all and they will soon correct themselves. • Show a good man his error, and he turns it to a virtue; but an ill, it doubles his fault. ◆ 過ちて改めざる是を過ちと謂う ◆ 過ちは改むる に憚る事なかれ ◆ 地に倒るる者は地によりて立つ

## 君子の学は善を留むること無く、問いを宿すること無し

[In the learning of a man of virtue, there is no halting of good nor stalling of questions.] 📖 This proverb is attributed to the Chinese Confucianist Xunzi. ● When good people apply themselves to learning, there will be no discrepancy between what they have learned and what they practice; as soon as they have learned how to do good they will put their knowledge into action; as soon as they find a lacuna in their knowledge they will ask the right questions. ● He cannot be virtuous that is not rigorous. ◆ 心の欲する所に従えども矩を踰えず

## 君子は危うきに近寄らず

[Men of virtue will not draw near to danger.] 📖 This proverb is taken from the *Analects* of Confucius. ● Good people will be careful about how they speak and act, and thus avoid dangerous situations. ● Discretion is the better part of valor. ● Danger is next neighbor to security. = 聖人は危うきに近寄らず ◆ 危ない事は怪我の内 ◆ 三十六計逃ぐるに如かず ◆ 重宝を抱くる者は夜行せず ◆ ❷ 馬鹿さしじ がれば二がえ馬鹿 ≠ 盲蛇に怖じず

## 君子は九度思いて一度言う

[A man of virtue will think nine times and speak once.] 📖 This proverb is taken from the *Analects* of Confucius. ● Good people will turn something over in their mind many times before they finally speak. ● Little said is soon amended. ◆ 一寸の舌に五尺の 身を損ず ◆ 言わぬが花 ◆ 口数の多い者は襤褸を出す ◆ 口は災いの元 ◆ 言葉多ければ恥多し ◆ 三寸の舌に五尺の身を亡ぼす ◆ 舌は禍の根 ◆ 沈黙は金、雄弁は銀 ◆ 禍は口から

## 君子は其の罪を憎んで其の人を憎まず

[Men of virtue hate the sin but not the sinner.] ● Good people believe that crimes must be condemned but that those who commit them should be forgiven. ● One hates not the person, but the vice. = 其の罪を憎んで其の人を憎まず

# ケ

##### けいかい　けいび
### 警戒は警備なり

[A warning is a defense.] ● Notice of a looming danger allows one to take precautions. ● Forewarned is forearmed. ♦ 銭有る時は銭無き日を思え ♦ 治に居て乱を忘れず

##### げい　み　たす　　ほど　ふ　し　あ
### 芸が身を助ける程の不仕合わせ

[Accomplishments are a misery as deep as they are helpful.] ☞ This is a parody on the proverb 芸は身を助ける. ● Those who have mastered an art or skill solely to fill one's idle hours with merriment during times of plenty, may find those same skills vital for earning a living in the lean years that are the result of one's prodigal living. ● Art brings bread. = 若い時の遊芸が用に立つ ♦ 芸は身を助けぬ籠の鶉 ♦ 芸は身を助ける

##### けいぐん　　いっかく
### 鶏群の一鶴

[One crane among a flock of hens.] ● Among a crowd of ordinary people, one with talent will stand out. ● Triton amongst the minnows. = 掃き溜めに鶴 ♦ 一文は無文の師

##### けいこう　　　ぎゅうご　　　なか
### 鶏口となるも牛後となる勿れ

[Better be the beak of a hen than the rear of a cow.] ● Rather than play a minor part in a major event, it is better to play a leading role in a minor event. Similarly, rather than be an unimportant member of a large group, it is better to be the leader of a small group. ● Better be a chicken's head than an ox's rump. ● Better be first in a village than second in Rome. = 大鳥の尾より小鳥の頭 = 鯛の尾より鰯の頭 ≠ 鰯の頭より鯛の尾

##### けいし　　あ　やす　じんし　あ　がた
### 経師は遇い易く人師は遇い難し

[It is easy to meet a teacher of the Buddhist scriptures; it is difficult to meet a teacher of people.] ● Those who lecture from the Buddhist scriptures are easy to find, but it is difficult to find those who can teach one the proper way to live. = 経師を得るは易く心の師を得るは難し

**け**

## 経師を得るは易く心の師を得るは難し

[It is easy to find a teacher of the Buddhist scriptures; it is difficult to obtain a teacher of the heart.] ● Those who lecture from the Buddhist scriptures are easy to find, but it is difficult to find those who know the proper way to live. = 経師は遇い易く人師は遇い難し

## 芸は道に依りて賢し

[Every person is clever in their own art.] ● Someone who has mastered an art or a skill will be better in practicing it than the average person. ● Every man must labor in his own calling. ● Every man to his trade. = 鹿つきの山は猟師知り、魚つきの浦は網人知る ◆ 海の事は漁父に問え ◆ 海老踊れども川を出でず ◆ 鴉が鵜の真似 ◆ 酒は酒屋に茶は茶屋に ◆ 田作る道は農に問え ◆ 餅は餅屋

## 芸は身に付く

[Accomplishments stay with a person.] ● While fame and fortune are fleeting, mastery of an art is a treasure for life. ● Art holds fast when all else is lost. ◆ 芸は身を助ける ◆ 芸が身を助ける程の不仕合わせ ◆ 芸は身を助けぬ籠の鶉 ◆ 若い時の遊芸が用に立つ

## 芸は身を助けぬ籠の鶉

[Its accomplishments do not save the quail in the cage.] ● No matter how beautiful its song, the caged quail does not have the power to free itself. By extension, those esteemed for their accomplishments are not necessarily freed by them; indeed, they might be trapped by them. ◆ 芸が身を助ける程の不仕合わせ ◆ 芸は身を助ける ◆ 若い時の遊芸が用に立つ

## 芸は身を助ける

[Accomplishments can save a person.] ● Those who have mastered a skill may earn a living by practicing it. ● Art brings bread. ◆ 芸が身を助ける程の不仕合わせ ◆ 芸は身を助けぬ籠の鶉 ◆ 若い時の遊芸が用に立つ

## 下戸の建てたる蔵も無し

[No teetotaler ever became a millionaire.] ● Both work and pleasure should be enjoyed in good measure. • All work and no play makes Jack a dull boy.

### 芥子の中に須弥山有り

[Mount Sumeru within a poppy seed.] ✍ Mount Sumeru (須弥山) in Buddhist lore is said to stand at the center of the world and tower over all that surrounds it. • Small and apparently insignificant things may contain great wonders. • Great oaks grow from little acorns. • A forrest in an acorn.

### 下衆無い上﨟は成らず

[No court lady without a vulgar fellow.] • Without the labor of people of low rank the court could not be splendid. By extension, high and low are both necessary and inseparable.

### 下衆の後知恵

[The afterwit of the vulgar fellow.] • It is always easy to come up with good ideas after a crisis has passed. Conversely, to know how to handle a crisis when it happens is a skill possessed only by the above-average. • It is easy to be wise after the event. • Afterwit is a fool's wit. = 腰抜け武士の後思案

### 下衆の一寸鈍間の三寸馬鹿の開けっ放し

[The one *sun* of the vulgar fellow, the three *sun* of the dunce and the leaving open of the idiot.] ✍ The Japanese *sun* (寸) is a traditional unit of measurement still used by Japanese craftsmen. One *sun* is roughly three centimeters. • When an uncivilized person passes through a Japanese sliding door, he may leave it open by one *sun*; a dunce will leave it open by three *sun*; an idiot will fail to close it altogether. = 鈍間の一寸馬鹿の三寸

### 下駄も仏も同じ木の切れ

[*Geta* and the Buddha are both from wood.] ✍ *Geta* (下駄) are traditional Japanese wooden clogs. • Though people may differ in status, are all of the same flesh and should be treated accordingly. • Clogs and effigies are all of the same wood. ♦ 冥途の道に王無し

## 外面女菩薩内心女夜叉

[Outwardly a female *bodhisattva*, inwardly a female *yaksa*.] ✍ In Buddhist lore the *bodhisattva* (菩薩) is a saintly being, while a *yaksa* (夜叉) is a spirit who lives in the forests and preys on people's souls. ● Used to describe women whose outer appearance and deportment suggest a kind and benign nature, but whose true character is cruel and malign. • An angel without, a devil within. ≠ 糠の中にも粉米

## 蹴る馬も乗り手次第

[Even a kicking horse (may be broken in) depending on the handler.] ● Even difficult people may change their attitude when approached in the right manner. = 癖ある馬に乗りあり ↑ 門脇の姥にも用有り ↑ 枯れ木も山の賑わい ↑ 愚者も千慮に一徳あり ↑ ❷ 時に遭えば鼠も虎となる ↑ 馬鹿と鋏は使い様 ↑ 馬鹿も一芸 ↑ ❷ 用いる時は鼠も虎となる ↑ 野郎と鋏が使い様

## 喧嘩過ぎての棒乳切り

[Cutting the clubs after the fight.] ● To try to remedy a problem when it is too late. • Lock the stable door after the horse is stolen. • After death, the doctor. After meat, mustard. = 戦を見て矢を矧ぐ = 賊去って張弓 = 賊の後の棒乳切り = 敵を見て矢を矧ぐ = 泥棒を捕らえて縄を綯う = 難に臨んで兵を鋳る = 盗人を見て縄を綯う = 火を失して池を掘る ↑ 後の祭 ↑ 六日の菖蒲、十日の菊 ↑ 盆過ぎての鯖商い

## 喧嘩に被る笠は無し

[There is no hat that will protect one from quarrels.] ● No matter how much one may try to make the right arrangements, disputes may still arise. • There is no preparing for calamities. ↑ 雨が降れば土砂降り ↑ 泣き面に蜂が刺す ↑ 二度ある事は三度ある ↑ ❷ 目の寄る所へ玉が寄る ↑ 弱り目に崇り目

## 現在の因果を見て過去未来を知る

[Knowing the past and future by observing today's cause and effect.] ● Today we suffer or enjoy the results of yesterdays actions; tomorrow we may suffer or enjoy the results of today's actions. Thus we can know the past and the future by carefully observing the results and actions of today. • Things present are judged by things past. ◆ 古きを温ねて新しきを知る ◆ 来を知らんと欲する者は往を察す ≠ 昔は昔、今は今

## 現在の甘露は未来の鉄丸なり

[Today's nectar is tomorrow's bullet.] ● Those who are living it up today may suffer the consequences of their indulgence tomorrow. • After pleasure comes pain. • Every pleasure has a pain. = 楽しみは苦しみの種 = 夏歌う者は冬泣く = 楽は苦の種 ◆ 苦有れば楽有り ◆ 喜び有れば憂い有り ◆ 楽有れば苦有り ≠ 苦を知らぬ者は楽を知らぬ ≠ 苦は楽の種 ≠ 楽しみは憂いに生ず

## 賢者も千慮の一失

[Even the intelligent may fail once in a thousand ponderings.] ● Even those who seem complete masters of their craft may sometimes get it wrong. • Homer sometimes nods. • A good marksman may miss. = 王良も時として馬車を覆す = 河童の川流れ = 弘法にも筆の誤り = 猿も木から落ちる = 知者にも千慮の一失 = 上手の手から水が漏れる = 竜馬の躓き

# コ

## 子有れば万事足る

[To have children is the fulfillment of all things.] ● The joy and comfort of having children is sufficient to make up for all other difficulties of life. • Children are poor men's riches. ◆ 子を持って知る親の恩 ≠ ❷ 子が無くて泣く者は無い

## 恋いたほど飽いた

[One tires of a person to the degree that one loves them.] ✍ Koi (恋) stands for romantic love, which is often selfish, whereas ai (愛) stands for emotional love, which is usually altruistic. ● Those who fall in love passionately tend to fall out of love with equal passion. • Hot love is soon cool. ◆ 近惚れの早飽き ◆ 熱し易いは冷め易し

### 恋と戦は手段を選ばず

[Love and war do not discriminate between methods.] ✍ *Koi* (恋) stands for romantic love, which is often selfish, whereas *ai* (愛) stands for emotional love, which is usually altruistic. ● The strength of emotions aroused in love and war may cause people to behave immorally. • All is fair in love and war. = 恋は手段を選ばず

### 恋に上下の隔て無し

[There is no distinction between high and low when it comes to love.] ✍ *Koi* (恋) stands for romantic love, which is often selfish, whereas *ai* (愛) stands for emotional love, which is usually altruistic. ● Love is a universal emotion that can affect every one at every level of society. • Love makes men equal. • Love levels all ranks. = 愛は宮殿にも藁屋にも住む

### 恋に同伴は邪魔

[In love, company is a nuisance.] ✍ *Koi* (恋) stands for romantic love, which is often selfish, whereas *ai* (愛) stands for emotional love, which is usually altruistic. ● Two people deeply in love prefer to be on their own. • Love likes no fellowship. • Three is a crowd.

### 恋の至極は忍ぶ恋

[The pinnacle of love is secret love.] ✍ *Koi* (恋) stands for romantic love, which is often selfish, whereas *ai* (愛) stands for emotional love, which is usually altruistic. ● Forbidden love inspires the deepest passion. • Stolen sweets are best. ♦ 会わねば愛しさいや優る

### 恋の山には孔子の倒れ

[On the mountain of love Confucius stumbles.] ✍ *Koi* (恋) stands for romantic love, which is often selfish, whereas *ai* (愛) stands for emotional love, which is usually altruistic. ● In love, even a sage may be disappointed at times.

### 恋は思案の外

[Love is beyond reflection.] ✍ *Koi* (恋) stands for romantic love, which is often selfish, whereas *ai* (愛) stands for emotional love, which is usually altruistic. ● Those who are deeply in love will not listen to reason. • Love and reason do not go together. • One cannot love and be wise. • Love is without reason. = 色は思案の外 ♦ 愛屋烏に及ぶ ♦ 止めて止まらぬ恋の道 ♦ 惚れた病に薬無し ♦ 惚れ病と馬鹿の治る薬は無い

## 恋は手段を選ばず

[Love is not selective in its methods.] ✍ *Koi* (恋) stands for romantic love, which is often selfish, whereas *ai* (愛) stands for emotional love, which is usually altruistic. ● The strength of emotions aroused by love causes people to behave inappropriately or irrationally. • All is fair in love (and war). = 恋と戦は手段を選ばず

## 恋は盲目

[Love is blind.] ✍ *Koi* (恋) stands for romantic love, which is often selfish, whereas *ai* (愛) stands for emotional love, which is usually altruistic. ☞ This proverb derives from its English equivalent. ● True love prevents one from seeing faults in the person loved. • Love is blind. = 惚れた欲目

## 光陰に関守無し

[There is no keeper at the barrier of time.] ● It is not within the power of humans to stop or reverse time. • Time and tide wait for none. = 月日に関守無し ♦ 光陰人を待たず ♦ 歳月人を待たず ♦ 盛年重ねて来たらず ♦ 若い時は二度無い ♦ 若きは二度と無し

## 光陰人を待たず

[Time waits for no one.] 📖 This proverb is taken from the *Taiheiki*, a 14th-century Japanese historical epic. ● Time will pass regardless of one's plans, and opportunities that are missed now are lost forever. • Time and tide wait for none. = 歳月人を待たず ♦ 光陰に関守無し ♦ 月日に関守無し ♦ 盛年重ねて来たらず ♦ 若い時は二度無い ♦ 若きは二度と無し

## 光陰矢の如し

[Time is like an arrow.] ● Time passes much faster than one would

wish. ● Time flies like an arrow. = 光陰流水の如し = 歳月流るる如し
♦ 光陰夢の如し

## 光陰夢の如し

[Time is like a dream.] ● All experiences in life are fleeting and soon only vaguely remembered. ● All that we see or seem is but a dream within a dream. ● We are such stuff as dreams are made on, rounded with a little sleep, ♦ 光陰矢の如し ♦ 歳月流るる如し

## 光陰流水の如し

[Time is like a flowing river.] ● Time passes steadily and inexorably and no power can stop it. ● Time flies like an arrow. = 光陰矢の如し = 歳月流るる如し ♦ 光陰夢の如し

## 後悔先に立たず

[Repentance never comes beforehand.] ● By the time one repents one's words or actions it is usually too late. ● Repentance comes too late. ● It is no use crying over spilt milk. ● What is done cannot be undone. ♦ 五十にして四十九年の非を知る ♦ 死んだ子の年を数える ♦ 後悔は知恵の糸口 ♦ 覆水盆に返らず ♦ 流水源に返らず

## 後悔は知恵の糸口

[Repentance is the start of wisdom.] ● Only when one admits and regrets one's folly does one begin to learn. ● Never too late to repent. = 五十にして四十九年の非を知る ♦ 後悔先に立たず ♦ 懺悔は十罪ばを滅す

## 好機逸す可からず

[One should not let go of a good opportunity.] ● When opportunity beckons one should not fail to seize the moment. ● Make hay while the sun shines. ♦ 一寸の光陰軽んず可からず ♦ 逢うた時に笠を脱げ ♦ 善は急げ ♦ 時は得難くして失い易し ♦ 時を得る者は昌え、時を失う者は亡ぶ

## 巧言令色鮮し仁

[Flattery and servile looks, little virtue.] 📖 This proverb is taken

こ

from the *Analects* of Confucius. ● Pleasing words and winning appearance often disguise a lack of character. ● Much eloquence, little conscience. ● Fair without, false within. ▶ 衣ばかりで和尚は出来ぬ ▶ 衣を染めんより心を染めよ ▶ 鞘が無くても身は光る ▶ 数珠ばかりで和尚が出来ぬ ▶ 人肥えたるが故に尊からず ▶ 見目より心 ▶ 山高きが故に貴からず

## 孝行のしたい時分に親は無し

[At the moment one wants to practice filial piety there are no parents.] ● When children finally reach an age where they understand the sacrifices their parents have made on their behalf and eager to express their gratitude their parents may have passed away. ▶ 子を持って知る親の恩

## 高山の巓には美木無し

[There are no fair trees on the summit of high mountains.] ● People who attain high social status will be exposed to greater public scrutiny, and when they are afflicted by scandal, the degree of public pressure will be commensurate. ● Great winds blow upon high hills. ● High regions are never without storms. ▶ ❶ 大きい家に大きい風が吹く ▶ 高木風に憎まる ▶ 高木風に妬まる ▶ 高木は風に折らる ▶ 大木は風に折らる ▶ ❷ 出る杭は打たれる ▶ 大名の下には久しく居るべからず ▶ 誉れは誇りの基

## 孔子に論語

[Teaching the *Analects* to Confucius.] ☞ The *Analects*, or *Lun-yu* (論語), are a collection of Confucius' sayings compiled by his pupils shortly after his death. ● Describes someone trying to teach a lesson to an expert. ● A sow teaching Minerva. ● Teach your grandmother to suck eggs. = お釈迦様に経を聞かせる = 釈迦に説法

## 好事魔多し

[Good things, many devils.] ● It seems always that just when everything is going according to plan that troubles tend to arise. ● Lights are followed by shadows. ▶ 勝って兜の緒を締めよ ▶ 百里を行く者は九十を半ばとす

## 好事門を出でず

[Good news does not leave the gate.] Words, good deeds, or a good reputation often inspire jealousy so are not quickly passed along.
• The evil than men do lives after them, the good is oft interred with their bones. = 悪事千里を走る ◆ 手形は残れど足形は残らず ◆ 人は一代、名は末代 ◆ 身は一代、名は末代 ≠ 蔭徳有れば陽報有り

## 孝立てば則ち忠遂ぐ

[Those who are filial achieve loyalty.] ☞ This deeply Confucian view of the organization of society prevailed throughout Japan's feudal era and may still be observed. ● In displaying filial piety toward their parents, children will automatically show their loyalty toward those whom their parents serve. = 忠臣を孝子の門に求む ◆ 貞女は孝女の門に出づ

## 狡兎死して走狗烹らる

[Boil the hound when the cunning rabbit is dead.] ● Even something of great use will be discarded when no longer needed. • Vows made in storms are forgotten in calms. • Danger past and God forgotten. • The peril past, the saint mocked. = 魚を得て筌を忘る = 飛鳥尽きて良弓蔵る ◆ 暑さ忘れて蔭忘る ◆ 雨晴れて笠を忘る ◆ 苦しい時の神頼 ◆ 恐い時の仏頼み ◆ 災害は忘れた頃にやって来る ◆ 喉元過ぎれば熱さを忘れる ◆ 病治りて薬師忘る

## 郷に入っては郷に従え

[When entering a district, do as the district does.] ● To avoid trouble and to achieve one's goals one should obey the laws of the place one is in. • When in Rome, do as the Romans do. = 里に入りては里に従う = 俗に入っては俗に従え = 其の国に入れば其の俗に従う ◆ 国に入っては先ずその法を聞 ◆ 境に入っては禁を問え

## 甲に適するものは乙にも適する

[What is suitable for the one is suitable for the other.] ● Things that are beneficial to oneself are likely to be beneficial to others, too. • What is sauce for the goose is sauce for the gander. ≠ 甲の薬は乙の毒

## 甲の薬は乙の毒

[What is medicine for one is poison for the other.] ● A remedy that may prove helpful to one person may prove harmful to another. • One man's meat is another man's poison. ≠ 甲に適するものは乙にも適する

## 高飛の鳥も美食に死す

[Even high-flying birds find their death in dainty food.] ● Like the bird who is lured from the sky with bait, so noble and high-minded people may be led astray by worldly desires or the sordid temptations of the gutter.

## 好物に祟りなし

[There is no evil in food one likes to eat.] ● There is no harm in eating food one enjoys. Similarly, one does not tire from work that one enjoys. • Content works all ambrosia. = 得食に毒無し

## 弘法にも筆の誤り

[Even Kōbō may err in his writing.] ☞ Kōbō Daishi, better known by the name of Kūkai (774-835), was the founder of the Shingon school of Buddhism and is known for his mastery of the art of calligraphy. ● Even those who seem complete masters of their craft may sometimes get it wrong. • Homer sometimes nods. • A good marksman may miss. = 王良も時として馬車を覆す = 河童の川流れ = 賢者も千慮の一失 = 猿も木から落ちる = 知者にも千慮の一失 = 上手の手から水が漏れる = 竜馬の躓き

## 弘法は筆を択ばず

[Kōbō is not particular about his (writing) brush.] ☞ Kōbō Daishi, better known by the name of Kūkai (774-835), was the founder of the Shingon school of Buddhism and is known for his mastery of the art of calligraphy. ● Those who are masters of their craft will be able to make a masterpiece, even with inferior tools. • A poor craftsman quarrels with his tools. = 能書筆を択ばず = 名人は筆を択ばず = 名筆は筆を択ばず = 良工は材を択ばず ♦ 下手な番匠木の難を言う ♦ 下手の道具調べ

## 高木風に憎まる／妬まる

[Great trees are the envy of the wind.] ● Important people often incur envy that can bring them down. • Tall trees catch much wind. • The highest in court, the nearest the gallows. = 大木は風に折らる = ❷ 出る杭は打たれる ▶ ❶ 大きい家に大きい風が吹く ▶ 高山の巓には美木無し ▶ 高木は風に折らる ▶ 大名の下には久しく居るべからず ▶ 誉れは誇りの基

## 高木は風に折らる

[Great trees are broken by the wind.] ● Important people often incur envy that can bring them down. • Tall trees catch much wind. • The highest in court, the nearest the gallows. = 高木風に憎まる = ❷ 出る杭は打たれる ▶ ❶ 大きい家に大きい風が吹く ▶ 高山の巓には美木無し ▶ 高木風に妬まる ▶ 大木は風に折らる ▶ 大名の下には久しく居るべからず ▶ 誉れは誇りの基

## 紺屋の白袴

[The dyer's white *hakama*.] ✍ The *hakama* (袴) is a trousered skirt, a traditional garment worn by Japanese men. ● Those who use their skills to make a living usually do not have the time or means to use those skills to satisfy their own needs. • The shoemaker's children go barefoot. • The tailor's wife is worst clad. = 耕す者は食わず、織る者は着ず = 駕籠舁き駕籠に乗らず = 大工の掘っ立て ▶ 医者の不養生

## 亢竜 悔い有り

[A dragon (which ascends the heavens in rain) repents.] ● Those who reach the pinnacle of success can look forward only to decline. • Those who climb high fall heavily. • Pride goes before a fall. ▶ 驕る平家久しからず

## 呉越 同舟

[Go and Etsu in the same boat.] ✍ Go and Etsu are the Japanese names for the ancient Chinese states of Wu and Yue, which were bitter rivals during the Spring and Autumn period (770-476BC). 📖 Attributed to the Chinese general Sun Tzu. In his classic *The Art of War*, the general expounds: "The men of Wu and the men of Yue

こ

are enemies, yet were they to cross a river in the same boat and be caught in a storm, they would come to each other's aid, just as the left hand works together with the right." ● Exceptional circumstances may force one to forge ties with those with whom one would prefer not to associate under normal conditions. • Adversity makes strange bedfellows.

## 碁が強ければ将棋も強い

[Strong at *go*, strong at *shōgi*.] ✍ *Go* (碁) and *shōgi* (将棋) are Japanese board games that have their Western equivalents in checkers (draughts) and chess. ● Those who excel in one field tend to do well in related fields. ≠ 碁で勝つ者は将棋で負ける ≠ 碁で負けて将棋で勝つ

## 子が無くて泣く者は無い

[No one to cry without children.] ❶ When one has no children, there will be no one to grieve over one's hardships or to mourn one's death. ❷ When one has no children, one is free of the burden and worry that children may bring. • Children are certain cares, but uncertain comforts. = 子は三界の首枷 ≠ 子有れば万事足る

## 黄金と侍は朽ちても朽ちぬ

[Although bullion and samurai may lose their shape, they do not lose their luster.] ● Like gold bullion that has become misshapen through years of use, samurai will not lose their value, even when decrepit with old age. = 侍と黄金は朽ちても朽ちぬ

## 故郷忘じ難し

[One's home town is hard to forget.] ● Those who leave the town they grew up in will always feel a yearning for home. • Home is where the heart is. • East or west, home is best. ◆ 越鳥南枝に巣をかけ、胡馬北風に嘶く ◆ 住めば都 ◆ 代馬北風に依る

## 焦げたる木には火が付きやすい

[A charred tree easily catches fire.] ● Love between those who have been separated by fate easily blazes anew. • Old pottage is sooner heated than made fresh. = 焼け木杭に火が付く ♦ 友と酒は古い程良し ♦ 本木に勝る末木無し

## 虎穴に入らずんば虎子を得ず

[One cannot obtain the tiger's cub without entering the tiger's den.] ☞ Since a tiger protects its offspring like a treasure, the expression 虎の子 is a metaphor for something of great value. ● In order to attain something precious it is often necessary to take great risks. ● Nothing ventured, nothing gained. ● Faint heart never won fair lady/castle. = 虎の穴に入らねば虎の子を得られぬ ♦ 死を先んずる者は必ず生ず ♦ 蒔かぬ種は生えぬ ♦ 身を捨ててこそ浮かぶ瀬も有れ ♦ 物は試し

## 此処ばかりに日は照らぬ

[The sun does not only shine here.] ● The sun does not shine on one person only but on people everywhere; if good or ill can happen in one place, they can happen somewhere else too. ● The sun shines upon all alike. ● The sun rises in the morning in every country. ♦ 江戸中の白壁は皆旦那 ♦ 尺も短き所あり、寸も長き所あり ≠ 入り船に良い風は出船に悪い ≠ 出船に良い風は入り船に悪い

## 心焉に在らざれば視れども見えず

[If the mind is absent, one cannot see, even though one looks.] ● When one is distracted or distraught, one may look at something, but not mentally record what one sees. ● The eye is blind if the mind is absent.

## 心正しければ事正し

[If the heart is right, the thing is right.] ● If one acts for noble reasons, the product of one's actions will be good. ● Handsome is that handsome does. = 源清ければ流れ清し ♦ 巧言令色鮮し仁 ♦ 鞘が無くても身は光る ♦ 曲がれる枝に曲がれる影 ♦ 見目より心 ♦ 歪み八石直ぐ九石

## 心の師となるとも心を師とせざれ

[Become the teacher of one's heart but do not make the heart one's teacher.] ● Though one may train the heart like a teacher trains pupils, one should not let one's emotions rule one's actions. ● Wise men have their mouth in their heart, fools their heart in their mouth.

## 心の欲する所に従えども矩を踰えず

[Follow what one's heart desires without transgressing what is right.] ☞ This proverb is taken from perhaps the most well known passages in Confucius' *Analects*. The whole description, in the translation of James Legge, runs as follows: "At fifteen, I had my mind bent on learning; at thirty, I stood firm; at forty, I had no doubts; at fifty, I knew the decrees of heaven; at sixty, my ear was an obedient organ for the reception of truth; at seventy, I could follow what my heart desired, without transgressing what was right." ● To have reached a level of moral enlightenment where one's actions are in perfect harmony with the dictates of heaven. ♦ 君子の学は善を留むること無く、問いを宿すること無し

## 乞食にも三の理屈

[Beggars, too, have their share of reason.] ● Those who have fallen on hard times have their own way of making sense out of their unsatisfactory existence. ♦ 盗人にも三の理 ♦ 盗人の昼寝も当てが有る

## 乞食の子も三年経てば三歳になる

[Even the child of a beggar will become three when three years have passed.] ● No matter what one's social background, everyone advances in age uniformly. = 三年経てば三つになる

## 乞食は天下話し

[Beggars talk of the whole country.] ● Unimportant people tend to talk about important matters in the belief that it will make them look important. ● Small people love to talk of great people. = 自慢高慢馬鹿の内

## 乞食も雇えば冷や飯を食わず

[Even employed beggars will turn up their nose at cold rice.] ● Even the lowliest person may become impudent when given too much credit. Hence, when one hires someone, one should take care not to overindulge them, lest they become haughty. • Set a beggar on horseback and he'll ride a gallop. = 雇う乞食は冷や飯を食わず = 雇う法師は味噌を嫌う ▶ 門脇の姥にも用有り ▶ 枯れ木も山の賑わい ▶ 癖ある馬に乗りあり ▶ 蹴る馬も乗り手次第 ▶ 馬鹿と鋏は使い様 ▶ 貧乏人も三年置けば用に立つ ▶ 野郎と鋏が使い様 ▶ 湯腹も一時、松の木柱も三年 ▶ 割れ鍋も三年置けば用に立つ

### 乞食を三日すれば止められぬ

[If one has been a beggar for three days one cannot give up.] ● The slothful habit of a life of dependency is hard to shake off. • Once a beggar, always a beggar. = 三年乞食すれば生涯忘れられぬ = 三日乞食すれば一生止められぬ

### 五十歩をもって百歩を笑う

[Fifty steps laughing at a hundred steps.] ☞ This proverb is based on the words of Mencius, who described the folly of a soldier who has retreated fifty steps, yet laughs at the cowardice of a soldier who has retreated a hundred steps. ● Laughing at the mistakes of others is folly, since sooner or later we all make mistakes. • The pot calling the kettle black. = 猿の尻笑い = 目糞が鼻糞を笑う = 目脂が鼻垢を笑う ▶ 己れを責めて人を責むるな ▶ 近くて見えぬは睫 ▶ ❷ 遠きを知りて近きを知らず ▶ 人の頭の蠅を追うより我が頭の蠅を追え ▶ 人の一寸我が一尺 ▶ 人の七難より我が十難 ▶ 人を知る者は知なり、自ら知る者は明なり ▶ 我が頭の蠅を追え ▶ 我が身の上は見えぬ

### 腰抜け武士の後思案

[The afterwit of the cowardly warrior.] ● It is easy to speak brave words when danger has passed, but it is bold action in the face of danger that counts. • It is easy to be wise after the event. = 下衆の後知恵

### 瞽者は文章の観に与ること無し

[The blind cannot take part in the appreciation of a composition.] 📖 This proverb is taken from the works of Zhuangzi. ● Only those who have have cultivated the senses and possess a sufficient refinement of taste can appreciate the value and beauty of fine art. ◆ ❶ 大声里耳に入らず

## 五十にして四十九年の非を知る

[At fifty, one knows the faults of forty-nine years.] ● Only upon maturity does one begin to see the mistakes of one's past life (when it is too late to correct them). • It is no use crying over spilt milk. • What is done cannot be undone. ＝ 後悔は知恵の糸口 ◆ 後悔先に立たず ◆ 五十にして天命を知る ◆ 死んだ子の年を数える ◆ 提灯持ち後に立たず ◆ 覆水盆に返らず ◆ 流水 源 に返らず

## 五十にして天命を知る

[At fifty, one knows the decree of heaven.] ☞ This proverb is taken from perhaps the most well known passages in Confucius' *Analects*. The whole description, in the translation of James Legge, runs as follows: "At fifteen, I had my mind bent on learning; at thirty, I stood firm; at forty, I had no doubts; at fifty, I knew the decrees of heaven; at sixty, my ear was an obedient organ for the reception of truth; at seventy, I could follow what my heart desired, without transgressing what was right." ● Only when one has reached the age of fifty will one know what role or fate one has been dealt in life. ◆ 五十にして四十九年の非を知る

## 国家昏乱して忠臣あり

[When a state is in turmoil, there will be loyal retainers.] 📖 This proverb is attributed to the Chinese Daoist Laozi. ● When a country is in danger and without strong leadership, capable people who love their country will rise to lead it. Similarly, people of quality tend to come to the fore in times of trouble. • The night bring out the stars. ＝ 国乱れて忠臣 現わる ◆ 家貧しくして孝子顕わる

## 言葉多き者は品少なし

[Many words, little grace.] ● Those who are always talking have no sense of good manners. • Empty vessels make the greatest sound. ◆ 浅瀬に仇波 ◆ 音無き川は水深し ◆ 静かに流れる川は深い ◆ 能ある鷹は爪を隠す

## 言葉多ければ恥多し

[The more the words, the greater the shame.] ● The more one argues, the more one will be embarrassed when proven wrong. When one has made a *faux pas*, it is often better to remain quiet than risk yet more embarrassment by defending oneself. ● Least said, soonest mended. = 口数の多い者は襤褸を出す ♦ 口は災いの元 ♦ 君子は九度思いて一度言う ♦ 三寸の舌に五尺の身を亡ぼす ♦ 舌は禍の根 ♦ 沈黙は金 ♦ 禍は口から

## 子供の狂いは泣き狂い、大人の狂いは死に狂い

[The madness of children is crying madness, the madness of adults is dying madness.] ● The mischief done by children will end in tears, the mischief done by adults will end in death.

## 碁で勝つ者は将棋で負ける

[Those who win at *go* lose at *shōgi*.] ✍ *Go* (碁) and *shōgi* (将棋) are traditional Japanese board games that have their Western equivalents in checkers (draughts) and chess. ● Those who excel in one field tend to underperform in others. Similarly, those who gain in one area are prone to lose in others. = 碁で負けて将棋で勝つ ≠ 碁が強ければ将棋も強い

## 碁で負けて将棋で勝つ

[Lose at *go* and win at *shōgi*.] ✍ *Go* (碁 ) and *shōgi* (将 棋 ) are traditional Japanese board games that have their Western equivalents in checkers (draughts) and chess. ● Those who excel in one field may underperform in others. Similarly, those who gain in one area may lose in others. = 碁で勝つ者は将棋で負ける ≠ 碁が強ければ将棋も強い

## この君にしてこの臣あり

[As a lord must be a lord, so a vassal must be a vassal.] 📖 From the *Analects* of Confucius. ● As leaders must strive to live up to the responsibilities of their positions, so their followers must strive to live up to the requirements of theirs. ● Like master, like servant. ● Like lord, like chaplain. = 君君たり臣臣たり ♦ 蛙の子は蛙 ♦ 父も父なら子も子だ ♦ 瓜の蔓に茄子はならぬ

## 子の恥は親の恥

[A child's shame is the parent's shame.] ● The disreputable behavior of a child will inevitably tarnish the name of those who raised it. ● Well for him who has good children. ◆ 子が無くて泣く者は無い ◆ 子は三界の首枷

## 子は生むも心は生まぬ

[Though one may give birth to a child, one cannot give birth to its heart.] ● Though parents can expect their children to resemble them in physical appearance, they should not expect them to be similar in character. ◆ 鳶が鷹を生む ◆ 鳶の子鷹にならず ◆ 鶏が鷹を生む

## 子は三界の首枷

[Children are the neck-shackles of the Three Worlds.] ☞ In Buddhist lore the Three Worlds are those of the past, present, and future, as well as those of desire, form, and formlessness. ● In every stage of their progress from infant to adult, children are a constant source of worry to their parents. ● Children are certain cares, but uncertain comforts. = 子が無くて泣く者は無い ◆ 子の恥は親の恥

## 虎豹の駒は食牛の気あり

[Young tigers and panthers have an appetite for oxen.] ● Great people will show signs of their exceptional talents at an early age. ● One may know the lion by its claws. = 虎の子は地に落つれば牛を食う気あり ◆ 栴檀は双葉より芳し ◆ 実の生る木は花から知れる ◆ 実を見て木を知れ ≠ 大器晩成 ≠ ❷ 早く熟すれば早く腐る

## 小股取っても勝つが得

[Victory can also be obtained by tripping someone up.] ✍ The expression 小股を取る literally means to "grab someone in the crotch," but its idiomatic meaning is "to trip someone up." ☞ This expression is still used to describe a technique in *sumō* (Japanese wrestling) by which a momentarily off-balance wrestler is grabbed in the crotch by his belt and thrown over. Since this technique relies on using a lapse in the opponent's defense—rather that the attacker's superior strength—it is considered to be a less honest means to victory. ● Victory must at times be obtained by less honorable means. ◆ 三十六計瞞すに上無し

## 転がる石には苔は生えない

[A rolling stone gathers no moss.] ❶ Those who remain active and buoyant will retain their youthful vigor. ● A rolling stone gathers no moss. ❷ Those who keep changing their course in life (whenever the going gets rough) are not likely to accomplish anything. ● A rolling stone gathers no moss. = 転石苔を生ぜず

## 殺す神あれば助ける神あり

[If there are gods that kill, there are gods that help.] ● In life one may encounter many vicissitudes, and even in the very midst of danger rescue may be at hand. ● Fortune's wheel is always turning. ● The world is as kind as it is cruel. ● When one door is shut, another is open. = 禍福は糾える縄の如し = 沈む瀬あれば浮かぶ瀬あり = 捨てる神はあれば助ける神あり ◆ 入り船あれば出船あり ◆ 有為転変は世の習い ◆ 昨日の敵は今日の味方 ◆ 昨日の友は今日の仇 ◆ 昨日の情けは今日の仇 ◆ 昨日の花は今日の夢 ◆ 昨日の淵は今日の瀬 ◆ 今日の味方は明日の敵 ◆ 損をする者あれば得をする者がある ◆ 天道人を殺さず

## 転ばぬ先の杖

[The walking stick before one falls.] ● Rather than wait until difficulties arise, one should try to prepare for them. ● Look before you leap. = 濡れぬ前の傘 ◆ 明日は雨人は泥棒 ◆ 石橋を叩いて渡る ◆ 備え有れば憂い無し ◆ 人を見たら泥棒と思え ◆ 火を見れば火事と思え

## 衣ばかりで和尚は出来ぬ

[One cannot become a Buddhist priest merely by (wearing) the robe.] ● One cannot acquire someone's desirable qualities merely by imitating their outward appearances. Similarly, one cannot solely rely on outward appearances to make a sound judgment. ● The cowl does not make the monk. = 数珠ばかりで和尚が出来ぬ ◆ 衣を染めんより心を染めよ ◆ 人肥えたるが故に尊からず ◆ 見目より心 ◆ 山高きが故に貴からず

## 衣を染めんより心を染めよ

[Rather than dye one's robes, dye one's heart.] ● One cannot become a good person merely by improving one's outward appearance. ● The cowl does not make the monk. ♦ 衣ばかりで和尚は出来ぬ ♦ 人肥えたるが故に尊からず ♦ 見目より心 ♦ 山高きが故に貴からず

## 恐い時の仏頼み

[The invoking of gods in times of distress.] ● When times turn hard people turn to their gods; when times are good they forget them. ● Vows made in storms are forgotten in calms. ● Danger past and God forgotten. ● The peril past, the saint mocked. = 苦しい時の神頼み ♦ 暑さ忘れて蔭忘る ♦ 雨晴れて笠を忘る ♦ 叶わぬ時の神叩き ♦ 狡兎死して走狗烹らる ♦ 災害は忘れた頃にやって来る ♦ 喉元過ぎれば熱さを忘れる ♦ 病治りて薬師忘る

## 子を持って知る親の恩

[To understand paternal kindness by having children.] ● Only by having children can one truly know the depth of paternal love. ● He that has no children knows not what love is. ♦ 子有れば万事足る ♦ 孝行のしたい時分に親は無し ♦ 他人の飯を食わねば親の恩は知らぬ

## 困難は徳の基

[Hardship is the foundation of virtue.] ● It is especially when one is confronted with difficult moral decisions that one has the opportunity to lay the foundation of a virtuous life. ● Failure is the foundation of success. ● Failure teaches success. ♦ 失敗は成功の基

# サ

## 才有れども用いざれば愚人の如し

[To have talent and not to use it is tantamount to being an idiot.] ● Those who have a talent have a moral obligation to use it for their own benefit, as well as the good of the community. = 蒔かぬ種は生えぬ ♦ 逸物の鷹も放さねば捕らず ♦ 猿を檻に置けば豚と同じ

▶ ❶ 千両の鷹も放さねば知れぬ ▶ 百貫の鷹も放さねば捕らず ▶ 身を捨ててこそ浮かぶ瀬も有れ ▶ 物は試し

## 災害は忘れた頃にやって来る

[Disaster comes round by the time it is forgotten.] ● Immediately after disaster has struck, people will fear its recurrence and busy themselves in preparing for the worst. After the memory of suffering has faded, people tend to drop their guard, so that when disaster strikes a second time, the effects are as devastating as the first time. ● Vows made in storms are forgotten in calms. ▶ 暑さ忘れて蔭忘る ▶ 雨晴れて笠を忘る ▶ 苦しい時の神頼み ▶ 恐い時の仏頼み ▶ 喉元過ぎれば熱さを忘れる ▶ 病治りて薬師忘る

## 細工は流々、仕上げをご覧じる

[A carpenter has many methods, observe the product.] ● There are many ways to accomplish a task, so instead of criticizing the way in which someone goes about it, it is better to wait and give one's opinion on the final product. ● The end crowns the work. ▶ 田から行くも畦から行くも同じ

## 歳月流るる如し

[Time flows like (a river).] ● Time passes relentlessly and irrevocably. ● Time flies like an arrow. ● Time flies. ＝ 光陰流水の如し ＝ 光陰矢の如し

## 歳月人を待たず

[Time does not wait for people.] ● Time will pass regardless of one's plans, and opportunities that are missed now are lost forever. ● Time and tide wait for none. ＝ 光陰人を待たず ▶ 光陰に関守無し ▶ 月日に関守無し ▶ 盛年重ねて来たらず ▶ 若い時は二度無い ▶ 若きは二度と無し

## 宰相とならずんば則ち良医となれ

[If one cannot become a (prime) minister, one should become a good doctor.] ● If one cannot relieve the suffering by grand means, one should at least try by more modest means.

## 財少なければ悲しみ少ない

[If one has little wealth, one has little sorrow.] ☞ This proverb derives from its English equivalent. If one has few possessions, one will have little cause to worry over how to keep them safe. • Little wealth, little sorrow. ♦ 金持ち苦労多し ♦ 金持ちと貧乏者はじっとしていられない

## 財を盗む者は盗人なり、国を盗む者は諸侯

[Those who steal property are robbers; those who steal countries are feudal lords.] ● Those who commit crimes that fall within the confines of the law (of a state) are brought to justice, but those who commit even greater crimes go unpunished. • Little thieves are hanged, but great ones escape. • One murder makes a criminal, a million a hero. = 一州も誅八州も誅 = 鍵を盗む者は誅せられ、国を盗む者は諸侯となる = 金を奪う者は殺され、国を奪う者は王となる

## 境に入っては禁を問え

[When crossing the border, first learn the laws.] ● To avoid trouble and to achieve one's goals one should obey the laws of the place one is in. • When in Rome, do as the Romans do. = 国に入っては先ずその法を聞く ♦ 郷に入っては郷に従え ♦ 里に入りては里に従う ♦ 俗に入っては俗に従え ♦ 其の国に入れば其の俗に従う

## 先勝ち

[The first win.] ● Those who take the initiative are often able to dictate conditions and so gain the upper hand. • First come, first served. = 先にすれば人を制し、後るる時は制せらるる = 先んずれば人を制す = 早い者勝ち ♦ 先勝ちは糞勝ち ♦ 始めの勝ちは糞勝ち

## 先勝ちは糞勝ち

[The first victory is a hollow victory.] ● Winning the war is more important than winning a battle. It is important to keep the final goal in sight and not get carried away by initial success. • He laughs best who laughs last. • All's well that ends well. = 始めの勝ちは糞勝ち ♦ 先勝ち ♦ 先にすれば人を制し、後るる時は制せらるる ♦ 先にすれば人を制し、後るる時は制せらるる ♦ 先んずれば人を制す ♦ 早い者勝ち

## 先にすれば人を制し、後るる時は制せらるる

[Those who lead will rule, those who are late are ruled.] ● Those who take the initiative will attain a position of advantage and so eventually command others; those who are late will lose the advantage and so eventually have to accept the rule of others. ● The first blow is half the battle. = 先勝ち = 先んずれば人を制す = 早い者勝ち ◆ 先勝ちは糞勝ち ◆ 始めの勝ちは糞勝ち

## 先んずれば人を制す

[Those who lead will rule.] ● Those who take the initiative will attain a position of advantage and so eventually command others. ● The first blow is half the battle. = 先勝ち = 先にすれば人を制し、後るる時は制せらるる = 早い者勝ち ◆ 先勝ちは糞勝ち ◆ 始めの勝ちは糞勝ち

## 策士策に溺れる

[The trickster will fall by his own schemes.] ● Those who think they can exploit others by ruses will eventually be the victim of their own scheming. ● Craft brings nothing home. ◆ 狩人も罠に掛かる ◆ 人を取る亀人に取られる ◆ 人を呪わば穴二つ

## 酒口に入る者は舌いず

[Where *sake* goes into the mouth tongues comes out.] ● Drinking causes most people to become talkative and say things that in sober moments they would never discuss. ● When wine sinks, words swim. ● He speaks in his drink what he thought in his draught. ◆ 酒は気違い水 ◆ 酒は本心を現わす

## 酒中国に江戸女、住まい京都に武士薩摩

[For *sake*, Chugoku; for women, Edo; for living, Kyoto; and for warriors, Satsuma.] ☞ This proverb stems from the Edo period (1600-1867), when the best *sake* was considered to be that produced in the Chugoku region (the western part of the main island of Honshū), the most beautiful women were considered to be those who lived in Edo (modern-day Tokyo), the most pleasant place to live in was considered to be Kyoto, and the best warriors were considered to be

さ

those who came from the province of Satsuma (the western part of modern-day Kagoshima prefecture). ● The best things in life are never to be found in one location.

## 酒と朝寝は貧乏の近道

[*Sake* and morning lie-ins are the short road to poverty.] ● Ruining one's health and career by dissipation in *sake* and oversleeping are the surest way to poverty. • Drink less and go home by daylight. • Wine ever pays for his lodgings. ▶ 朝謡は貧乏の相 ▶ 稼ぐに追い付く貧乏無し ▶ 勤勉は福の神 ▶ 好きの道には薦被る

## 酒と女と博打には錠おろせ

[Keep *sake*, women, and gambling behind locks.] ● Drinking, womanizing, and gambling are the three vices that may lead to one's ruin. • Gaming, women and wine, while they laugh, they make men pine. • Play, women, and wine undo men laughing. • Wine and wenches empty men's purses. ≠ 酒は憂いを払う玉箒

## 酒は憂いを払う玉箒

[*Sake* sweeps away sorrow like a broom.] 📖 This proverb is taken from a poem by the 11th century Chinese poet Su Shi. ● The soothing effect of intoxication will help to alleviate the anxieties of heart and mind. ≠ 酒と女と博打には錠おろせ

## 酒は気違い水

[*Sake* is madness water.] ● When people drink too much they will say and do irrational things. • When wine is in, wit is out. ▶ 酒口に入る者は舌いず

## 酒は酒屋に茶は茶屋に

[For *sake*, the *sake* shop; for tea, the tea shop.] ● In all arts, crafts, and trades there are professionals and it is best not to dabble in their fields but rather rely on their expertise. • Every man to his trade. = 海の事は漁父に問え = 餅は餅屋 = 田作る道は農に問え ▶ 海老踊れども川を出でず ▶ 鴉が鵜の真似 ▶ 芸は道に依りて賢し ▶ 鹿つきの山は猟師知り、魚つきの浦は網人知る

### 酒は百毒の長

[*Sake* is chief among a hundred poisons.] ● Among all the poisonous agents to which the human body is exposed alcohol is the most malignant. ♦ 薬も過ぎれば毒となる ≠ 酒は百薬の長

### 酒は百薬の長

[*Sake* is chief among a hundred drugs.] ● When indulged in with moderation, alcohol is better for the body and soul than any medicine. ● Wine is the panacea of all ills ● Good wine makes good blood. ♦ 薬も過ぎれば毒となる ≠ 酒は百毒の長

### 酒は本心を現わす

[*Sake* reveals the heart.] ● Alcohol will cause people to drop their guard and say whatever is on their mind, thereby revealing their true colors. ● Soberness conceals what drunkenness reveals. ● In wine there is truth. ● In vino veritas. ● Wine is the mirror of the mind. ♦ 酒口に入る者は舌いず

### 差し金無くては雪隠も建たぬ

[Without a ruler not even a closet can be built.] ● No task can be accomplished without the necessary tools and procedures. ● Mete and measure make all men wise. ♦ 網無くて淵をのぞくな ♦ 種の無い手品は使われぬ ♦ 一目の網は以て鳥を得べからず

### 座して食らえば山も空しい

[If one sits and eats, even a mountain (of riches) will be to no avail.] ● A life that consists of mere idleness and indulgence has an unlimited capacity to consume wealth. ● Idleness makes the fullest purse empty. = 居て食らえば山も空し

### 里に入りては里に従う

[When entering a district, do as the district does.] ● To avoid trouble and to achieve one's goals one should obey the laws of the place one is in. ● When in Rome, do as the Romans do. = 郷に入っては郷に従え = 俗に入っては俗に従え = 其の国に入れば其の俗に従う ♦ 国に入っては先ずその法を聞 ♦ 境に入っては禁を問え

111

## 里の金には詰まるが習い

[It is the way of the world that money in the pleasure quarters is always short.] ✍ *Sato* (里), here, has the meaning of pleasure quarters. ● Those who spend their time solely in the pursuit of pleasure will eventually inevitably run out of money. ♦ 振られて帰る果報者

## 侍と黄金は朽ちても朽ちぬ

[Samurai and bullion, even though they lose their shape, they do not lose their luster.] ● Like gold bullion that has lost its shape over time, samurai will not lose their value, even when they have grown old. = 黄金と侍は朽ちても朽ちぬ

## 侍は食わねど高楊枝

[Though they have not eaten, samurai will hold their toothpicks high.] ● Though they may not have had anything to eat, samurai will act as if they have had a good meal, as it is beneath their dignity to complain. = 武士は食わねど高楊枝 ♦ 猿も食わねど高楊枝じ ≠ 兵法より食い方

## 去る跡へ行くとも、死に跡へ行くな

[Go where the wife has left, but not where the wife has died.] ● When a man has been left by his wife, he is likely to love his new wife; when he has lost his wife, he is likely to continue to mourn her memory. Hence, a woman who seeks a husband who has been maried before should marry a divorcee, but not a widower. = 住に跡へ行くとも、死に跡へ行くな

## 猿の尻笑い

[The buttock-laugh of apes.] ● Laughing at the mistakes of others is folly, since no one is above reproach and sooner or later one is apt to make a mistake oneself. ● The pot calling the kettle black. = 五十歩をもって百歩を笑う = 目糞が鼻糞を笑う = 目脂が鼻垢を笑う ♦ 己れを責めて人を責むるな ♦ 猿の尻笑い ♦ 近くて見えぬは睫 ♦❷ 遠きを知りて近きを知らず ♦ 人の頭の蠅を追うより我が頭の蠅を追え ♦ 人の一寸我が一尺 ♦ 人の七難より我が十難 ♦ 我が頭の蠅を追え ♦ 我が身の上は見えぬ

# 猿も木から落ちる

[Monkeys, too, fall from trees.] ● Even those who seem complete masters of their craft may sometimes get it wrong. ● Homer sometime nods. ● A good marksman may miss. = 王良も時として馬車を覆す = 河童の川流れ = 賢者も千慮の一失 = 弘法にも筆の誤り = 知者にも千慮の一失 = 上手の手から水が漏れる = 竜馬の躓き

# 猿も食わねど高楊枝じ

[A monkey, too, though he has not eaten, will hold its toothpick high.] ☞ This proverb is a parody on the old proverbs 武士は食わねど高楊枝 and 侍は食わねど高楊枝. ● If monkeys act as if they have had a good meal, even though they have not had anything to eat, how much more are humans obliged to hold their heads high in the face of hardships. ♦ 侍は食わねど高楊枝. ♦ 武士は食わねど高楊枝

# 去る者は日々に疎し

[Those who depart are (more) neglected with every day.] ● When people leave a group they tend to be soon forgotten. Similarly, those who have passed away will be forgotten with time. ● Out of sight, out of mind. ● Long absent, soon forgotten.

# 猿を檻に置けば豚と同じ

[A monkey placed in a pen is the same as a pig.] ● People with talent who are deprived of the freedom to develop it will over time lose it and become like those who have none. ♦ 逸物の鷹も放さねば捕らず ♦ 才有れども用いざれば愚人の如し ♦ ❶ 千両の鷹も放さねば知れぬ ♦ 百貫の鷹も放さねば捕らず ♦ 身を捨ててこそ浮かぶ瀬も有れ ♦ 蒔かぬ種は生えぬ ♦ 物は試し

# 触らぬ神に祟り無し

[There is no curse from gods that are left alone.] ● Where there is no relation between things there can be no harmful effects. Hence it is better not to meddle in other people's affairs, as it may only be the cause of trouble. ● Far from Jupiter, far from thunder. ● Let sleeping dogs lie. = 触らぬ蜂は刺さぬ = 知らぬ神に祟り無し ♦ 薮を突ついて蛇を出すな

## 触らぬ蜂は刺さぬ

[The bee that is left alone does not sting.] ● It is better not to meddle in other people's affairs, lest they may take offense and cause trouble. • Let sleeping dogs lie. • Far from Jupiter, far from thunder. = 触らぬ神に祟り無し = 知らぬ神に祟り無し ♦ 薮を突いて蛇を出すな

## 鞘が無くても身は光る

[Though the scabbard is lacking, the blade shines.] ☞ During the first centuries of Japan's feudal era and roughly up until the middle of the 13th century, Japanese warriors wore their long swords, or *tachi* (太刀), suspended from their waist by means of girdles on top of their elaborate armor. Clear for all to admire, the scabbards, or *saya* (鞘), of warriors of high rank were usually highly decorated with gold leaf. Later, with the introduction of firearms, the heavy armor became obsolete and the Japanese warrior changed to a lighter attire. Instead of the one suspended long sword they now began to carry two swords—a long one, the *katana* (刀) and a short one, the *wakizashi* (脇差)—close to their body by tucking both into their belt or *obi* (帯). With this change, the urge to decorate the *saya*, which was now largely obscured by the warrior's garment, inevitably diminished. ● Even though the outward appearance may be poor the content is good. • All is not gold that glitters. ♦ 巧言令色鮮し仁 ♦ 衣ばかりで和尚は出来ぬ ♦ 衣を染めんより心を染めよ ♦ 数珠ばかりで和尚が出来ぬ ♦ 人肥えたるが故に尊からず ♦ 見目より心 ♦ 山高きが故に貴からず

## 三会行かぬは客の恥

[Refrain from going a third time is to the customer's shame.] ☞ This proverb has its origin in the many licensed quarters of feudal Japan, where it was considered bad style to discontinue the frequenting of a prostitute after the second time. ● If, following a first visit, a customer fails to show up a second time, the poor quality of the establishment may be to blame. If he fails to show up a third time, it is either because he is not a loyal customer or because he has no money, either way the shame is his.

さ

## 懺悔は十罪ばを滅す

[Penitence undoes the ten sins.] ☞ The ten sins in Buddhist teaching are the taking of life (殺生), stealing (偸盗), lewdness (邪淫), lying (妄語), duplicity (両舌), slander (悪口), sophistry (綺語), avarice (貪欲), anger (瞋恚), and holding wrong views (on cause and effect) (邪見). ● To recognize one's sins and to repent is the first step on the road to a virtuous life. ● A fault confessed is half redressed. ♦ 後悔は知恵の糸口

## 三尺下がって師の影を踏まず

[Keep three *shaku* behind the master so as not to tread on his shadow.] ✍ The Japanese *shaku* (尺) is an old unit of measurement still used by Japanese craftsmen. One *shaku* (尺) corresponds to roughly thirty centimeters. ● Used to express the reverence that is paid to teachers. ● He that teaches himself has a fool for his master. = 師の影は七尺下がって踏まず = 弟子七尺去って師の影を踏まず

## 三十馬鹿と八月青田は治らない

[The thirty-year-old fool and the green rice field in August do not mend.] ● Like the rice field that has failed to turn golden yellow by August, those who have not shed their immature ideas by the age of thirty will never reach maturity. ♦ 阿呆に付ける薬無し ♦ 馬鹿に付ける薬無し ♦ 惚れ病と馬鹿の治る薬は無い

## 三十六計騙すに上無し

[Deception is the best among the thirty-six tactics.] ✍ The thirty-six tactics (三十六計) are part of the ancient Chinese teachings on the art of war. ● The best way to gain the upper hand over one's enemy is by deception. ♦ 小股取っても勝つが得

## 三十六計逃ぐるに如かず

[Among the thirty-six tactics, none is equal to escape.] ✍ The thirty-six tactics (三十六計) are part of the ancient Chinese teachings on the art of war. ● In war, what counts is to win the war, not the battle, so the decision to retreat is not a sign of cowardice, but of the will to fight and win the next battle. Similarly, when one is in

さ

acute danger and does not know what to do, the best thing is to run away. ● He that fights and runs away may live to fight another day. ♦ 危ない事は怪我の内 ♦ 君子は危うきに近寄らず ♦ 重宝を抱く者は夜行せず ♦ 聖人は危うきに近寄らず ♦ ❷ 馬鹿さしじがれば二がえ馬鹿 ♦ 盲蛇に怖じず

## 三寸の舌に五尺の身を亡ぼす

[A tongue of three *sun* may destroy a body of five *shaku*.] ✍ The Japanese *sun* (寸) is a traditional unit of measurement still used by Japanese craftsmen. One *sun* is roughly three centimeters; a *sun* is ten *bu* (分) and a tenth of a *shaku* (尺). ● A thoughtless remark made in an unguarded moment may well lead to one's undoing. ● The tongue talks at the head's cost. = 一寸の舌に五尺の身を損ず = 口は災いの元 = 舌は禍の根 = 禍は口から ♦ 言わぬが花 ♦ 口数の多い者は襤褸を出す ♦ 言葉多ければ恥多し ♦ 沈黙は金、雄弁は銀

## 山賊の罪を海賊があげる

[The crimes of a mountain bandit will be raised by a pirate.] 📖 This proverb is taken from the *Taiheiki*, a 14th-century Japanese historical epic. ❶ If people have no common interests to bind them together, nothing will unite them, even if they share some characteristics. ● There is no love lost between sailors and soldiers. One false knave accuses another. = 海賊が山賊の罪をあげる ❷ Used when people point out the mistakes in others, while ignoring their own shortcomings. ● The pot calling the kettle black. ♦ 五十歩をもって百歩を笑う ♦ 猿の尻笑い ♦ 目糞が鼻糞を笑う ♦ 目脂が鼻垢を笑う

## 山中の賊を破るは易く心中の賊を破るは難し

[To conquer the mountain rebel is easy; to conquer the rebel within is difficult.] ● It is easy to point out the mistakes in others, but to look critically at oneself and correct one's own faults is far more difficult. ● He that is master of himself will soon be master of others. = 人に勝たんと欲する者は必ず先ず自ら勝つ ♦ 己れを責めて人を責むるな ♦ 近くて見えぬは睫 ♦ 人の頭の蠅を追うより我が頭の蠅を追え ♦ 人の一寸我が一尺 ♦ 人の七難より我が十難 ♦ 我が頭の蠅を追え ♦ 我が身の上は見えぬ

## 三度目には芽が出る

[Buds come forth on the third time.] ● It may take several unsuc-cessful attempts before one finally succeeds in an endeavor. ● Third time lucky. ● The third is a charm. ● The third pays for all.

## 三人寄れば公界

[When three people gather, it is public.] ● When something is dis-cussed or done in the presence of more than two people, it will be difficult to keep it secret. ● Murder will out. ● The truth will out. ◆ 氏素性は争えないもの ◆ 隠すこと千里 ◆ 隠すことは現わる ◆ 天知る地知る我知る人知る

## 三人寄れば文殊の知恵

[When three people gather, the wisdom of Manjusri.] ☞ Manjusri is the bodhisattva of wisdom and intellect. ● The combined intelligence of several people may help to solve problems too daunting for one. ● Two heads are better than one. ● As many heads, as many wits.

## 三年乞食すれば生涯忘れられぬ

[If one has been a beggar for three years one cannot forget it in a lifetime.] ● Once one has grown used to begging for a living it is hard to give it up. Similarly, the slothful habit of a life of dependency is hard to shake off. ● Once a beggar, always a beggar. = 乞食を三日すれば止められぬ = 三日乞食すれば一生止められぬ

## 三年先の事を言えば鬼が笑う

[Talk of things three years ahead and the devil will laugh.] ● No one can predict what tomorrow may bring, so to talk of one's expectations for the future is to tempt providence. ● Nobody knows what tomorrow may bring. ● Nobody knows the 'morrow. = 明日の事を言えば鬼が笑う = 三日先の事を言えば鬼が笑う= 来年の事を言えば鬼が笑う ◆ 一寸先は闇 ◆ 知者も面前に三尺の闇あり ◆ 人の行方と水の流れ ◆ 水の流れと人の末

## 三年経てば三つになる

[If three years pass one will be three years older.] ● In life, nothing

117

is constant and everything is subject to change. Similarly, we all advance in age uniformly (no matter what our social background). = 乞食の子も三年経てば三歳になる

## 三枚うら冠らぬうちは人の運が分からぬ

[As long as the three rear planks are not placed (on the coffin), one cannot know someone's fate.] ☞ The three closing planks were used to fortify crudely crafted coffins. ● Only after someone is laid to rest can one sum up the accomplishments of their life. ● Call no man great before he is dead. = 棺を蓋いて事定まる

# シ

## 爺はしんどする、子は楽をする、孫の代は乞食する

[The old man labors hard, the child lives at ease, and the grandchildren go begging.] ● The belief in working hard for a living tends to fade with each generation that is brought up in luxury. ● The father buys, the son builds, the grandchild sells, and his son begs. = 親は苦労する、子は楽をする、孫は乞食する ▶ 前人樹を植えて後人涼を得

## 鹿つきの山は猟師知り、魚つきの浦は網人知る

[The hunter knows the mountain with deer; the fisherman knows the inlet with fish.] 📖 This proverb is taken from the *Genpei jōsuiki*. ● Someone who has mastered an art or a skill will be better in practicing it than the average person. ● Every man must labor in his own calling. ● Every man to his trade. = 芸は道に依りて賢し ▶ 海の事は漁父に問え ▶ 海老踊れども川を出でず ▶ 鴉が鵜の真似 ▶ 酒は酒屋に茶は茶屋に ▶ 田作る道は農に問え ▶ 餅は餅屋

## 鹿を遂う者は山を見ず

[Those who pursue the deer do not see the mountain.] ❶ Those engrossed in a single pursuit will lose sight of everything else. ● The hunter in pursuit of a deer sees no hills. ❷ Those who are enslaved by avarice or lust will lose their appreciation of life's other pleasures.

## 鹿を死するや音を択ばず

[The dying deer does not care what sound (it calls out).] ● People in desperate straits will lose their sense of decorum. ♦ 窮鳥 枝を選ばず ♦ 逃げる者は道を選ばず ♦ 礼儀は富足より生り、盗賊は飢寒より起こる

## 敷き居を跨げば七人の敵がある

[When one crosses the threshold, there will be seven foes.] ● When children leave the parental home to make a living for themselves, there will be many difficulties lying in wait. ● Man is to man a wolf.

## 地獄にも鬼ばかりではない

[Even in hell there are not only devils.] ● Even in times of trouble one does not merely encounter heartless people, but one encounters compassionate people, too. ● The devil is not so black as he is painted. = 浮き世に鬼は無い = 人に鬼は無い = 渡る世間に鬼は無い ≠ 人を見たら泥棒と思え

## 地獄の沙汰も金次第

[The judgement of hell, too, is dictated by money.] ● In all walks of life greed is a defining force. ● Money makes the mare go round. ● Money is the best lawyer. = 仏の沙汰も銭 ♦ 愛は多能で有り、金は万能で有る ♦ 金の世の中 ♦ 金は世界の回り物 ♦ 金は天下の回り持ち ♦ 人間万事金の世の中

## 獅子の子落とし

[The dropping of a lion's cub.] ☞ This proverb derives from an ancient belief that lions dropped their cubs into a deep ravine to rear only those that survived. ● Rather than pamper and spoil one's children, one should make them experience the hardships of life so that they may grow into capable adults. ● Home-keeping youth have ever homely wits. ● Spare the rod and spoil the child. = 可愛い子には旅をさせよ ♦ 祖母育ちは三百安い

## 獅子は小虫を食わんとてもまず勢いをなす

[When a lion intends to eat a small insect it will do so with vigor.]

119

● When talented people set out to do even a trivial task, they will do everything in their power to make it a success.

## 獅子人を噛むに牙を露わさず

[When a lion bites a human being it does not expose its fangs.] ● Shrewd people do not make a display of their talents, so that (when those around them have become complacent) they may use them to greater advantage. • Cats hide their claws. • Who knows most says least. • Still waters run deep. = 逸物の猫は爪を隠す = 泣かぬ猫は鼠を取る = 鼠を取る猫は爪を隠す = 能ある鷹は爪を隠す ◆ 浅瀬に仇波 ◆ 言葉多き者は品少なし ◆ 静かに流れる川は深い

## 静かに流れる川は深い

[Quietly flowing rivers are deep.] ● People who are quiet and composed in manner often have great depth of character. • Still waters run deep. • Who knows most says least. = 音無き川は水深し ◆ 浅瀬に仇波 ◆ 言葉多き者は品少なし ◆ 能ある鷹は爪を隠す

## 沈む瀬あれば浮かぶ瀬あり

[If there are rapids that pull things under, there will be rapids that push things up.] ● In life, there are many vicissitudes; one moment one is drowning in troubles, the next moment one is basking in the sun. • Fortune's wheel is always turning. The world is as kind as it is cruel. • When one door is shut, another is open. = 禍福は糾える縄の如し = 殺す神あれば助ける神あり = 捨てる神はあれば助ける神あり ◆ 入り船あれば出船あり ◆ 有為転変は世の習い ◆ 昨日の敵は今日の味方 ◆ 昨日の友は今日の仇 ◆ 昨日の情けは今日の仇 ◆ 昨日の花は今日の夢 ◆ 昨日の淵は今日の瀬 ◆ 今日の味方は明日の敵 ◆ 損をする者あれば得をする者がある

## 親しき隣は遠き兄弟に優る

[A close neighbor is better than a distant sibling.] ● In times of trouble, a sympathetic neighbor may be a greater source of comfort than a relative who lives far away. • A near neighbor is better than a distant cousin. = 京の妹に隣代えず = 遠い親類より近くの他人 ◆ ❷ 近火で手を焙れ

## 親しき中にも垣を作れ

[Even between close friends, put up a fence.] ● No matter how close one's friendship, one should always maintain a degree of reserve. • A hedge between keeps friendship green. • Love your neighbor, yet pull not down your hedge. • Familiarity breeds contempt. = 良い中には垣をせよ ♦ 遠きは花の香 ♦ 隣りの花は赤い

## 舌は禍の根

[The tongue is the origin of disaster.] ● A remark made in an unguarded moment may cause irreparable damage. • Little said is soon amended. = 一寸の舌に五尺の身を損ず = 口は災いの元 = 三寸の舌に五尺の身を亡ぼす = 禍は口から ♦ 言わぬが花 ♦ 口数の多い者は襤褸を出す ♦ 君子は九度思いて一度言う ♦ 言葉多ければ恥多し ♦ 沈黙は金、雄弁は銀

## 日月明らかならんと欲すれば浮雲之を覆う

[When the sun and moon desire to shine, drifting clouds will cover them.] ❶ The virtue of a wise ruler may at times go unnoticed through the scheming of dishonest courtiers. ≠ 君に争臣有れば、身不義に陥らず ❷ There will always be obstacles that jeopardize an enterprise.

## 日月一物の為にその明を晦くせず

[The sun and moon do not dim their light for one object.] ❶ Enlightened rulers cannot make exemptions for one subject alone, but have to let their benevolence shine on all subjects in equal measure. • The sun shines upon all alike. ❷ It is impossible to do anything in absolute secrecy, and sooner or later everyone will know about it. • Murder will out. • The truth will out. ♦ 氏素性は争えないもの ♦ 隠すこと千里 ♦ 隠すことは現わる ♦ 三人寄れば公界 ♦ 天知る地知る我知る人知る

## 日月は曲がられる穴を照らさず

[The sun and moon do not light up a crooked hole.] ✍ The verb *magaru* (曲がる), meaning "to twist," has the connotation of corruption. ● The benevolence of the gods is not bestowed on those who live dishonest lives. • He that hates the light does ill.

## 七珍万宝の随一は人の命と人の誠

[Greatest among the seven treasures are human life and human sincerity.] ✍ The seven treasures (七宝) according to Buddhist lore are gold (金), silver (銀), lapis lazuli (瑠璃), quartz (玻璃), mother of pearl (真珠層), coral (珊瑚), and agate (瑪瑙). ● Among all the treasures a human being may possess, life and sincerity are foremost. ◆ 武士に二言は無い ◆ 礼繁きの者は実心衰うるなり

## 失敗は成功の基

[Failure is the foundation of success.] ● It is only by learning the cause of failure that one can lay the foundations for success. ● Failure is the foundation of success. ● Failure teaches success. ◆ 困難は徳の基

## 品物を誉める人に買うた例なし

[There is no instance of those who praise an article buying it.] ● People who merely praise a product without voicing any points of criticism have no intention of eventually buying it. ● Praise without profit puts little in the pot. = 誉める人は買わぬ

## 師の影は七尺下がって踏まず

[Keep seven *shaku* behind the master so as not to tread on his shadow.] ✍ The Japanese *shaku* (尺) is an old unit of measurement still used by Japanese craftsmen. One *shaku* (尺) corresponds to roughly thirty centimeters. ● Used to express the reverence that is paid to teachers. ● He that teaches himself has a fool for his master. = 三尺下がって師の影を踏まず = 弟子七尺去って師の影を踏まず

## 死馬の骨を買う

[Buy the bones of a dead horse] ☞ This proverb is taken from a Chinese anecdote in which King Zhao of Zhou, a man known for his love of animals, sends his retainer out with a thousand pieces of gold in search of a horse that will run a thousand *ri* (roughly equivalent to three hundred miles) in one day. The retainer returns with the bones of a dead horse, for which he has paid half the money put into his care. Outraged, the king asks him why he has spent such an amount on a pile of horse bones. To this the retainer replies "if it is known that the King spends so much even on the bones of a dead horse, the people will realize that the King is serious about his pursuit of a good horse and flock to the court with their best horses." As the retainer predicted, within a year the king had acquired three horses that met his requirements. ● One in search of perfection should still treat the imperfect with consideration. ◆ 隗より始めよ

## 師は針の如し、弟子は糸の如し

[A teacher is like a needle; a disciple is like the thread.] ☞ In traditional Japan young men learned a trade by being attached to a craftsman or teacher (師) as an apprentice (弟子). Apprentices would start with menial tasks and gradually learn the secrets of a craft by closely following the teacher's instructions. ● In the same way as the thread follows a needle's movement precisely, so should the pupil follow the guidance of his master. ● Jack is as good as his master. ◆ 君と共にする一夜の話は十年の書を読むに優る ◆ 千日の勤学より一時の名匠

## 士は文武を左右にす

[A gentleman has full command of the civil and the martial.] ☞ During Japan's feudal era, much emphasis was placed on the acquisition of civil skills as well as martial skills, as is borne out by the popular expression 文武両道, "the dual way of civil and martial accomplishments," a concept that is Chinese in its origin. ● In order to become a well-rounded individual, it is vital that one develop both one's civil as well as one's martial skills. = 文武は車の両輪 = 武を右にし文を左にす ◆ 文は人也 ◆ 馬子にも衣裳 ≠ 文は武に優る

## 死は易うして生は難し

[Death is easy, life is difficult.] ● It is easy to avoid hardships by taking one's life, but to go on living and endure those hardships is much more difficult. = 生は難く死は易し

## 自慢高慢馬鹿の内

[Pride and arrogance are found among fools.] ● Those who think highly of themselves are blind to the superiority of others. • The fool thinks he is wise, but the wise man knows himself to be a fool. • Self-praise is no recommendation. • The first chapter of fools is to esteem themselves wise. = 乞食は天下話し ♦ 馬鹿も有ればこそ、利口も引き立つ ♦ 下手があるので上手が知れる

## 鴟目大なれど観ること鼠に若かず

[The eyes of an owl are large but are not equal to those of a mouse.] ● Though an owl may have large eyes, a mouse has superior vision. By extension, even those whose presence seems of no consequence may have their part to play in the greater scheme of things. • For the want of a nail the shoe was lost, for the want of a shoe the horse was lost, for the want of a horse the battle was lost. ♦ 門脇の姥にも用有り ♦ 枯れ木も山の賑わい ♦ 愚者も千慮に一徳あり ♦ 癖ある馬に乗りあり ♦ 蹴る馬も乗り手次第 ♦ ❷ 時に遭えば鼠も虎となる ♦ 馬鹿と鋏は使い様 ♦ 馬鹿も一芸 ♦ 貧乏人も三年置けば用に立つ ♦ ❷ 用いる時は鼠も虎となる ♦ 野郎と鋏が使い様 ♦ 湯腹も一時、松の木柱も三年 ♦ 割れ鍋も三年置けば用に立つ

## 駟も舌に及ばず

[Even a four-horse chariot cannot keep up with the tongue.] ● A verbal *faux pas*, once uttered, cannot be recalled. • A word and a stone let go cannot be called back. = 過言一度出ずれば駟も舌に及ばず

## 釈迦に説法

[Preaching to Sakyamuni.] ☞ Sakyamuni, literally "sage of the Sakya [clan]," is an alternate name for the Buddha. His teachings formed the basis of Buddhism, one of the world's four major religions. ● Used when someone is trying to teach a lesson to an expert. • A sow teaching Minerva. • Teach your grandmother to suck eggs. = お釈迦様に経を聞かせる = 孔子に論語

## 釈迦も銭ほど光る

[Sakyamuni, too, shines in proportion to its wealth.] ☞ Images and effigies of Buddha are often gilded, so the more money it acquires (through donations) the brighter it will shine, just as a person will gain in attractiveness with wealth. ● The worldly power of money vies with the spiritual power of Buddha. • No penny, no paternoster. = 阿弥陀の光も金次第 ♦ 金の光は阿弥陀ほど ♦ 地獄の沙汰も金次第 ♦ 仏の光より金の光

## 尺の木も必ず節目あり、寸の玉も必ず瑕あり

[In one *shaku* of wood there will be a joint, in one *sun* of jewel there will be a flaw.] ✍ The Japanese *shaku* (尺) is an old unit of measurement still used by Japanese craftsmen. One *shaku* (尺) corresponds to roughly thirty centimeters. One *shaku* is ten *sun* (寸). ● We live in an imperfect world, comprised of imperfect things. • In evil there is odds. ♦ 寸善 尺 魔の世の中 ♦ 寺の隣に鬼が住む ♦ 寺の門前に鬼が住む

## 尺も短き所あり、寸も長き所あり

[A *shaku* has its short points; a *sun* has its long points.] ✍ The Japanese *shaku* (尺) is an old unit of measurement still used by Japanese craftsmen. One *shaku* (尺) corresponds to roughly thirty centimeters. One *shaku* is ten *sun* (寸). ● All things have their merits and demerits; something that is inappropriate in one situation it may be appropriate in another. ♦ 入り船に良い風は出船に悪い ♦ 門脇の姥にも用有り ♦ 枯れ木も山の賑わい ♦ 愚者も千慮に一徳あり ♦ 乞食も雇えば冷や飯を食わず ♦ 出船に良い風は入り船に悪い ♦ ❷ 時に遭えば鼠も虎となる ♦ 馬鹿と鋏は使い様 ♦ 馬鹿も一芸 ♦ 貧乏人も三年置けば用に立つ ♦ ❷ 用いる時は鼠も虎となる ♦ 雇う乞食は冷や飯を食わず ♦ 雇う法師は味噌を嫌う ♦ 野郎と鋏が使い様 ♦ 湯腹も一時、松の木柱も三年 ♦ 割れ鍋も三年置けば用に立つ

## 蛇にあらざれば蛇をしらず

[Those who are not among snakes do not know snakes.] 📖 This proverb is taken from the *Taikōki*. ● Those who are at home in a certain level of society will be familiar with the kind of people who move in it. Similarly, those who practice a certain trade will know the ruses by which fellow tradesmen try to outsmart each other or do their customers out of money. • One devil knows another. • The wicked know the ways of their own kind. = 蛇の道は蛇

## 蛇の道は蛇
じゃ みち へび

[On a the road of serpents, snakes.] ● Those who are at home in a certain level of society will be familiar with the kind of people who move in it. Similarly, those who practice a trade will know the ruses by which fellow tradesmen try to outsmart each other or do their customers out of money. ● One devil knows another. ● The wicked know the ways of their own kind. = 蛇にあらざれば蛇をしらず

**し**

## 沙弥から長老にはなれぬ
しゃ み ちょうろう

[One does not become a doyen (directly) from being an acolyte.] ● One cannot expect to achieve something in life overnight, but only through long and dedicated effort. = 始めから長老にはなれぬ ▶ 一朝一夕の故に非ず ▶ 馬に乗るまで牛に乗れ ▶ ❷ 将を射んと欲すれば先ず馬を射よ ▶ 千里の道も一歩より始まる ▶ 高きに登るは低きよりす ▶ 始めの一歩、末の千里 ▶ ❷ 人を射んとせば先ず馬を射よ

## 舎を道端に作れば三年にして成らず
しゃ みちばた つく さんねん な

[A house built along the roadside will not be finished in three years.] ● If one builds a house along the roadside, many people who pass by will stop to give advice, causing plans to be changed and the completion of the house to be delayed. By extension, one should stick to one's plan and not be distracted by unsolicited advice. = 家を道端に作れば三年成らず ▶ 船頭多くて船山に上る

## 重宝を抱く者は夜行せず
じゅうほう いだ もの やこう

[Those who carry a priceless treasure do not travel by night.] ● Those who have great ambitions will refrain from embarking on frivolous and dangerous enterprises. ● Danger is next neighbor to security. ▶ 危ない事は怪我の内 ▶ 君子は危うきに近寄らず ▶ 三十六計逃ぐるに如かず ▶ 聖人は危うきに近寄らず ▶ ❷ 馬鹿さしじがれば二がえ馬鹿 ▶ 盲蛇に怖じず

## 柔 能く剛を制する、弱 能く強を制する
じゅう よ ごう せい じゃく よ きょう せい

[The yielding control the unyielding well; the weak control the strong well.] ☞ This concept from Chinese martial philosophy is one of the pillars of Japanese martial arts. For example, the art of *jūdō*

(柔道), where we find the character *ju* (柔), meaning soft or pliable. The practitioner of *jūdō* will initially yield to an attack but only to use the force contained in the attack to unbalance or throw the opponent. ● Those who initially yield to a stronger but less flexible opponent may eventually be victorious by absorbing the blows and thus exhaust their opponent. ● She stoops to conquer. = 茶碗を投げば綿で抱えよ ▶ 木強ければ折れ易し ▶ 強き木はむず折れ ▶ 柳に風折れなし ▶ 柳に風折れなし ▶ 柳の枝に雪折れ無し

## 主が主なら家来も家来

[If a master is a master, a vassal is a vassal.] ● If a master sets a good example, his servants will have an incentive to conduct themselves well. ● Like master, like man. = 蛙の子は蛙 = この君にしてこの臣あり = 父も父なら子も子だ

## 数珠ばかりで和尚が出来ぬ

[One cannot become a Buddhist priest merely with a string of beads.] ● One cannot attain someone's superior qualities merely by imitating their outward appearances. Similarly, one cannot solely rely on outward appearances to make a sound judgment. ● The cowl does not make the monk. = 衣ばかりで和尚は出来ぬ = 衣を染めんより心を染めよ ▶ 人肥えたるが故に尊からず ▶ 見目より心 ▶ 山高きが故に貴からず

## 朱に交われば赤くなる

[When one mingles with red one will become red.] ● The circles in which people move will have an influence on their character; if they keep bad company they will become bad; if they keep good company they will become good. ● He that touches pitch shall be defiled. ▶ 強将の下に弱卒無し ▶ 麻に連るる蓬 ▶ 大木の下に小木育つ ▶ 勇将の下に弱卒無し ▶ 良将の下に弱卒無し

## 小過を許して賢才を挙ぐ

[Pardon the small transgressions, raise the intelligence.] 📖 This proverb is taken from the *Analects* of Confucius. ● In order to get the best out of those who work under them, leaders should overlook people's minor shortcomings and develop their intelligence. ◆ 麻に連るる蓬 ◆ 強将の下に弱卒無し ◆ 大樹の下に美草無し ◆ 大木の下に小木育つ ◆ 勇将の下に弱卒無し ◆ 良将の下に弱卒無し

## 上交 諂わず下交驕らず

[Do not curry favor with the high; do not be haughty to the low.] ● The proper way to conduct oneself is to treat everybody in the same way, without trying to ingratiate oneself with the high and mighty, and without looking down on the low and humble. ◆ 富んでは驕る、貧しきは諂う

## 正直の頭に神宿る

[The gods dwell in the head of the honest.] 📖 This proverb is taken from the *Soga monogatari*. ● The gods will come to the aid of those who are honest. • God dwells in an honest heart.

## 正直の儲けは身に付く

[Honestly gotten gains stick to the body.] ● Wealth that is gained by legal means is not subject to any claims and so tends to accumulate. • Ill-gotten goods seldom prosper. = 不義の富貴は浮雲の如 ◆ 悪銭身に付かず

## 正直は最善の策

[Honesty is the best plan.] ☞ This proverb derives from its English equivalent. ● Rather than resorting to various tricks and stratagems, the best way to achieve one's aims in life is to be honest. • Honesty is the best policy. ◆ 正しき者は艱難多し ≠ 商人と屏風は曲がらねば世に立たぬ ≠ 商売と屏風は曲がらぬと立たぬ ≠ 屏風と商人は真直ぐにては立たぬもの

## 小人 閑居して不善をなす

[Small people who lead a life of leisure will do wrong.] ● Those who have no moral firmness will not have the discipline to use their spare time to do good. • An idle brain is the devil's workshop. Idleness is the root of all evil. • The devil finds mischief for idle hands to do. ◆ 良馬は鞭影を見て行く

## 上手の手から水が漏れる

[Water will spill (even) from the skilled hand.] ● Even those who seem complete masters of their craft may sometimes get it wrong. • Homer sometime nods. • A good marksman may miss. = 王良も時として馬車を覆す = 河童の川流れ = 賢者も千慮の一失 = 弘法にも筆の誤り = 猿も木から落ちる = 知者にも千慮の一失 = 竜馬の躓き

## 小節を規る者は栄名を成す能わず

[Those who observe trifles do not achieve fame.] ● Those who are diverted by minor details will lose sight of the larger picture and fail to achieve their aims. = 小利を見れば則ち大事成らず ♦ 明日の百より今日の五十 ♦ あの世千日この世の一日 ♦ 大取りより小取り ♦ 末始終より今の三十 ♦ 後の千金より今の百文 ≠ ❷ 大事の前の小事

## 少年 老い易く学成り難しく

[Youth become old easily, but learned with difficulty.] ● Though age is acquired without effort, knowledge is acquired only through hard study. • Art is long, life is short. ♦ 学問に王道無し ♦ 学問に近道無し

## 少年 学ばざれば老後に知らず

[What is not learned in youth is not known in old age.] ● Those who fail to apply themselves to their studies in their youth will have to endure hardships in old age due to their lack of education. • Reckless youth makes rueful age. • Lazy youth, lousy age. ♦ 一生の計は幼きにあり ♦ 始めが大事

## 商売と屏風は曲がらぬと立たぬ

[Business and folding screens won't stand unfolded.] ✍ The *byōbu* (屏風), or Japanese folding screen, will only stand up when partially folded. As in English, the verb *magaru* (曲がる), "to bend" or "to twist," has the connotation of crookedness and corruption. ● Trade will only flourish with a slight degree of dishonesty. • There is knavery in all trades, but most in tailors. = 商人と屏風は曲がらねば世に立たぬ = 屏風と商人は真直ぐにては立たぬもの ♦ 正しき者は艱難多し ≠ 正直は最善の策

## 生は難く死は易し

[Life is difficult; death is easy.] ● It is easy to avoid hardships by taking one's life, but to go on living and endure the hardships of life is more difficult. = 死は易うして生は難し

## 勝負は時の運

[In victory and defeat, the luck of the moment.] 📖 This proverb is taken from the *Taiheiki*, a 14th-century Japanese historical epic. ● The outcome of a contest is often more the result of good or bad luck than talent or power. ♦ 運は天にあり

## 小勇は血気の怒りなり、大勇は理儀の怒りなり

[Small courage is hot-blooded anger; great courage is rightful anger.] ● Courage that is the result of the flaring of hot tempers is easily cowed; courage rooted in moral indignation is unyielding and wins through.

## 小利を見れば則ち大事成らず

[Those who have (only) an eye for small gains will fail to accomplish great feats.] 📖 This proverb is taken from the *Analects* of Confucius. ● Those who cannot resist making the most of minor opportunities will lose sight of the larger picture and never be able to achieve great things. Similarly, when one sets out to accomplish an important objective one should not be distracted by the lure of small profit. = 小節を規る者は栄名を成す能わず ♦ 明日の百より今日の五十 ♦ あの世千日この世の一日 ♦ 一文惜しみの百知らず ♦ 大取りより小取り ♦ 末始終より今の三十 ♦ 後の千金より今の百文 ≠ 一銭を笑う者は一銭に泣く ≠ ❷ 大事の前の小事

## 将を射んと欲すれば先ず馬を射よ

[If one would shoot a general, first shoot his horse.] ❶ The best way to deal a decisive blow to an opponent is to destroy what they chiefly depend upon. ❷ Those who want to achieve greatness should lay the foundation for success by honing their skills on less ambitious goals. ● He that would the daughter win, must with the mother first begin. = 馬に乗るまで牛に乗れ = 高きに登るは低きより

す＝人を射んとせば先ず馬を射よ ◆ 一朝一夕の故に非ず ◆ 沙弥から長老にはなれぬ ◆ 千里の道も一歩より始まる ◆ 始めから長老にはなれぬ ◆ 始めの一歩、末の千里

## 将を畏るる者は勝ち、敵を畏るる者は敗る

[Those who fear the general will win, those who fear the enemy will lose.] ● If one fears (and therefore obeys) the generals of one's allies and remains firm in the face of the enemy, one will win in battle; if one fears one's enemy and lacks faith in the generals of one's allies one will lose.

## 知らざるを知らずとせよ

[Make that which is unknown, unknown.] 📖 This proverb is taken from the *Analects* of Confucius. ● One should not pretend to know things of which one is ignorant, but clearly state what one knows and what one does not know. ◆ 聞くは一時の恥、聞かぬは末代の恥 ◆ 問うは一時の恥、問わぬは末代の恥

## 知らぬが仏

[Ignorance is Buddha.] ● The ignorant are not perturbed by life's injustices and thus, in their serenity, resemble the Buddha. ● He that knows nothing doubts nothing. ● Where ignorance is bliss, 'tis folly to be wise.

## 知らぬ神に祟り無し

[There is no curse from gods one does not know.] ● Where there is no relation between things there can be no harmful effects. Hence it is better not to meddle in other people's affairs, lest it may only be the cause of trouble. ● Far from Jupiter, far from thunder. ● Let sleeping dogs lie. ＝ 触らぬ神に祟り無し ＝ 触らぬ蜂は刺さぬ ◆ 薮を突いて蛇を出すな

## 知る者は言わず言う者は知らず

[The knowing do not talk; the talking do not know.] 📖 This proverb is attributed to the Chinese Daoist Laozi. ● Those who have a deep understanding of things will not comment on them without good

131

reason. By contrast, those who have a superficial understanding of things will comment on them rashly. • A wise head makes a close mouth. • The wise remain silent and let the fools chatter. • Who knows most says least. ◆ 愚者の雄弁は沈黙なり ◆ 雀の千声鶴の一声 ◆ 沈黙は愚者の機知である

## 死を先んずる者は必ず生ず

[Those who face death will surely live.] ● Those who are willing to risk their lives to achieve their goals will certainly succeed. • Nothing ventured, nothing gained. • Faint heart never won fair lady/castle. = 身を捨ててこそ浮かぶ瀬も有れ ◆ 糧を捨てて船を沈む ◆ 清水の舞台から飛び降りる ◆ 虎穴に入らずんば虎子を得ず ◆ 虎の穴に入らねば虎の子を得られぬ ◆ 背水の陣

## 死を知りて避けざるは勇なり

[To know death, but not to yield, is courage.] ● To know that one's actions may result in death, yet to carry on in the knowledge that they are necessary and worthy is true courage.

## 字を知るは憂いの始め

[The knowledge of a (Chinese) character is the beginning of grief.] ● It is only when one has mastered the written word and able to read (the classics) that one can begin to fathom the tragedy of life. • Much learning, much sorrow. = 人生字を識るは憂患の始め

## 人間万事塞翁が馬

[People and all things are like Saio's horse.] ☞ An ancient Chinese folk tale relates how the horse of an old man (翁) from Sai (塞), near the Great Wall, one day ran away to Mongol territory. A few days later the mare returned accompanied by a beautiful stallion and gave birth to a foal. When the foal had grown strong enough the old man's son rode it and fell off, breaking his leg. Shortly after, Sai was invaded by a marauding Mongol army. Most of Sai's young men were killed but the old man's son was spared since he had been incapacitated by his fall from the horse that was reared by the Mongol stallion. ● An apparent evil may in hindsight prove to be a blessing in disguise. Conversely, an apparent blessing may in hindsight prove to be an evil in disguise. • A joyful evening may follow a sorrowful morning. ▶ 雨降って地固まる

# 信言は美ならず、美言は信ならず

[Truthful words have no beauty; beautiful words have no truth.] ● Words spoken from the heart will be plain and straightforward; flowery words may impress but contain no truth and should not be believed. • Fair words and foul deeds cheat wise men as well as fools. • Fine words dress ill deeds. ▶ 甘言が愚人を喜ばしむ ▶ 口に蜜有り腹に剣有り ▶ 追従する者陰にて誹る ▶ 天子将軍の事でも陰では言う ▶ 天子将軍も障子の内 ▶ 耳の楽しむ時は慎むべし

# 人事を尽くして天命を待つ

[Do all that is humanly possible and await the decree of heaven.] ● One should leave no stone unturned to achieve one's goals but whether one's efforts will bear fruit is ultimately in the hands of fate. • Man proposes, God disposes. ＝ 運は天にあり、鎧は胸にあり ▶ 果報は寝て待て

# 人心の異なるその面の如し

[The hearts of people are as different as their faces.] ● In the same way that people differ in outward appearance, so will they differ in their inward natures. • So many men, so many minds. ＝ 人の心は区々だ

# 人生字を識るは憂患の始め

[In life, the knowledge of a (Chinese) character is the beginning of grief.] ● It is only when one has mastered the written word and able to read (the classics) that one can begin to fathom the tragedy of life. • Much learning, much sorrow. ＝ 字を知るは憂いの始め

# 死んだ子の年を数える

[Counting the years of the child that has died.] ● There is no turning back time, so no use dwelling on how things might have been. • It is no use crying over spilt milk. • What is done cannot be undone. ♦ 後悔先に立たず ♦ 五十にして四十九年の非を知る ♦ 提灯持ち後に立たず ♦ 覆水盆に返らず ♦ 流水源に返らず

## 心頭を滅却すれば火もまた涼しい

[When one extinguishes the heart and mind, even fire will be cool.] ☞ In 1582, following his victory over Takeda Katsuyori's forces, Oda Nobunaga destroyed the Enri temple—which held the remains of Katsuyori's father, Takeda Shingen—by setting fire to the temple and all who were in it. It is said that while young and old were driven back into the fire by Nobunaga's men, the temple's abbot, Kaisen, sat himself down with a fan to speak these immortal words, upon which he, too, was consumed by the flames. ● If one has the mental power to achieve perfect serenity, there is no limit to the hardships one can endure. ● He that endures is not overcome. ♦ 死は易うして生は難し ♦ 生は難く死は易し

## 仁は過ぐべく義は過ぐべからず

[There can be no excess in benevolence; there should be no excess in justice.] ● Benevolence is by nature a positive force, so there should be no limit to the compassion one shows toward others. Justice, by contrast, should be applied with care, since too strict an adherence to the letter of the law will lead to an undue tendency to punish people. ♦ 蔭徳有れば陽報有り ♦ 蔭徳は果報の来る門口 ♦ 徳は才の主才は徳の奴

## 辛抱する木に金がなる

[Money grows on the tree of patience.] ● If one continues to work hard, over time one will eventually create wealth. ● Everything comes to him who waits. = 果報は寝て待て ♦ 運は天にあり、牡丹餅は棚にあり ♦ 堪忍は無事長久の基 ♦ 待てば海路の日和あり ≠ 株を守りて兎を待つ

## 信用は無形の財産

[Credit is wealth without form.] ● To enjoy the trust of others is a treasure that cannot be expressed in money. ● Credit is better than gold.

# ス

## 末始終より今の三十

[Rather today's thirty than (wait until) the end of ends.] ● It is better to seize the opportunity of the moment and make a modest profit rather than wait for great gains and make no profit at all. ● A bird in the hand is worth two in the bush. ● Better an egg today than a hen tomorrow. ＝ 明日の百より今日の五十 ＝ ❶ 近火で手を焙れ ＝ 後の千金より今の百文 ＝ 来年の百両より今年の一両 ♦ あの世千日この世の一日 ♦ 大取りより小取り ♦ 聞いた百文より見た一文 ≠ 小節を規る者は栄名を成す能わず ≠ 小利を見れば則ち大事成らず

## 末は野となれ山となれ

[Let (the place) become a wild plain or a mountain.] ● Used by or with respect to those who wash their hands of something and do not care what happens afterwards. ● After me the deluge. ＝ 後は野となれ山となれ

## 好き連れは泣き連れ

[Loving company is crying company.] ● Those who (elope and) marry against the wishes of their parents will regret their deed. ♦ 縁と浮世は末を待て ♦ 縁と月日の末を待て

## 過ぎたる猶及ばざるが如し

[To exceed is the same as falling short.] 📖 This proverb is taken from the *Analects* of Confucius. ● Moderation in all things is wise; to do something in excess may be just as ineffective as not doing anything. ● Overdone is worse than undone. ＝ 及ばざるは過ぎたるより勝れり ♦ 薬も過ぎれば毒となる

## 好きの道には薦被る

[The wearing of straw (hats) for the favorite road.] ✍ In the old days beggars could not afford anything better than a straw hat. Consequently, the verb *komokaburu* (薦被る), or "the wearing of straw," became synonymous with poverty. Nowadays, the word *komokaburi* (薦被り) is used for a *sake* cask wrapped in a rush mat, though it may still be used to indicate a beggar. ❶ Those who take the easy road in life will soon fall into poverty. = 好く道より破る ♦ 酒と朝寝は貧乏の近道 ❷ Used by those who are happy to suffer the hardships that come with the pursuit of what they like to do most. ≠ 道は好む所によって安し

## 空き腹にまずい物無し

[There is no bad food for an empty stomach.] ● Those in dire straits are willing to try any means to help improve their situation. ● Hunger is the best sauce. ● Hunger is not dainty. = 飢えては食を択ばず ♦ 飢えたる犬は棒を恐れず

## 隙間の風は寒い

[The draft through a crevice is cold.] ● The consequences of a small oversight can be great. ● The devil is in the detail.

## 好く道より破る

[The favorite road leads to destruction.] ● Those who choose the easy road in life invite disaster. ● A hobby may be ridden to death. = ❶ 好きの道には薦被る ♦ 酒と朝寝は貧乏の近道 ≠ 道は好む所によって安し

## 進むこと早きものは退くこと急なり

[Those who are quick in their progress make a sudden retreat.] ● Those who hurry to make great strides in a short period of time are also the first to give up. = 進む者は退き易し

## 進む者は退き易し

[Those who make progress easily retreat.] ● Those who hurry to make great strides in a short period of time are also the first to turn back at any obstacle. = 進むこと早きものは退くこと急なり

## 雀の千声鶴の一声

[The cry of a thousand sparrows, the cry of one crane.] ● One word of a wise person is worth more than a thousand words of a fool. Equally the words of one wise person are worth more than the babble of a thousand fools. ♦ 愚者の雄弁は沈黙なり ♦ 知る者は言わず言う者は知らず ♦ 沈黙は愚者の機知である

## 雀 百まで踊り忘れず

[A sparrow will remember its dance till it reaches a hundred.]
● What is leaned early in life is retained in old age. • What is learned in the cradle is carried to the grave. • The child is the father of the man. = 老いたる馬は路を忘れず

## 捨てる神はあれば助ける神あり

[If there are gods that forsake one, there are gods that assist one.]
● The world is a vast place with many people, and if one is deserted by one person at one moment, one may be rescued by another person at another moment. • Fortune's wheel is always turning. • The world is as kind as it is cruel. • When one door is shut, another is open. = 禍福は糾える縄の如し = 殺す神あれば助ける神あり = 沈む瀬あれば浮かぶ瀬あり ♦ 入り船あれば出船あり ♦ 有為転変は世の習い ♦ 昨日の敵は今日の味方 ♦ 昨日の友は今日の仇 ♦ 昨日の情けは今日の仇 ♦ 昨日の花は今日の夢 ♦ 昨日の淵は今日の瀬 ♦ 今日の味方は明日の敵 ♦ 損をする者あれば得をする者がある ♦ 天道人を殺さず

## 脛に傷持てば笹原走る

[Those with a scar on their shin will run through a plain of bamboo grass.] ☞ This proverb is a pun on the expression 脛に傷持つ, the idiomatic meaning of which is "to have a guilty conscience," yet the literal meaning of which is "to have a scar on one's shin." Thus, people with a guilty conscience will not be at peace with themselves and always be on tenterhooks. ● Someone who is wounded on the shin will not be able to walk leisurely (but be forced to run) through a field of hard and prickly bamboo grass. • He who is guilty believes all men speak ill of him. • Quiet conscience sleeps. • A guilty conscience needs no accuser. = 足に傷持てば笹原走る

## 墨は餓鬼に摩らせ、筆は鬼に持たせよ

[Let a little devil rub the ink; let the Devil hold the brush.] ✍ *Sumi* (墨) is a high-grade Indian ink that comes in a hard, thin stick,

**す**

which is rubbed against an ink stone (硯), filled with a little water in order to produce ink. ● When writing calligraphy, one should rub the ink without applying too much force and save one's energy and vigor for the composition. = 墨を摩るは病児の如くし、筆を把るは壮夫の如くす

## 墨を摩るは病児の如くし、筆を把るは壮夫の如くす

[Rub the ink like a weak infant; wield the brush like a man in his prime.] ✍ *Sumi* (墨) is a high-grade Indian ink that comes in a hard thin stick, which is rubbed against an ink stone (硯), filled with a little water in order to produce ink. ● When writing calligraphy, one should rub the ink without applying too much force and save one's energy and vigor for the composition. = 墨は餓鬼に摩らせ、筆は鬼に持たせよ

## 住めば都

[If one lives in a place it is the capital.] ● Once people have rooted in a place, they often prefer it above any other. • An Englishman's home is his castle. • Home is where the heart is. • East or west, home is best. ▶ 越鳥南枝に巣をかけ、胡馬北風に嘶く ▶ 故郷忘じ難し ▶ 代馬北風に依る

## するは一時名は末代

[To do something is temporal; fame is eternal.] ❶ To do what is necessary may be a momentary burden; not to do what is necessary will be an eternal disgrace. ❷ The hardships one endures to accomplish a great work will pass, the fame that will accrue is eternal. ▶ 手形は残れど足形は残らず ▶ 虎は死して革を止め、人は死して名を残す ▶ 人は一代、名は末代 ▶ 身は一代、名は末代

## 寸善尺魔の世の中

[We live in a world in which for one *sun* of goodness there is one *shaku* of evil.] ✍ The Japanese *sun* (寸) is a traditional unit of measurement still used by Japanese craftsmen. One *sun* is roughly three centimeters; a *sun* is ten *bu* (分) and a tenth of a *shaku* (尺). ● We live in an imperfect world, in which for every good deed done

138

many crimes are committed. ● In evil there is odds. ◆ 寺の隣に鬼が
住む ◆ 寺の門前に鬼が住む

## 寸を与えれば尺を望む

[Give someone a *sun* and they will covet a *shaku*.] ✍ The Japanese
*sun* (寸) is a traditional unit of measurement still used by Japanese
craftsmen. One *sun* is roughly three centimeters; a *sun* is ten *bu* (分
) and a tenth of a *shaku* (尺). ● What is granted as a concession is
often interpreted as an invitation to take all. ● Give someone an
inch and they'll take a mile. = 鉈を貸して山を伐られる = 庇を貸し
て母屋を取られる ◆ 有るが上にも欲しがるのが人情 ◆ 有るは嫌な
り、思うは成らず ◆ 昨日に優る今日の花 ◆ 千石を得て万石を恨む ◆
成るは嫌なり、思うは成らず ◆ 隴を得て蜀を望む

# セ

## 性相近し、習い相遠し

[Nature is close; learning is distant.] ● People's innate character
will change little with time, but their acquired learning will differ
greatly as time goes by. ◆ 愚は書を得て賢となり、賢は書に因って利
あり ◆ 貧しき者は書に因って富み、富める者は書に因って貴し

## 井蛙は以って海を語るべからず

[The frog in the well cannot speak of the ocean.] 📖 This proverb is
attributed to the Chinese philosopher Zhuangzi. ● Those who share
a world of limited scope can talk only of small matters and will
never be able to fathom the depths of the minds of great people.
● Home-keeping youth have ever homely wits. = 井魚は共に大を語
るべからず ◆ 井の中の蛙大海を知らず ◆ 燕雀は天地の高きを知らず
◆ 大海知らぬ井の蛙 ◆ 夏の虫氷を笑う

## 生あるものは必ず滅ぼす

[That which has life will inevitably perish.] ● All living things must
sooner or later die, such is life. ● He that is once born, once must die.
● Man is mortal. ● All living things are bound to die. = 生は死の始め

**せ**

## 井魚は共に大を語るべからず

[The fish in the well cannot speak with each other of the world at large.] ● Those who share a world of limited scope can talk only of small matters and will never be able to fathom the depths of the minds of great people. • Home-keeping youth have ever homely wits. = 井蛙は以って海を語るべからず ♦ 井の中の蛙大海を知らず ♦ 燕雀は天地の高きを知らず ♦ 大海知らぬ井の蛙 ♦ 夏の虫氷を笑う

## 精神一到何事かならざらん

[If it is done with unity of spirit nothing is impossible.] ● If one applies oneself to something wholeheartedly there is nothing that one cannot do. • Where there is a will there is a way. = 為せば成る = 石に立つ矢 = 一念岩をも徹す = 一念天に通ず = 為せば成る ♦ 石の上にも三年 ♦ 泥棒も十年

## 聖人に師無し

[Sages have no teachers.] ● Good people need no teachers, since in their wisdom, they will go through life and adopt from others what is good and discard what is bad. • By other's faults wise men correct their own. ♦ 前車の覆るは後車の戒め ♦ 人のふり見て我がふり直せ

## 聖人は危うきに近寄らず

[Sages will not draw near to danger.] ● Good people will be careful about how they speak and act, and thus avoid danger. • Discretion is the better part of valor. • Danger is next neighbor to security. = 君子は危うきに近寄らず ♦ 危ない事は怪我の内 ♦ 三十六計逃ぐるに如かず ♦ 重宝を抱く者は夜行せず ♦ ❷ 馬鹿さしじがれば二がえ馬鹿 ≠ 盲蛇に怖じず

## 急いた蟹は穴を失う

[The hurrying crab will miss its hole.] ● Those who lose their composure and try to reach their goal in a hurry will fail. • Haste makes waste. • The hasty angler loses the fish. = 慌てる蟹は穴へ入れぬ ♦ 焦ると損する ♦ 急いては事を仕損じる ♦ 急がば回れ ♦ 短気は損気

## 急いては事を仕損じる

[Hurrying will lead to failure.] ● Doing something in a hurry without proper thought or preparation will inevitably lead to failure. ● Patient men win the day. ● Haste makes waste. = 焦ると損する ♦ 慌てる蟹は穴へ入れぬ ♦ 急がば回れ ♦ 短気は損気

## 盛年重ねて来たらず

[The prime of one's life never comes round a second time.] ● One is only young once, and to miss the chances of youth is to have the window of life closed on one forever. ● Time and tide wait for none. = 若い時は二度無い = 若きは二度と無し ♦ 光陰に関守無し ♦ 光陰人を待たず ♦ 歳月人を待たず ♦ 月日に関守無し

## 生は死の始め

[Life is the beginning of death.] ● All living things must sooner or later die, and thus the beginning of life is the beginning of death, and no sooner has one been born or one begins to die. ● Man is mortal. All living things are bound to die. = 生あるものは必ず滅ぼす

## 世間の口に戸は立てられぬ

[One cannot put a door in the mouth of the public.] ● People will talk, and once a rumor or scandal has entered the public domain, before long it will be known by all. ● People will talk. = 人の口に戸は立てられぬ ♦ 一犬虚を吠ゆれば万犬実を伝う ♦ 流言は知者に止まる ≠ 人の噂も七十五日 ≠ 世の取り沙汰も七十五日

## 世上の毀誉は善悪にあらず

[The praise and slander of the world do not lie in good and bad.] ● The degree in which things are valued in the world bears no relation to their intrinsic good and bad qualities. Similarly, the way one is perceived in the public eye bears little relation to one's true character.

## 背に腹は換えられない

[One cannot exchange one's back with one's stomach.] ● Some things are more important than others, and it may be necessary to sacrifice something important for something that is of even greater value. ● Close is my shirt, but closer is my skin. ♦ 海老で鯛を釣る ♦ 雁は八百、矢は三文

## 銭有る時は銭無き日を思え

[In times when one has money, do not forget the day one had none.] ● When one has or comes into money one should remember what it was like to go without and spend sensibly. ● In fair weather prepare for foul. ♦ 警戒は警備なり ♦ 治に居て乱を忘れず

## 千石万石も飯一杯

[A thousand *koku*, ten thousand *koku*, one bowl of boiled rice.] ✍ A *koku* (石) is the traditional Japanese measure for rice yields, equivalent to approximately 180 liters, considered an average person's annual consumption. ● No matter how much one may accumulate in life, to live comfortably one requires only a few basic necessities. ● Sufficient unto the day is the evil thereof. ● He is rich enough that wants nothing. = 千畳敷で寝ても畳一枚 = 千畳 万畳 只一畳 ♦ 起きて三尺寝て六尺 ♦ 起きて半畳寝て一畳

## 千石を得て万石を恨む

[Obtain a thousand *koku*, yet feel resentment at ten thousand.] ✍ A *koku* (石) is the traditional Japanese measure for rice yields, equivalent to approximately 180 liters, considered an average person's annual consumption. ☞ As Japan's staple food, rice in feudal times was the immediate agent of wealth and power, since the amount of rice a domain yielded was commensurate with the number of troops its lord could maintain. The estates of the *hatamoto* (旗本), the enfeoffed bannermen who directly served the *shōgun*, might have yields anywhere between one thousand and three thousand *koku*, while those of the powerful *daimyō* (大名), or warlords could range from a hundred thousand *koku* to well over a million. ● Those who obtain what they have set their eyes on are often tempted to acquire more. ● Avarice knows no bounds. = 隴を得て蜀を望む ♦ 有るが上にも欲しがるのが人情 ♦ 有るは嫌なり、思うは成らず ♦ 昨日に優る今日の花 ♦ 成るは嫌なり、思うは成らず

## 前車の覆るは後車の戒め

[The overturning of the preceding cart is a warning to the following cart.] ● A good way to improve oneself is to observe the mistakes made by others and correct one's behavior to avoid making similar mistakes. • One man's fault is another's lesson. • Learn wisdom by the follies of others. • It is good to learn at other men's cost. • By other's faults wise men correct their own. • Learn wisdom from the folly of others. = 人のふり見て我がふり直せ ♦ 木は規に依って直く人は人に依って賢し

## 千畳敷で寝ても畳一枚

[Though one may sleep in a room with a thousand *tatami*, only one *tatami* is needed.] ✍ The *tatami* (畳) is a thick mat of woven straw of roughly one hundred and eighty by ninety centimeters. ● No matter how much one may accumulate in life, to live comfortably requires only a few basic necessities. = 千石万石も飯一杯 = 千畳万畳只一畳 ♦ 起きて三尺寝て六尺 ♦ 起きて半畳寝て一畳

## 千畳 万畳只一畳

[A thousand *tatami*, ten thousand *tatami*, just one *tatami*.] ✍ The *tatami* (畳) is a thick mat of woven straw of roughly one hundred and eighty by ninety centimeters. ● No matter how much one may accumulate in life, to live comfortably one requires only a few basic necessities. = 千石万石も飯一杯 = 千畳敷で寝ても畳一枚 ♦ 起きて三尺寝て六尺 ♦ 起きて半畳寝て一畳

## 前人樹を植えて後人涼を得

[Those who go before plant the tree; those who come after gain the coolness.] ● The benefits enjoyed by one generation are obtained through the efforts of the previous generation. Similarly, by the labor of the present generation future generations will be able to live in comfort. ♦ 親は苦労する、子は楽をする、孫は乞食する ♦ 爺はしんどする、子は楽をする、孫の代は乞食する

## 栴檀は双葉より芳し

[The sandalwood tree is fragrant from the moment it buds.]

**せ**

● People with exceptional talents tend to manifest them already in early youth. ● Genius displays itself even in childhood. = 実の生る木は花から知れる ♦ 虎豹の駒は食牛の気あり ♦ 虎の子は地に落つれば牛を食う気あり ♦ 流れを汲みて源を知る ♦ 実を見て木を知れ ≠ 大器晩成 ≠ ❷ 早く熟すれば早く腐る

### 船頭馬方お乳の人

[Skippers, packhorse drivers, and wetnurses.] ✍ An *umakata* (馬方) is a packhorse driver. An *o-chi* (お乳) is an old word for wetnurse. ☞ This proverb hails back to a time when skippers, packhorse drivers, and wetnurses were hard to come by. That demand, combined with the power they exercised over the passengers, cargo, and infants in their care, apparently caused many to assume airs somewhat above their station. ● Used to describe the demanding and bullying nature of those who have a little authority over others. = 馬方船頭お乳の人

### 船頭多くて船山に上る

[When there are too many skippers the ship will run into a mountain.] ● When too many persons are in control of a project it will become impossible to get all the various policies to be consistent with each other, causing the project to fail. ● Too many cooks spoil to broth. ♦ 家を道端に作れば三年成らず ♦ 舎を道端に作れば三年にして成らず

### 千日取り越すとも一日延ばすな

[Anticipate by a thousand days, but do not delay by one.] ● To do something well in advance is wise; to postpone things to tomorrow which should be done today is folly. ● Procrastination is the thief of time.

### 千日の勤学より一時の名匠

[Rather than a thousand days of diligent learning, one hour with a great teacher.] ● Rather than try to acquire knowledge by reading widely on one's own, one should seek the guidance of a great teacher, since they will know what is worthwhile to learn and how to correctly interpret the teachings of the sages. ● In every art it is good to have a master. = 君と共にする一夜の話は十年の書を読むに優る ◆ 師は針の如し、弟子は糸の如し

## 善人の敵となるとも悪人を友とすな

[Even though one may become the enemy of a good person, one should never befriend a bad person.] ● The loss of influence of a good person will not corrupt one's character too much; the continued negative influence of friendship with a bad person, however, will. ● Better an open enemy than a false friend. ● A false friend is worse than an open enemy. ● Better be alone than in bad company. ◆ 麻に連るる蓬 ◆ 朱に交われば赤く¥}なる ◆ 知者の敵とはなるとも愚者の友とはなるべからず ◆ 白砂は泥に在りて之と皆黒し

## 善は急げ

[Hurry when doing good.] ● When one has an opportunity to do good (and thus accumulate *karma*) one should not waste a moment. ● Make hay while the sun shines. ◆ 一寸の光陰軽んず可からず ◆ 逢うた時に笠を脱げ ◆ 好機逸す可からず

## 千里の馬はあれども一人の伯楽は無し

[There will be a thousand-*ri*-horse, but not a Hakuraku.] ✍ The *ri* (里 ) is an ancient Chinese measurement of distance, the equivalent of 0.3 miles. With time, it came to denote the distance one could walk in an hour, and during the Edo period (1600–1867) it was officially defined as 36 *chō*, or about 2.44 miles. Hakuraku, or Bai Lo in Chinese, was a famous Chinese connoisseur of horses who lived during the Spring and Autumn period (770-476BC). ● In every age there will be people with talent, but not every age brings forth those who are able to recognize those talents and foster them. ● Workmen are easier found than masters. ◆ 強将の下に弱卒無し ◆ 勇将の下に弱卒無し ◆ 良将の下に弱卒無し

## 千里の道も一歩より始まる

[A journey of a thousand *ri* starts with one step.] ✍ The *ri* (里) is an ancient Chinese measurement of distance, the equivalent of 0.3

miles. With time, it came to denote the distance one could walk in an hour, and during the Edo period (1600–1867) it was officially defined as 36 *chō*, or about 2.44 miles. ● No matter how ambitious the goal, one must begin with the (small) tasks at hand. Similarly, the greatest accomplishments often have humble beginnings (so one should not despair at what appears to be modest progress). • Everything must have a beginning. • Step by step one goes a long way. ＝ 始めの一歩、末の千里 ◆ 一朝一夕の故に非ず ◆ 馬に乗るまで牛に乗れ ◆ 沙弥から長老にはなれぬ ◆ ❷ 将を射んと欲すれば先ず馬を射よ ◆ 高きに登るは低きよりす ◆ 始めから長老にはなれぬ ◆ ❷ 人を射んとせば先ず馬を射よ

### 千両の鷹も放さねば知れぬ

[Even (the talent of) a thousand-*ryō* falcon cannot be known unless it is set free.] ✍ The *ryō* (両) is an ancient Japanese unit of measurement for the weighing of silver and gold. During the Meiji period (1868–1912) the *ryō* became synonymous with the *yen* (円). ❶ No matter how skillful or useful something or someone may seem, unless put to the test, there is no knowing their true value. ＝ 逸物の鷹も放さねば捕らず ＝ 百貫の鷹も放さねば捕らず ◆ 猿を檻に置けば豚と同じ ◆ 盤根錯節に遭いて利器を知る ◆ 雪圧して松の操を知る ❷ Money is not the measure of all things.

# ソ

### 相談は年寄り、喧嘩は若者

[For counsel, old men; for quarrels, young men.] ● Old people, who have learned to control their emotions, are more inclined to settle disputes by reason; young people, who are easily excited, are more inclined to resort to violence. • Old men for counsel, young men for war. • An old wise man's shadow is better than a young buzzard's sword. ◆ 相手の無い喧嘩は出来ない

### 象は兎の小道に遊ばず

[Elephants do not wander onto the small paths of rabbits.] ● Great people will not be found in the company of or behave in the same

146

way as commoners, but will move in their own spheres and behave according to their own rules. • Great ships must have deep waters. • Great would have none great, and the little all little. = 大魚は小池に棲まず = 呑舟の魚は枝流に泳がず ♦ 大人は小目を遣わず ≠ 河海は細流を択ばず ≠ 大海は細流を択ばず

## 然うは問屋が卸さない

[The wholesaler does not sell them that cheap.] ● Things seldom are as easy as one would hope. • Things seldom go as one wishes. • If wishes were horses, beggars would ride. = 儘にならぬが浮世の習い ♦ 有るが上にも欲しがるのが人情 ♦ 有るは嫌なり、思うは成らず ♦ 成るは嫌なり、思うは成らず

## 惻隠の心は仁の端なり

[A heart with sympathy is the beginning of benevolence.] 📖 This proverb is taken from the works of Mencius. ● Those who see the suffering of others and take pity have taken the first step on the road of charity. • Pity's akin to love.

## 賊去って張弓

[The stringing of a bow after the rebels have departed.] ● To try to remedy a problem when it is too late. • Lock the stable door after the horse is stolen. • After death, the doctor. • After meat, mustard. = 戦を見て矢を矧ぐ = 喧嘩過ぎての棒乳切り = 賊の後の棒乳切り = 敵を見て矢を矧ぐ = 泥棒を捕らえて縄を綯う = 難に臨んで兵を鋳る = 盗人を見て縄を綯う = 火を失して池を掘る ♦ 後の祭 ♦ 六日の菖蒲、十日の菊 ♦ 盆過ぎての鯖商い

## 俗に入っては俗に従え

[When going among the commoners, do as the commoners do.] ● When among people with their own customs it is only by acting in accordance to those customs that one will avoid trouble and achieve one's goals. • When in Rome, do as the Romans do. = 郷に入っては郷に従え = 里に入りては里に従う = 其の国に入れば其の俗に従う ♦ 国に入っては先ずその法を聞 ♦ 境に入っては禁を問え

## 賊の後の棒乳切り

[The cutting of clubs after the rebels.] ● To try to remedy a problem when it is too late. ● Lock the stable door after the horse is stolen. ● After death, the doctor. ● After meat, mustard. = 戦を見て矢を矧ぐ = 喧嘩過ぎての棒乳切り = 賊去って張弓 = 敵を見て矢を矧ぐ = 泥棒を捕らえて縄を綯う = 難に臨んで兵を鋳る = 盗人を見て縄を綯う = 火を失して池を掘る ♦ 後の祭 ♦ 六日の菖蒲、十日の菊 ♦ 盆過ぎての鯖商い

## 袖振り合うも他生の縁

[A chance meeting, too, is the karma of another life] ● All experiences in life are preordained, and even a chance encounter while traveling or an event that seems of little significance is karma. ● A meeting by chance is preordained. = 躓く石も縁

## 備え有れば憂い無し

[If preparations are made, there will be no grief.] ● If one is prepared for the worst there is no reason to fear what tomorrow may bring. ● Providing is preventing. ♦ 明日は雨人は泥棒 ♦ 石橋を叩いて渡る 運は天にあり、鎧は胸にあり ♦ 転ばぬ先の杖 ♦ 濡れぬ前の傘 ♦ 人を見たら泥棒と思え ♦ 火を見れば火事と思え

## 其の域に入らざれば之を知らず

[If one does not enter the area one cannot know what it contains.] ● If one is not willing to risk new experiences one cannot expect to gain any new understanding. Similarly, one cannot know the value of a certain stage (of enlightenment or progress) without first having attained it. ♦ 糠の中にも粉米

## 其の一を知りて其の二を知らず

[Know one but not know two.] ● Used to describe those who know one fact yet are unable to deduce a second that logically follows. ● To look on only one side of the shield. = 一を知って二を知らず ♦ 遠きを知りて近きを知らず ♦ 人を知る者は知なり、自ら知る者は明なり ≠ ❷ 一葉落ちて天下の秋を知る ≠ 一を聞いて十を知る ≠ 瓶中の氷を見て天下の寒さを知る

## 其の樹を陰とする者は其の枝を折らず

[Those who wish to use the tree for its shade will not break its branches.] ● Those who rely on the hospitality or kindness of others will avoid causing them harm. ● He is an ill guest that never drinks to his host. ♦ 居候三杯目にはそっと出し

## 其の国に入れば其の俗に従う

[When entering a country, comply with its customs.] ● To avoid trouble and to achieve one's goals one should obey the laws of the place one is in. ● When in Rome, do as the Romans do. = 郷に入っては郷に従え = 里に入りては里に従う = 俗に入っては俗に従え ♦ 国に入っては先ずその法を聞 ♦ 境に入っては禁を問え

## 其の罪を憎んで其の人を憎まず

[Hate the sin but do not hate the sinner.] ● Crimes must be atoned for but we must recognize our common humanity and try to understand and rehabilitate those who commit them. = 君子は其の罪を憎んで其の人を憎まず

## 空飛ぶ雁を吸い物に当てる

[Reserve the flying wild goose for one's soup.] ● Used in instances where people make plans based on their expectations of an uncertain future. ● Don't count your chickens before they are hatched. ● Sell the lion's skin before one has caught the lion. = 捕らぬ狸の皮算用 = 儲けぬ前の胸算用

## 空吹く風と聞き流す

[Ignore (something) along with the blowing wind.] ● Used in cases where advice or good counsel is totally ignored. ● In one ear and out the other. = 馬の耳に念仏 = 蛙の面に水 = 馬耳東風 ♦ 猫に小判 ♦ 豚に真珠

## 損をする者あれば得をする者がある

[If there are those who suffer a loss, there are those who make a profit.] ● Even though one may incur a loss today, tomorrow one may well make a profit. ● It is an ill wind that blows nobody good.

• When one door is shut, another is open. ♦ 入り船あれば出船あり ♦ 有為転変は世の習い ♦ 禍福は糾える縄の如し ♦ 殺す神あれば助ける神あり ♦ 沈む瀬あれば浮かぶ瀬あり ♦ 捨てる神はあれば助ける神あり ♦ 出船に良い風は入り船に悪い

# タ

**た**

## 大海知らぬ井の蛙

[The frog in the well that does not know the ocean.] ● Those who prefer the comfort of home and never travel do not know what the world has to offer, and thus will miss opportunities to live fuller lives. Similarly, those who fail to inquire into other people's thinking will become the self-complacent prisoners of their own limited knowledge and narrow-mindedness. • Home-keeping youth have ever homely wits. = 井の中の蛙大海を知らず = 燕雀は天地の高きを知らず ♦ 井蛙は以って海を語るべからず ♦ 井魚は共に大を語るべからず ♦ 夏の虫氷を笑う

## 大海の底は測りつべし人の心は測るべからず

[The floor of the ocean can be measured; the hearts of people cannot be measured.] ● All physical objects have their limits and can be measured. The hearts of people, by contrast, are unfathomable, and one can never know how much compassion or cruelty they may hold.

## 大海は細流を択ばず

[The ocean does not single out small streams.] ● Great people are big-hearted and can get along with all sorts of people. = 河海は細流を択ばず ♦ 大人は小目を遣わず ≠ 象は兎の小道に遊ばず ≠ 大魚は小池に棲まず ≠ 呑舟の魚は枝流に泳がず

## 大器晩成

[Great talents mature late.] 📖 This proverb is attributed to the Chinese Daoist Laozi. ● Exceptional gifts or talents often take a long time to fully develop. • Soon ripe, soon rotten. = 早く熟すれば早く

150

腐る ≠ 虎豹の駒は食牛の気あり ≠ 栴檀は双葉より芳し ≠ 虎の子は地に落つれば牛を食う気あり

## 大魚は小池に棲まず

[Large fish do not dwell in small ponds.] ● Great people will not be found in the company of commoners nor meddling in trifling affairs. ● Great ships must have deep waters. ● Great would have none great, and the little all little. = 象は兎の小道に遊ばず ≠ 呑舟の魚は枝流に泳がず ◆ 大人は小目を遣わず ≠ 河海は細流を択ばず ≠ 大海は細流を択ばず

## 大賢は愚なるが如し

[A great sage is like a fool.] ● People of great wisdom will refrain from flaunting their knowledge, thus creating the impression that they lack intelligence. ● It is wisdom to sometimes seem a fool. = 大知は愚の如し ◆ 大巧は拙なるが如し

## 大工の掘っ立て

[The carpenter's hovel.] ● Those who use their skills to make a living usually do not have the time or means to use those skills to satisfy their own needs. ● The shoemaker's children go barefoot. ● The tailor's wife is worst clad. = 耕す者は食わず、織る者は着ず = 駕籠舁き駕籠に乗らず ◆ 医者の不養生

## 大巧は拙なるが如し

[A great craftsman is like a blunderer.] 📖 This proverb is attributed to the Chinese Daoist Laozi. ● Great craftsmen will not flaunt their skills in public and thus create the impression that they do not possess much skill. ● It is wisdom to sometimes seem a fool. ◆ 大賢は愚なるが如し ◆ 大知は愚の如し

## 大巧は為さざる所に在り

[Great talent lies in the unaccomplished.] ☞ This proverb is well illustrated by Japanese ceramics, especially the seemingly crudely fashioned tea bowls or *chawan* (茶碗) that are used in the Japanese tea ceremony. ● The superiority of a truly great piece of art is

た

found not in ostentation or grand design, but in the unassuming refinement of its details. Similarly, the real genius of craftsmen or artists lies in their understanding of the beauty of imperfection.

## 大巧を成す者は衆を計らず

[Those who accomplish great things do not consult the people.]
● People who achieve greatness follow their own instincts and do not consult others on the wisdom of their actions. Similarly, great leaders will not be led astray by the unsolicited meddling of those around them. ▶ 英雄人を欺く ▶ 燕雀安んぞ鴻鵠の志を知らんや ▶ 名将は名将を知る

## 大巧を論する者は小過を録せず

[Those who consider great feats do not record small errors.] ● When one is about to reward someone for an outstanding achievement, one should not make an issue of small errors that were made in the process.

## 大山の高きは一石に非ず

[The height of the mountain is not found in one stone.] ● The realization of a great project requires the unity of thought and the concerted effort of a large number of ordinary people. Similarly, it may take many small efforts to accomplish a task, but once completed the result may be impressive. ● Many a little makes a mickle. ▶ ● 塵も積もれば山と成る

## 大山も蟻穴より崩る

[Great mountains may crumble through an ant hole.] ● The slightest negligence may result in an irreversible loss of the greatest magnitude. Similarly, the greatest of enterprises may come to naught through the tiniest of oversights. ● A small leak will sink a ship. = 蟻の穴から堤も崩れる ▶ ❷ 蛍火をもって酒弥山を焼く

## 大事の前の小事

[The small matter in the face of the large matter.] ❶ In a major undertaking it is important to pay careful attention to all the minor

た

details. ● The devil is in the detail. ♦ 隙間の風は寒い ❷ In order to achieve a great objective, it may be necessary to sacrifice objectives of less importance. ● Throw out a lobster and pull in a whale. ● Throw a sprat to catch a herring. ● Give an egg to gain an ox. ● You may lose a fly to catch a trout. 海老で鯛を釣る ♦ 雁は八百、矢は三文 ♦ 背に腹は換えられない

## 大樹の下に美草無し

[Fresh grass does not grow below large trees.] ● Those who are in the service of talented people will feel overawed by their superiority and be discouraged from achieving greatness for themselves. Similarly, talented people will not gather in places where those talents are frustrated. ● Great trees keep down the little ones. ≠ 麻に連るる蓬 ≠ 朱に交われば赤くなる ≠ 大木の下に小木育つ ≠ 強将の下に弱卒無し ≠ 勇将の下に弱卒無し ≠ 良将の下に弱卒無し

## 大人は赤子の心を失わず

[Great people do not lose the heart of an infant.] 📖 This proverb is taken from the works of Mencius. ❶ Great people have the purity of heart of infants, and it is that which makes them virtuous. ● Great men are children at heart. ❷ Great leaders treat their subjects with the same affection they would bestow on their own infants and thus gain their loyalty. ♦ 大人は小目を遣わず

## 大人は小目を遣わず

[Great people do not use small eyes.] ❶ Great people are magnanimous. ♦ 大人は赤子の心を失わず ❷ Great people do not meddle in trifling affairs. ● A great ship asks deep waters. ♦ 河海は細流を択ばず ♦ 象は兎の小道に遊ばず ♦ 大海は細流を択ばず ♦ 大魚は小池に棲まず ♦ 呑舟の魚は枝流に泳がず

## 大声里耳に入らず

[A great voice does not enter the public ear.] ❶ Sophisticated music is not readily appreciated by commoners. ♦ 瞽者は文章の観に与ること無し ❷ The words of the great are not easily understood by commoners.

## 大象も女の髪には繋がれる

[Even an elephant can be tied with the hair of a woman.] ● The sway a woman can hold over men who are bewitched by her charms can be more powerful than any other force. ● One hair of a woman draws more than a hundred yoke of oxen. = 女の髪の毛には大象も繋がる

## 大知は愚の如し

[A great intellect is like a fool.] ● People of great wisdom will refrain from flaunting their knowledge, thus creating the impression that they lack intelligence. ● It is wisdom to sometimes seem a fool. = 大賢は愚なるが如し ♦ 大巧は拙なるが如し

## 鯛の尾より鰯の頭

[Rather than the tail of a sea bream, be the head of a sardine.] ● Rather than play a minor part in a major event, it is better to play a leading role in a minor event. Similarly, rather than be an unimportant member of a large group, it is better to be the leader of a small group. ● Better the head of a pike than the tail of a sturgeon. ● Better be first in a village than second in Rome. = 大鳥の尾より小鳥の頭 = 鶏口となるも牛後となる勿れ ≠ 鰯の頭より鯛の尾

## 大の虫を生かして小の虫を殺す

[Kill the small insect to give life to the big insect.] ● In order to achieve something great, it may be necessary to sacrifice things of less importance. ● Throw out a lobster and pull in a whale. ● Throw a sprat to catch a herring. ● Give an egg to gain an ox. ● You may lose a fly to catch a trout. ♦ ❷ 大事の前の小事 ♦ 海老で鯛を釣る ♦ 雁は八百、矢は三文 ♦ 背に腹は換えられない

## 代馬北風に依る

[A horse from Dai will respond to the northern wind.] ☞ Dai was a northern province in ancient China. ● Those who are far from their family and friends will grow homesick with the faintest reminder of home. ● Home is where the heart is. ● East or west, home is best. = 越鳥南枝に巣をかけ、胡馬北風に嘶く ♦ 故郷忘じ難し ♦ 住めば都

## 大木の下に小木育つ

[Small trees are raised below large trees.] ● Those who are in the service of people with power will benefit from their influence and be able to develop their talents unhampered. ▶ 強将の下に弱卒無し ▶ 勇将の下に弱卒無し ▶ 良将の下に弱卒無し ≠ 大樹の下に美草無し

## 大木は風に折らる

[Great trees are broken by the wind.] ● Great people are the envy of others, which, when too strong may even bring them down. ● Tall trees catch much wind. ● The highest in court the nearest the gallows. = 高木は風に折らる = ❷ 出る杭は打たれる ▶ ❶ 大きい家に大きい風が吹く ▶ 高山の巓には美木無し ▶ 高木風に憎まる ▶ 高木風に妬まる ▶ 大名の下には久しく居るべからず ▶ 誉れは謗りの基

## 大名の病は行き倒れも同然

[An ailing *daimyō* is alike a dead person in the street.] ☞ This proverb is evocative of Japan's feudal period, when the feudal lords, or *daimyō* (大名) had absolute power over those who dwelled in their domains. They were so much feared that when they fell ill, their physicians would often refrain from taking drastic measures for fear of hurting the patient and risking their own lives, preferring instead to pass the buck on to someone else. This led the hapless patients to be compared to the *yukidaore* (行き倒れ), the anonymous travelers found collapsed and dying in the street, who were often sent from village to village, since no one wanted to bear the burden of their treatment. ● When something goes wrong, nobody is keen to take the responsibility of setting things right for fear of being blamed if they fail.

## 大名の下には久しく居るべからず

[One should not remain under a great name long.] 📖 This proverb is taken from the *Taiheiki*, a 14th-century Japanese historical epic. ● Those who reach a position of fame are wise to leave that position before the envy of others causes their downfall. ● After honor and state follow envy and hate. ● Envy is the companion of honor. ● The brighter the moon the more the dogs howl. ▶ ❶ 大きい家に大きい風

た

155

が吹く ◆ 高山の巓には美木無し ◆ 高木風に妬まる ◆ 高木風に憎まる ◆ 高木は風に折らる ◆ 大木は風に折らる ◆ ❷ 出る杭は打たれる ◆ 誉れは謗りの基

## 大欲は無欲に似たり

[Avarice resembles unselfishness.] ❶ Those who set out to make huge gains will be willing to make great investments to achieve them, which may give the impression that they are generous. ❷ If one sets the stakes too high, one may fail, so that the result will be the same as if one had not entertained any ambitions at all. • Grasp all, lose all. = 欲の深い鷹は爪を抜ける ◆ 虻蜂取らず ◆ 一念は継ぐとも二念は継ぐな ◆ 二足の草蛙は履けぬ ◆ 二兎を追う者は一兎をも得ず ≠ 一挙両得 ≠ 一石二鳥

## 倒れる事は必ず傾く方に有り

[The falling will assuredly be in the direction of the leaning.] ❶ If one perseveres in something long enough one will eventually be successful. • Constant dripping wears away the stone. ◆ 雨垂れ石を穿つ ◆ 斧を研いで針にする ◆ ❷ 塵も積もれば山と成る ◆ 点滴石をも穿つ ❷ Those who are biased or perverted will sooner or later come to grief. • As a man lives so shall he die, as a tree falls, so shall it lie.

## 高きに登るは低きよりす

[Those who (want to) climb high should start low.] ● Those who set their aims high should realize that they have a long way to go and that in order to lay a solid foundation it is better to begin modestly. • He who would climb a ladder must begin at the bottom. • Learn to speak before you sing. = 馬に乗るまで牛に乗れ = ❷ 将を射んと欲すれば先ず馬を射よ = ❷ 人を射んとせば先ず馬を射よ ◆ 一朝一夕の故に非ず ◆ 沙弥から長老にはなれぬ ◆ 千里の道も一歩より始まる ◆ 始めから長老にはなれぬ ◆ 始めの一歩、末の千里

## 耕す者は食わず、織る者は着ず

[Those who till do not eat; those who weave are not dressed.] ● Those who use their skills to make a living often do not have the time or means to use those skills to satisfy their own needs. • The

た

shoemaker's children go barefoot. ● The tailor's wife is worst clad.
= 紺屋の白袴 ♦ 駕籠舁き駕籠に乗らず

## 田から行くも畔から行くも同じ

[It is the same, whether one goes through the rice field or along the ridge between rice fields.] ● Though the methods differ the end result may be the same. ● Many roads lead to Rome. ♦ 細工は流々、仕上げをご覧じる

## 薪を抱いて火を救う

[Use firewood to extinguish the fire.] ● Used to describe an action that has the opposite effect of what was intended. ● Take oil to extinguish a fire.

## 多芸は無芸

[Many accomplishments are no accomplishments.] ● Trying to be good at too many things will only lead to a superficial and useless mastery of them. ● Jack of all trades and master of none. ● He who commences many things finishes but few. ♦ 何でも来いに名人無し ♦ 百様を知って一様を知らず ♦ 万能足りて一心足らず

## 正しき者の道は朝日の如し

[The road of the righteous is like the morning sun.] 📖 This proverb is a direct translation from the *Old Testament*. ● The life of those who are honest is bright, full of opportunity, and stable. ≠ 正しき者は艱難多し

## 正しき者は艱難多し

[The righteous have many hardships.] ● In a world rife with vice and corruption, those who try to live an honest life are confronted with many difficulties. ● Honesty may be dear bought, but can never be an ill pennyworth. ♦ 商売と屏風は曲がらぬと立たぬ ♦ 曲がれねば世が渡らぬ ≠ 正しき者の道は朝日の如し

## 立ち寄れば大木の陰

[When halting at a place, stop under the shade of a large tree.]

● When one marries or enters the service of a master, one should attach oneself to a wealthy person. • It is good sheltering under an old hedge. ◆ 富む家に痩せ犬無し

## 田作る道は農に問え

[For the (right) way to cultivate a rice field ask the farmer.] ● In all arts, crafts, and trades there are professionals and it is best to rely on their expertise. • Every man to his trade. = 海の事は漁父に問え = 酒は酒屋に茶は茶屋に = 餅は餅屋 ◆ 海老踊れども川を出でず ◆ 鴉が鵜の真似 ◆ 芸は道に依りて賢し ◆ 鹿つきの山は猟師知り、魚つきの浦は網人知る

## 立つ鳥跡を濁さず

[A bird taking wing does not soil its tracks.] ● Those who leave office always seek to leave a favorable impression. • It is an ill bird that defiles its own nest. ≠ 後は野となれ山となれ

## 蓼食う虫も好き好き

[Even the insect that eats smartweed enjoys it.] ☞ This proverb is generally used to criticize what is perceived as someone's bad taste. ● The bitter taste of smartwood is no deterrent to some insects. Similarly, what is distasteful to one may be delightful to others. • There is no accounting for tastes. • Every man to his taste. • Some prefer nettles. Tastes differ. ◆ 人おのおの楽しみ有り ◆ 人は好き好き

## 棚から牡丹餅は落ちてこない

[*Botamochi* do not fall from shelves.] ✍ *Botamochi* (牡丹餅) are rice cake dumplings covered with bean jam. ☞ This proverb builds on the Japanese idiom 棚から牡丹餅, or "a *botamochi* from the shelf," which stands for a windfall or godsend. Rice cakes, or *mochi* (餅) are made by pounding steamed rice into cakes with a large and heavy wooden hammer, a time-consuming and and tiring process. ● No feat is accomplished without effort, and the greater the feat, the more effort is required. • No pains, no gains. = 牡丹餅は棚から落ちて来ず

## 他人の飯を食わねば親の恩は知らぬ

[If one has not eaten the food of others one does not know one's debt of gratitude toward one's parents.] ● Those who have not yet had the experience of leaving home and having to make a living among others, are not aware of the depth of their parents' love and support. ● God, and parents, and our master, can never be requited. ◆ 子を持って知る親の恩

## 種の無い手品は使われぬ

[There can be no magic without a seed.] ● No task can be accomplished without the right opportunity, preparation, or resources. ● Without bait fish are not caught. ◆ 網無くて淵をのぞくな ◆ 一目の網は以て鳥を得べからず ◆ 差し金無くては雪隠も建たぬ

## 楽しみは憂いに生ず

[Pleasure is born in grief.] ● True happiness is only found and fully appreciated by living through hardships and overcoming them. Consequently, if there is suffering today, there may be joy tomorrow. ● After pain comes pleasure. ● No cross, no crown. ● No pleasure without pain. = 苦は楽の種 = 苦を知らぬ者は楽を知らぬ ◆ 苦有れば楽有り ◆ 喜び有れば憂い有り ◆ 楽有れば苦有り ≠ 現在の甘露は未来の鉄丸なり ≠ 楽しみは苦しみの種 ≠ 夏歌う者は冬泣く ≠ 楽は苦の種

## 楽しみは苦しみの種

[Pleasure is the seed of pain.] ● Pain and pleasure are two inseparable aspects of life: if there is pleasure at present, there will be pain in the future. Similarly, the pleasure one has today may come at the cost of pain in the future. ● Unrest comes from rest. = 現在の甘露は未来の鉄丸なり = 夏歌う者は冬泣く = 楽は苦の種 ◆ 苦有れば楽有り ◆ 楽有れば苦有り ≠ 苦は楽の種 ≠ 苦を知らぬ者は楽を知らぬ

## 旅の恥は掻き捨て

[When on a journey, abandon one's shame.] ● Those who travel far away from home—to places where no one knows them and their actions will go unnoticed—will be tempted to do things that they would refrain from at home. • Once over the border, one may do anything.

## 旅は道連れ、世は情け

[On a journey, a fellow traveler; in life, kindness.] ● In life, the presence of kindness is as soothing as the company of a fellow traveler on the road. • No road is long with good company. • Company in distress makes trouble less. • A merry companion is a wagon in the way. = 人は情けの下に立つ ▶ 愛出ずる者は愛返り、福往く者は福来る ▶ 愛は愛を生む ▶ 仇も情けも我が身より出る ▶ 魚心有れば水心 ▶ 問い声良ければいらえ声良い ▶ 情けは人の為ならず ▶ 人は情けの下に立つ

## 玉磨かざれば光なし

[A gem when not polished does not sparkle.] ● No matter how much talent one may possess, if one does not study hard and try to improve oneself one will never reap its full benefits. • An uncut gem does not sparkle. = 瑠璃の光も磨きがら ▶ 逸物の鷹も放さねば捕らず ▶ 瓦も磨けば玉となる ▶ 才有れども用いざれば愚人の如し ▶ 猿を檻に置けば豚と同じ ▶ ❶ 千両の鷹も放さねば知れぬ ▶ 百貫の鷹も放さねば捕らず ▶ 蒔かぬ種は生えぬ ▶ 物は試し ≠ 瓦は磨いても玉にはならぬ ≠ 度場は伯楽に会わず

## 黙り虫壁を通す

[Silent worms pierce walls.] ❶ It is the modest who usually accomplish great feats. • Quietness is best, as the fox said when he bit off the cock's head. ❷ Those who have evil designs often keep a low profile. • Silent men, like silent waters, are deep and dangerous.

## 民は之に由らしむべし、之を知らしむべからず

[One should make the people act (according to one's will), but not inform them (of one's intentions).] 📖 This proverb is taken from the *Analects* of Confucius. ❶ It is possible to make people do what is right, but to make them understand what is right is difficult. ❷ One should make the people comply by way of order, but one need not expound the underlying policies. = 由らしむべし知らしむべからず

## 撓めるなら若木の内

[If one is to bend a tree, do it while it is young.] ● If a person's character is to be corrected, it should be done while they are still young. • Best to bend while it is a twig. • As a twig is bent the tree is inclined.

## 足ろ事を知る者は幸福なり

[Those who know their fill are fortunate.] ● Those who know how to be content with what they have are truly fortunate. • He is not rich who is not satisfied. • Contentment is natural wealth.

## 短気は損気

[A short temper is a harmful temper.] ● Those who easily lose their patience tend to harm their own cause. • Let patience grow in your garden always. • Haste makes waste. ◦ 焦ると損する ◦ 慌てる蟹は穴へ入れぬ ◦ 急がば回れ ◦ 急いた蟹は穴を失う ◦ 急いては事を仕損じる

# チ

## 知恵は万代の宝

[Wisdom is the treasure of ten thousand generations.] ● Someone's wisdom does not only benefit their own generation, but may be passed on and serve many generations to come. • Without wisdom wealth is worthless. ＝ 富は一生の財、知は万代の財 ◦ 一世の富貴死後までの文章

## 近火で手を焙れ

[Warm your hands at the closest fire.] ❶ Rather than wait for an opportunity to make great gains, it is better to seize the opportunity of the moment even if gains are modest. • A bird in the hand is worth two in the bush. • Better an egg today than a hen tomorrow. ＝ 明日の百より今日の五十 ＝ 末始終より今の三十 ＝ 後の千金より今の百文 ＝ 来年の百両より今年の一両 ◦ あの世千日この世の一日 ◦ 大取りより小取り ◦ 聞いた百文より見た一文 ≠ 小節を規る

者は栄名を成す能わず ≠ 小利を見れば則ち大事成らず ❷ Rather than rely only on a distant but close friend, one should cherish acquaintances that are less dear but close by. ● A near neighbor is better than a distant cousin. ◆ 京の妹に隣代えず ◆ 親しき隣は遠き兄弟に優る ◆ 遠い親類より近くの他人

## 近くて見えぬは睫

[Eyelashes, though near, are not seen.] ● It is easy to see the shortcomings of others, but to see one's own shortcomings is exceedingly difficult. ● We see not what sits on our own shoulder. = 我が身の上は見えぬ ◆ 己れを責めて人を責むるな ◆ 局に当たる者は惑う ◆ 五十歩をもって百歩を笑う ◆ 猿の尻笑い ◆ 堤灯持ちの足元暗し ◆ 灯台下暗し ● ❷ 遠きを知りて近きを知らず ◆ 人の頭の蠅を追うより我が頭の蠅を追え ◆ 人の一寸我が一尺 ◆ 人の七難より我が十難 ◆ 目糞が鼻糞を笑う ◆ 目脂が鼻垢を笑う ◆ 我が頭の蠅を追え

## 近惚れの早飽き

[Soon enamored, soon tired.] ● People who are easily enthused about something tend to lose interest with the same ease. ● Soon hot, soon cold. ● Hot love is soon cool. ◆ 熱し易いは冷め易し ◆ 恋いたほど飽いた

## 知者にも千慮に一失

[Even the wise may fail once in a thousand ponderings.] ● Even those who seem to know everything may sometimes get it wrong. ● Homer sometime nods. ● No man is wise at all times. = 王良も時として馬車を覆す = 河童の川流れ = 賢者も千慮の一失 = 弘法にも筆の誤り = 猿も木から落ちる = 上手の手から水が漏れる = 竜馬の蹟き

## 知者の敵とはなるとも愚者の友とはなるべからず

[Even though one may become the enemy of a wise person, one should never become the friend of a fool.] ● The loss of influence of a wise person will not affect one's character adversely; the negative influence of friendship with a fool, however, will. ● Better be alone than in bad company. ◆ 麻に連るる蓬 ◆ 善人の敵となるとも悪人を友とすな

## 知者も面前に三尺の闇あり

[Even to the wise it is dark ahead beyond three *shaku*.] ✍ The Japanese *shaku* (尺) is an old unit of measurement still used by Japanese craftsmen. One *shaku* (尺) corresponds to roughly thirty centimeters. ● The road of life is known to none and even the wise will not be able to see far into the future. ● A man's destiny is always dark. = 一寸先は闇 ♦ 明日の事を言えば鬼が笑う ♦ 三年先の事を言えば鬼が笑う ♦ 人の行方と水の流れ ♦ 水の流れと人の末 ♦ 三日先の事を言えば鬼が笑う ♦ 来年の事を言えば鬼が笑う

## 血筋は争えないもの

[Lineage is incontestable.] ● No matter how much one may try to hide one's own ancestry or to assume the name of another, the personal traits and characteristics that run in a family will eventually tell. ● Blood will tell. = 氏素性は争えないもの ♦ 隠すことは現わる ♦ 天知る地知る我知る人知る

## 父に諫むる子有ればその家必ず繁栄す

[If a father has a remonstrating son the house will prosper.] ● If a son has the courage to point out the injustices in his father's actions the rest of the family will benefit. = 木は縄に従って材なり、君は諫めに従って聖なり = 君に争臣有れば、身不義に陥らず >諫言耳に逆らう >忠言耳に逆らう >良薬口に苦し

## 父も父なら子も子だ

[If the father acts the father, the son will be a son.] ● If a father does his duty as a father, he can expect his son to do his duty as a son. ● Like father, like son. ● Like breeds like. = この君にしてこの臣あり

## 知徳は車の両輪の如し

[Knowledge and virtue are like the two wheels on a cart.] ● Knowledge and virtue are inseparable, since knowledge without virtue is dangerous and virtue without knowledge is impotent. ● A man of great memory without learning hath a rock and a spindle and no stuff to spin. ♦ 学んで思わざれば則ち罔し、思いて学ばざれば則ち殆うし

163

### 治に居て乱を忘れず

[In times of peace do not forget war.] ● Even in times of peace one should not forget the possibility of war. Instead, one should remain vigilant and prepared. ● In fair weather prepare for foul. ◆ 警戒は警備なり ◆ 銭有る時は銭無き日を思え

### 地に倒るる者は地によりて立つ

[Those who stumble to the ground rise up from the ground.] ● The same mistake that causes one's downfall may, through reflection and self-improvement, be the basis for one's recovery. ◆ 過ちて改めざる是を過ちと謂う ◆ 過ちは改むるに憚る事なかれ ◆ 君子の過ちは日月の食の如し

### 地の利は人の和に如かず

[The advantage of terrain is not equal to the harmony of people.] 📖 This proverb is attributed to Mencius. ● In all human endeavors, the most powerful force lies in the unity of men. ● Union is strength. ◆ 一条の矢は折るべし十条の矢は折り難し

### 茶碗を投げば綿で抱えよ

[If a teacup is thrown, catch it with cotton wool.] ● Those who initially yield to a stronger opponent may eventually be victorious by absorbing the blows and thus exhaust their attacker. ● She stoops to conquer. = 柔能く剛を制する、弱能く強を制する ◆ 木強ければ折れ易し ◆ 強き木はむず折れ ◆ 柳に風折れなし ◆ 柳の枝に雪折れ無し

### 忠言 耳に逆らう

[Good counsel is harsh to the ear.] ● To have one's shortcomings or mistakes pointed out is not a pleasant experience. ● If the counsel be good, no matter who gave it. ● He that will not be counselled cannot be helped. = 諫言耳に逆らう ◆ 良薬口に苦し

### 仲裁は時の氏神

[Mediation may at times be an *ujigami*.] 📖 *Ujigami* (氏神) are the guardian gods or spirits that protect a place connected to the Shintō religion. ● On occasions when tempers flare a soothing word or friendly gesture may help to diffuse the situation. ● Good words cool more than cold water. ● Good words cost naught. ● Good words anoint us, and ill do unjoint us. = 挨拶は時の氏神

## 忠臣は二君に仕えず

[A loyal retainer cannot serve two masters.] ● To be loyal to two masters with differing demands is impossible. ● No man can serve two masters. ◆ 忠臣を孝子の門に求む ◆ 良禽は木を択んで棲む

## 忠臣を孝子の門に求む

[Seek loyal retainers at the gate (of a house) with filial children.] ☞ This deeply Confucian view of the organization of society prevailed throughout Japan's feudal era and may still be observed in modern day Japan. ● Those who display filial piety toward their parents will prove loyal in their service of a master. ● A good son will make a good subject. = 孝立てば則ち忠遂ぐ ◆ 忠臣は二君に仕えず ◆ 良禽は木を択んで棲む

## 長者の万灯より貧者の一灯

[Rather the one lantern of a poor person than the ten thousand of a rich person.] 📖 This proverb is taken from the *Soga monogatari*. ● The gift of someone who can ill afford it should be esteemed above the gift of someone who easily can, since the measure of their sacrifice bears testimony to their sincerity. ● A poor man's penny is better appreciated that a rich man's pound. ● A 's mite. ◆ 貰う物なら夏も小袖

## 堤灯持ちの足元暗し

[It is dark at the feet of the lantern bearer.] ❶ Those who help others to solve their problems often find it difficult to deal with their own problems. ● Lookers-on see more than players. ◆ 局に当たる者は惑う ◆ 近くて見えぬは睫 ◆ ❷ 遠きを知りて近きを知らず ◆ 人を知る者は知なり、自ら知る者は明なり ◆ 我が身の上は見えぬ ❷ Those closest to one will often shy away from speaking their mind, so that one will remain ignorant of one's own shortcomings. ● The darkest place is under the candlestick. ● One must go into the country to hear what news at London. ● One must go abroad for news at home. 灯台下暗し

## 提灯持ち後に立たず

[The lantern bearer never comes behind.] ● By the time one repents one's words or actions it is usually too late. ● Repentance comes too late. ● It is no use crying over spilt milk. ● What is done cannot be undone. = ♦ 後悔先に立たず ♦ 五十にして四十九年の非を知る ♦ 死んだ子の年を数える ♦ 後悔は知恵の糸口 ♦ 覆水盆に返らず ♦ 流水 源に返らず

## 町内で知らぬは亭主ばかりなり

[The husband is the only one in the neighborhood not to know.] ● The husband is the last one to find out about his wife's infidelity. ● The good man is the last to know what is amiss at home. ● The cuckold is the last to know of it. = 間男を知らぬは亭主ばかり

## 一寸嘗めたが身の詰まり

[A mere taste will cause one's ruin.] ● A little indulgence in vice out of curiosity may ultimately lead to total ruin. ● From short pleasures, long repentance. ♦ 一年の快楽、百年の後悔を残す ♦ 見るに目の欲触るに煩悩

## 塵も積もれば山と成る

[Even dust when accumulated will form a mountain.] ● It may take many small efforts to accomplish a task, but the result may be formidable. ● Many a little makes a mickle. 大山の高きは一石に非ず
❷ Though it may take a long time, if one perseveres in something long enough, one may achieve one's aim. ● Constant dripping wears away the stone. = 雨垂れ石を穿つ = 斧を研いで針にする = 点滴石をも穿つ ♦ 石の上にも三年 ♦ 千里の道も一歩より始まる ♦ ❶ 倒れる事は必ず傾く方に有り ♦ 泥棒も十年 ♦ 始めの一歩、末の千里

## 珍客も三日目には居候

[After three days, even a welcome guest becomes a sponger.] ● Even the most welcome of guests becomes a burden to the host

ち

when they overstay their welcome. • The first day a guest, the third day a pest. • Fresh fish and new-come guests smell in three days. ♦ 居候三杯目にはそっと出し

## 沈黙は金、雄弁は銀

[Silence is gold; eloquence is silver.] ● Though eloquence is highly regarded, silence at the appropriate moment is even more valuable. • Speech is silver, silence is golden. • No wisdom like silence. = 雄弁は銀、沈黙は金 = 言わぬが花 ♦ 一寸の舌に五尺の身を損ず ♦ 口数の多い者は襤褸を出す ♦ 口は災いの元 ♦ 君子は九度思いて一度言う ♦ 言葉多ければ恥多し ♦ 三寸の舌に五尺の身を亡ぼす ♦ 舌は禍の根 ♦ 禍は口から

## 沈黙は愚者の機知である

[Silence is the wit of the fool.] ● It is better to say nothing than to embarrass oneself by commenting on something one knows little about. • Little said is soon amended. = 愚者の雄弁は沈黙なり ♦ 知る者は言わず言う者は知らず ♦ 雀の千声鶴の一声

# ツ

## 追従する者陰にて誹る

[Those who flatter speak ill behind one's back.] ● Those who flatter someone when in their presence will speak ill of them when they are with others. • He is a good friend that speaks well of us behind our backs. • A flatterer's throat is an open sepulcher. = 口に蜜有り腹に剣有り ♦ 甘言が愚人を喜ばしむ ♦ 信言は美ならず、美言は信ならず ♦ 天子将軍の事でも陰では言う ♦ 天子将軍も障子の内 ♦ 耳の楽しむ時は慎むべし

## 杖に縋るとも人に縋るな

[One can lean on one's walking stick, but one should not lean on people.] ● Unless there is compelling reason to do so, one should not rely on the help or hospitality of others. • He who depends on another dines ill and supps worse.

## 杖の下に回る犬は打てぬ

[One cannot hit a dog that lingers below the stick.] ● One cannot treat someone harshly who appeals for mercy. ● Mercy surpasses justice. = 棒の下に回る犬は打てぬ ♦ 窮鳥懐に入れば猟師も殺さず ♦ 飛ぶ鳥懐に入る時は狩人も助くる

## 月と鼈の差

[The difference between the moon and a turtle.] ● Used to indicate that two things are totally different. ● As different as chalk from cheese.

## 月は満つれば欠ける

[As the moon waxes, so it wanes.] ● In life there are ups and downs; what is on the rise today, may decline tomorrow. ● Every flow has its ebb. = 満つれば欠くる世の習い = 世は七下がり七上がり

## 月日に関守無し

[There is no keeper at the barrier of months and days.] ● Every day will be followed by another day and no one can stop or reverse time. ● Time and tide wait for no one. = 光陰に関守無し ♦ 光陰人を待たず ♦ 歳月人を待たず ♦ 盛年重ねて来たらず ♦ 若い時は二度無い ♦ 若きは二度と無し

## 角を矯めて牛を殺す

[To kill the ox by trying to straighten its horns.] ● Attempting to correct minor flaws in an area of little importance may cause irreparable damage in an area of great importance. ● To burn the house to frighten away the mouse. ● Throw out the baby with the bath water. = 枝を矯めて花を散らす = 枝を矯めんとして幹を枯らす = 仏を直すとて鼻を欠く ♦ 流れを汲みて源を濁す

## 躓く石も縁

[The stone on which one trips is also karma.] ● Even incidents that seem of little significance are preordained and deeply rooted in one's karma. ● A meeting by chance is preordained. = 袖振り合うも他生の縁

## 爪で拾って箕で零す

[Gather with the nails and shed with the basket.] ● Used to describe those who painstakingly amass a fortune, only to throw it away again carelessly. ● Penny wise and pound foolish. ● Spare at the spigot and let it out at the bunghole. ♦ 一文惜しみの百知らず ♦ 一銭を笑う者は一銭に泣く ≠ 大遣いより小遣い

## 強き木はむず折れ

[Strong trees will break sooner (than they bend).] ● Someone with a rigid character who tries to accomplish things by force is more likely to be frustrated than someone with a pliant and flexible character who can adapt to changing circumstances. ● Oaks may fall when reeds stand the storm. = 木強ければ折れ易し = 柳に風折れなし = 柳の枝に雪折れ無し ♦ 柔能く剛を制する、弱能く強を制する ♦ 茶碗を投げば綿で抱えよ

# テ

## 亭主の好きな赤烏帽子

[The husband's cherished red *eboshi*.] ✍ An *eboshi* (烏帽子) is a traditional Japanese headgear worn by nobles in court dress. ● When a man and wife have been married for a long time, they begin to resemble each other in their tastes. ● Husband's taste is his wife's. ♦ 似た者夫婦

## 貞女は孝女の門に出づ

[A virtuous woman comes from a house with filial daughters.] ☞ This deeply Confucian view of the order of society prevailed throughout Japan's feudal era and may still be felt today. ● If a woman shows filial piety toward her parents she will also be loyal to her husband. ● A good daughter will make a good wife. ♦ 孝立てば則ち忠遂ぐ

## 手形は残れど足形は残らず

[A hand print will remain; a foot print will not.] ● What is written down will be read by future generations; what is done will be lost with time. Similarly, someone's actions during their lifetime will go unnoticed by future generations unless they are recorded for posterity. • Written letter remains. ♦ ❷ するは一時名は末代 ♦ 虎は死して革を止め、人は死して名を残す ♦ 人は一代、名は末代 ♦ 身は一代、名は末代

## 敵を見て矢を矧ぐ

[Feathering one's arrows on seeing the enemy.] ● To try to remedy a problem when it is too late. • Lock the stable door after the horse is stolen. • After death, the doctor. • After meat, mustard. = 戦を見て矢を矧ぐ = 喧嘩過ぎての棒乳切り = 賊去って張弓 = 賊の後の棒乳切り = 泥棒を捕らえて縄を綯う = 難に臨んで兵を鋳る = 盗人を見て縄を綯う = 火を失して池を掘る ♦ 後の祭 ♦ 六日の菖蒲、十日の菊 ♦ 盆過ぎての鯖商い

## 弟子七尺去って師の影を踏まず

[The pupil keeps seven *shaku* behind the master so as not to tread on his shadow.] ✎ The Japanese *shaku* (尺) is an old unit of measurement still used by Japanese craftsmen. One *shaku* (尺) corresponds to roughly thirty centimeters. ● Used to express the reverence that is paid to teachers. • He that teaches himself has a fool for his master. = 三尺下がって師の影を踏まず = 師の影は七尺下がって踏まず

## 出船に良い風は入り船に悪い

[If the wind is fair to leave port, it will not be good to come into port.] ● Conditions that are favorable to do one thing may be unfavorable to do another. Similarly, every thing and situation will have its advantages and drawbacks. • The sun does not shine on both sides of the hedge at once. = 入り船に良い風は出船に悪い ♦ 尺も短き所あり、寸も長き所あり ≠ 此処ばかりに日は照らぬ

## 寺の隣に鬼が住む

[The devil lives next door to the temple.] ☞ In Japan it is not uncommon to find temples situated on the very edge of licensed quarters. ● We live in an imperfect world in which good and evil live side by side. ● In evil there is odds. ● The devil lurks behind the cross. = 寺の門前に鬼が住む ♦ 寸善尺魔の世の中

## 寺の門前に鬼が住む

[The devil lives before the gate of the temple.] ☞ In Japan it is not uncommon to find temples situated on the very edge of licensed quarters. ● We live in an imperfect world in which good and evil live side by side. ● In evil there is odds.● The devil lurks behind the cross. = 寺の隣に鬼が住む ♦ 寸善尺魔の世の中

## 出る杭は打たれる

[Nails that protrude are hit down.] ❶ Those who think or act differently from the group will be made to conform. ● The raised nail gets hammered down. ❷ Those who through their talents or achievements stand out from the rest tend to be envied and criticized. ● The raised nail gets hammered down. ● After honor and state follow envy and hate. ● Envy is the companion of honor. ● The brighter the moon the more the dogs howl. = 高木風に憎まる = 高木風に妬まる ♦ ❶ 大きい家に大きい風が吹く ♦ 高山の嶺には美木無し ♦ 高木は風に折らる ♦ 大木は風に折らる ♦ 大名の下には久しく居るべからず ♦ 誉れは誇りの基

## 天子将軍の事でも陰では言う

[Even divinely ordained generals will be spoken about behind their backs.] ● If the subject of conversation is not present, people will speak ill, even of the most important people. ● People will talk. ♦ 追従する者陰にて誹る ♦ 天子将軍も障子の内

## 天子将軍も障子の内

[Even divinely ordained generals are only so within the confines of shōji.] ✍ Shōji (障子) are the paper screens that divide the rooms of traditional Japanese buildings. ● If the subject of conversation is not present, people will speak ill even of the most important people. ● People will talk. ♦ 追従する者陰にて誹る ♦ 天子将軍の事でも陰では言う

### 天知る地知る我知る人知る

[Heaven knows, earth knows, you know, people know.] ● Even what is thought to be a well-hidden secret is known by everyone, and thus it will not pay to do wrong since, sooner or later, all will be exposed. = 隠すことは現わる ◆ 氏素性は争えないもの ◆ 血筋は争えないもの

### 転石苔を生ぜず

[A rolling stone gathers no moss.] ☞ This proverb derives from its English equivalent. ❶ Those who remain active and buoyant will retain their youthful vigor. • A rolling stone gathers no moss. ❷ Those who keep changing their course in life (whenever the going gets rough) are not likely to accumulate wealth or accomplish anything. • A rolling stone gathers no moss. = 転がる石には苔は生えない

### 点滴石をも穿つ

[Raindrops will wear down a stone.] ● If one perseveres in something long enough one will eventually be successful. • Constant dripping wears away the stone. = 雨垂れ石を穿つ = 斧を研いで針にする = ❷ 塵も積もれば山と成る ◆ 石の上にも三年 ◆ 千里の道も一歩より始まる ◆ ❶ 倒れる事は必ず傾く方に有り ◆ 泥棒も十年 ◆ 始めの一歩、末の千里

### 天道人を殺さず

[The way of heaven does not kill people.] ● Heaven is merciful and does not forsake those who turn their gaze upwards in their hour of need. Similarly, the gods look kindly upon those who keep to the straight and narrow. • God tempers the wind to the shorn lamb. ≠ 天網恢々疎にして漏らさず

### 天網恢々疎にして漏らさず

[Heaven's net is vast and coarse yet lets nothing through.] ● The laws of heaven are strict and those who commit crimes will not escape divine punishment. • Heaven's vengeance is slow but sure. ◆ 呑舟の魚を漏らす ≠ 天道人を殺さず

## 天を仰ぎて唾す

[Spit up into the sky.] ● Those who wish to cause harm to others will eventually harm themselves. • They hurt themselves who wrong others. • Curses, like chickens, come home to roost. = 狩人も罠に掛かる = 人を取る亀人に取られる = 人を呪わば穴二つ ♦ 策士策に溺れる

# ト

## 問い声良ければいらえ声良い

[If the voice that asks is good, the voice that answers is good.] ● The treatment one receives in life is often the product of one's own actions; if one approaches people with kindness one can expect to make friends, if one approaches people with hostility one can expect to make enemies. • Be a friend to make a friend. • He that soweth good seed shall reap good corn. • One never loses by doing good turns. • One good turn deserves another. = 仇も情も我が身より出る = 魚心有れば水心 ♦ 愛出ずる者は愛返り、福往く者は福来る ♦ 愛は愛を生む ♦ 旅は道連れ世は情け ♦ 情けは人の為ならず ♦ 人は情けの下に立つ

## 同気相求む

[Those with the same temperament seek each other out.] ● People in similar circumstances or people with the same kind of personality tend to be drawn together. • Birds of a feather flock together. • Like attracts like. = 牛は牛連れ = 馬は馬連れ = 類は友を呼ぶ = 友は類をもって集まる = ❶ 目の寄る所へ玉が寄る ♦ 鬼の女房に鬼神 ♦ 同病相憐れむ ♦ 不幸の際の伴侶は不幸を軽減す

## 灯台下暗し

[It is dark under the lighthouse.] ❶ Those who help others to solve their problems often find it difficult to deal with their own problems. • Lookers-on see more than players. ♦ 局に当たる者は惑う ♦ 近くて見えぬは睫 ♦ ❷ 遠きを知りて近きを知らず ♦ 人を知る者は知なり、自ら知る者は明なり ♦ 我が身の上は見えぬ ❷ Those closest to one will often shy away from speaking their mind, so that one will remain ignorant of one's own shortcomings. • The darkest place is under the candlestick. • One must go into the country to hear what news at London. • One must go abroad for news at home. = 堤灯持ちの足元暗し

## 問うは一時の恥、問わぬは末代の恥

[To ask may be a moment's shame; not to ask may lead to lifelong disgrace.] ● Rather than remain ignorant, it is better to endure temporary embarrassment and ask what one does not know. • He that nothing questioneth, nothing learneth. • Be brave to ask so as to learn. • Better ask than go astray. = 聞くは一時の恥、聞かぬは末代の恥 ♦ 知らざるを知らずとせよ

## 同病相憐れむ

[Those with the same disease pity each other.] ● Those who are afflicted by the same hardships often seek (consolation in) each other's company. • Misery makes strange bedfellows. • Misery loves company. = 不幸の際の伴侶は不幸を軽減す ♦ 牛は牛連れ ♦ 馬は馬連れ ♦ 鬼の女房に鬼神 ♦ 同気相求む ♦ 友は類をもって集まる = ❶ 目の寄る所へ玉が寄る ♦ 類は友を呼ぶ

## 灯滅せんとして光を増す

[A light that is about to die out will increase in luster.] ● Those who have fallen ill may experience a temporary restoration of powers when they are on the verge of death. Similarly, a movement or force may flare up temporarily when it is on the verge of extinction. • A lightning before death. = 灯火消えんとして光を増す

## 遠い親類より近くの他人

[A close neighbor rather than a distant relative.] ● In times of trouble, a sympathetic neighbor may be a greater source of comfort than a distant relative. • A near neighbor is better than a distant cousin. = 京の妹に隣代えず = 親しき隣は遠き兄弟に優る ♦ ❷ 近火で手を焙れ

## 遠きは花の香

[Far-off there is (only) the fragrance of flowers.] ● From afar things always look better than they actually are. • Far fowls have fair feathers. • The grass is always greener on the other side of the fence. • The neighbor's wife is always handsomest. • Better is the neighbor's hen than mine. = 隣りの花は赤い ♦ 親しき中にも垣を作れ ♦ 良い中には垣をせよ

## 遠きを知りて近きを知らず

[To know what is distant, but not know what is close.] ❶ Those who know much about lofty matters often know little about the mundane. ♦ 一を知って二を知らず ≠ 其の一を知りて其の二を知らず ❷ Those who understand the minds of others, do not necessarily know their own minds. • Know thyself. ♦ 近くて見えぬは睫 ♦ 我が身の上は見えぬ ♦ ● 堤灯持ちの足元暗し ♦ ● 灯台下暗し

## 時に遭えば鼠も虎となる

[At times, even a mouse becomes a tiger.] ❶ In times of great upheaval even small people may rise to the occasion and perform heroic feats. Similarly, even seemingly insignificant people may play a role of importance when given a chance. • A little body often harbors a great soul. • Put a coward on his metal and he will fight the devil. = 用いる時は鼠も虎となる ♦ 窮鼠猫を噛む ♦ 鼠窮して猫を噛み、人貧しゅして盗みす ❷ 門脇の姥にも用有り ❷ Even those whose presence seems of no consequence may have their part to play in the greater scheme of things. • For the want of a nail the shoe was lost, for the want of a shoe the horse was lost, for the want of a horse the battle was lost. = 用いる時は鼠も虎となる ♦ 枯れ木も山の賑わい ♦ 愚者も千慮に一徳あり ♦ 癖ある馬に乗りあり ♦ 蹴る馬も乗り手次第 ♦ 鴎目大なれど観ること鼠に若かず ♦ 馬鹿と鋏は使い様 ♦ 馬鹿も一芸 ♦ 貧乏人も三年置けば用に立つ ♦ 野郎と鋏が使い様 ♦ 湯腹も一時、松の木柱も三年 ♦ 割れ鍋も三年置けば用に立つ

## 時は得難くして失い易し

[Time is gained with difficulty and lost with ease.] ❶ The right moment to do something does not come around often, and when it does it is easily missed. • Strike while the iron is hot. • Make hay while the sun shines. ♦ 一寸の光陰軽んず可からず ♦ 好機逸す可から

175

ず ◆ 善は急げ ◆ 時を得る者は昌え、時を失う者は亡ぶ ❷ The time one is given on this earth is limited and each and every moment should be cherished and put to good use. • Get it while the getting is good. ◆ 一寸の光陰は沙裏の金

## 時を得る者は昌え、時を失う者は亡ぶ

[Those who seize the moment prosper; those who miss the moment perish.] 📖 This proverb is attributed to the Chinese Daoist Liezi. ● Those who seize the moment to advance themselves will do well; those who fail to seize that moment will miss the opportunity (to develop their talents) and fail. • Fortune knocks once at least at every man's gate. • Fortune favors the bold. ◆ 一寸の光陰軽んず可からず ◆ 好機逸す可からず ◆ 善は急げ ◆ ❶ 時は得難くして失い易し

## 読書は夜道の案内者

[Reading is the guide on one's nightly travels.] Through reading one may gain insight into things one does not yet understand. • Reading makes a full man. ◆ 読書 百遍 義自ずから見る

## 読書 百遍 義自ずから見る

[Reread a text a hundred times and you will see the meaning as a matter of course.] ● When one reads a text one does not understand often enough, one will eventually grasp its meaning. • Reading makes a full man. ◆ 読書は夜道の案内者

## 徳は孤ならず必ず隣あり

[Virtue does not stand alone but surely has a neighbor.] 📖 This proverb is taken from the *Analects* of Confucius. ● Those who are good never stand alone but will always find a willing ear or someone who is willing to lend a hand. • Good finds good.

## 徳は才の主才は徳の奴

[Virtue is the master of talent; talent is the servant of virtue.] ● The most important thing in a human being is to do good, and one's talents should always be employed in the service of doing good. • Virtue is its own reward.

176

## 毒を食らわば皿まで

[If one is to eat poison, eat the plate with it.] ● If one contemplates committing a crime, one might as well commit a great crime that will yield commensurate profits, since if caught one will be punished in either case. ● As well be hanged for a sheep as for a lamb. ● Over shoes, over boots. ● In for a penny, in for a pound. = 一州も誅八州も誅 ♦ 鍵を盗む者は誅せられ、国を盗む者は諸侯となる ♦ 金を奪う者は殺され、国を奪う者は王となる ♦ 財を盗む者は盗人なり、国を盗む者は諸侯

## 毒を以て毒を制す

[Use poison to suppress poison.] ● One who is poisoned may need to take another dangerous drug as an antidote. By extension, if one is to eradicate a vice or pest, it may be necessary to resort to measures of a similarly offensive nature. ● Like cures like. ♦ 盗人の番には盗人を使え

## 所変われば品変わる

[If the place changes, the article changes.] ● Each place has its own atmosphere, customs, and products, and as one travels one will notice the difference. ● So many countries, so many customs.

## 年寄りの言う事と牛の鞦は外れたことが無い

[The words of the old and the crupper of an ox do not slip.] ☞ The *shirigai* (鞦) is a strap (緒) that runs round the flanks of an ox, from the chest round to the tail to keep the shanks (轅) of a cart (車) in place. ● The words of the old and experienced are reliable and not dependent upon the changing fads and fashions that influence young people. ● An old man's sayings are seldom untrue. ♦ 相談は年寄り、喧嘩は若者 ♦ 年寄りの家には落ち度が無い

## 年寄りの家には落ち度が無い

[There are no mistakes in the homes of the old.] ● Families that have elderly—and thus more experienced and prudent—members are less likely to make rash decisions. ● An old man in a house is a good sign. ♦ 年寄りの言う事と牛の鞦は外れたことが無い

と

## 年寄りの物忘れ、若者の物知らず

[The forgetfulness of the old, the ignorance of the young.] ● Old people, though experienced, gradually lose their memory; young people, though their memory is sound, lack experience. ● The old forget, the young don't know.

## 隣りの火事に騒がぬ者無し

[There is no one who will not get excited at a fire next door.] ● Though we may remain indifferent about events that are distant and do not affect us, events that are closer to home and have a direct effect on our well-being tend to have our undivided attention. ● When next door is on fire it is high time to look to your own.

## 隣りの花は赤い

[The flowers next door are red.] ● From afar things always look better than they actually are. ● The grass is always greener on the other side of the fence. ● The neighbor's wife is always handsomest. = 遠きは花の香 ♦ 親しき中にも垣を作れ ♦ 良い中には垣をせよ

## 度場は伯楽に会わず

[A worn-out horse does not meet Hakuraku.] ☞ Hakuraku, or Bai Lo, was a famous Chinese connoisseur of horses who lived during the Spring and Autumn period (770-476BC). ● Those who have mediocre talents cannot expect to achieve recognition for their achievements. = 瓦は磨いても玉にはならぬ ♦ 千里の馬はあれども一人の伯楽は無し ≠ 瓦も磨けば玉となる

## 鳶が鷹を生む

[A kite begets a hawk.] ● Used when someone from a humble background attains greatness. ● A black hen lays white eggs. = 鵙が鷹を生む ≠ 蛙の子は蛙 ≠ 瓜の蔓に茄子はならぬ ≠ 鳶の子鷹にならず

## 鳶の子鷹にならず

[A kite's chick will not become a hawk.] ● People of humble birth cannot expect to attain high positions. Similarly, parents with mediocre talents cannot expect to bring forth children with exceptional talents. • The onion will not produce a rose. = 瓜の蔓に茄子はならぬ = 蛙の子は蛙 ≠ 鳶が鷹を生む ≠ 鵙が鷹を生む

## 飛ぶ鳥懐に入る時は狩人も助くる

[Even the hunter will spare the bird that seeks refuge at the bosom.] ● When someone in distress appeals for help, it is only human to offer assistance, even to an enemy. • Any port in a storm. = 窮鳥懐に入れば猟師も殺さず ♦ 杖の下に回る犬は打てぬ ♦ 棒の下に回る犬は打てぬ

## 富は一生の財、知は万代の財

[Riches are the treasure of one life; wisdom is the treasure of ten thousand generations.] ● One's wealth is the accumulation of a life's work; one's wisdom is drawn from all who came before. Similarly, upon death one's riches may pass to the next generation to spend, while wisdom will continue to accumulate for generations to come. • Without wisdom wealth is worthless. = 知恵は万代の宝 ♦ 一世の富貴死後までの文章

## 富は屋を潤し、徳は身を潤す

[Riches benefit the dwelling; virtue benefits one's station.] ● The more money one has, the more one's household will flourish; the more good one does, the higher one's status in life will be. ♦ 富む者仁ならず、仁なれば富まず

## 富を為せば仁ならず、仁を為せば富まず

[Those who amass riches have no benevolence; those who do good do not grow rich.] 📖 This proverb is taken from the works of Mencius. ● People who desire to accumulate wealth do so by sacrificing compassion; those who are benevolent are unselfish and will thus be unable to accumulate wealth. • Riches are but the baggage of virtue. = 富む者仁ならず、仁なれば富まず ♦ 富貴にして膳をなり易し、貧賤にして功をなし難し

## 富む家に痩せ犬無し

[No lean dogs in a wealthy household.] ● In the household of a wealthy family, one can expect all its members to be well off. ● Like master, like servant. ● Like lord, like chaplain. ◆ 立ち寄れば大木の陰

## 富む者仁ならず、仁なれば富まず

[Those who grow rich have no benevolence; those who are benevolent do not grow rich.] ● People who desire to accumulate wealth do so by sacrificing compassion; those who are benevolent are unselfish and will thus be unable to accumulate wealth. ● Riches are but the baggage of virtue. = 富を為せば仁ならず、仁を為せば富まず ◆ 富は屋を潤し、徳は身を潤す ◆ 富貴にして膳をなり易し、貧賎にして功をなし難し

## 止めて止まらぬ恋の道

[The road of love that cannot be stopped however one tries.] ● Those who are enslaved by love cannot help but follow the whims of their desire. ✍ *Koi* (恋) stands for romantic love, which is often selfish, whereas *ai* (愛) stands for emotional love, which is usually altruistic. ● Love laughs at locksmiths. ◆ 色は思案の外 ◆ 恋は思案の外 ◆ 惚れた病に薬無し ◆ 惚れ病と馬鹿の治る薬は無い

## 灯火消えんとして光を増す

[A light that is about to die out will increase in luster.] ● In those who have fallen ill there may be a temporary restoration of their powers when they are on the verge of death. Similarly, a movement or force may flare up temporarily when it is on the verge of extinction. ● A lightning before death. = 灯滅せんとして光を増す

## 友と酒は古い程良し

[Friends and *sake*, the older the better.] ● Friendship and *sake* grow more mature and enjoyable with the years. ● Old friends and wine are best. ◆ 焦げたる木には火が付きやすい ◆ 本木に勝る末木無し ◆ 焼け木杭に火が付く

## 友は類をもって集まる

[Friends gather by kind.] ● People in similar circumstances or

people with the same kind of personality tend to be drawn together.
• Birds of a feather flock together. • Like attracts like. = 牛は牛連
れ = 馬は馬連れ = 鬼の女房に鬼神 = 同気相求む = ❶ 目の寄る所へ玉
が寄る = 類は友を呼ぶ

## 捕らぬ狸の皮算用

[The counting of raccoon dog hides before they are caught.] ● Used
in instances where people make plans based on their expectations
of an uncertain future. • Don't count your chickens before they are
hatched. • Sell the lion's skin before one has caught the lion. = 儲
けぬ前の胸算用 = 空飛ぶ雁を吸い物に当てる

## 虎の穴に入らねば虎の子を得られぬ

[One cannot obtain the tiger's cub without entering the tiger's den.]
☞ This proverb builds on the idea that a tiger protects its offspring
like a treasure. Consequently, the expression 虎の子 is often used on
its own to denote a private treasure. ● In order to attain something
precious it is often necessary to take great risks. • Nothing ventured,
nothing gained. • Faint heart never won fair lady/castle. = 虎穴に入
らずんば虎子を得ず ♦ 死を先んずる者は必ず生ず ♦ 蒔かぬ種は生えぬ
♦ 身を捨ててこそ浮かぶ瀬も有れ ♦ 物は試し

## 虎の子は地に落つれば牛を食う気あり

[When a tiger cub falls to the ground (at birth) it will have an
appetite for beef.] ● Great people will show signs of their
exceptional talents at an early age. • One may know the lion by its
claws. = 虎豹の駒は食牛の気あり ♦ 栴檀は双葉より芳し ♦ 流れを汲
みて源を知る ♦ 実の生る木は花から知れる ♦ 実を見て木を知れ ≠ 大
器晩成 ≠ ❷ 早く熟すれば早く腐る

## 虎は死して革を止め、人は死して名を残す

[Tigers die to leave their skin; people die to leave their name.]
● The reputation one builds up during a lifetime, whether good or
bad, lasts beyond the grave. • Worthy men shall be remembered.
♦ ❷ するは一時名は末代 ♦ 手形は残れど足形は残らず ♦ 人は一代、名
は末代 ♦ 身は一代、名は末代

## 取らんとする者は先ずあ与う

[Those who intend to take should first give.] ● Those who intend to receive favors from others should first bestow favors on them. Similarly, if one intends to acquire something, it is prudent to first entrust it to another person's care. ● He who gives to another bestows on himself. ● The hand that gives gathers. ● He that gives lends. ◆ 参らすれば賜る

## 鳥なき里の蝙蝠

[A bat in a birdless village.] ● In a place where there is no one with talent even someone with mediocre gifts can make an impression. ● Where there are no dogs the fox is king. = 鼬無き間の貂誇り ◆ 一文は無文の師 ◆ 鶏群の一鶴 ◆ 掃き溜めに鶴

## 鳥は木を択べども木は鳥を択ばず

[A bird can choose a tree (to rest in); a tree cannot choose a bird.] 📖 This proverb is attributed to Confucius. ● Whilst servants have the freedom to work for whomever they deem worthy, masters have to make do with those who are willing to enter their service. ≠ 君、臣を選ぶのみに非らず、臣も亦君を選ぶ

## 鳥は翼に従って巣を作る

[A bird builds its nest to fit its wings.] ● Men should carve out their place in the world according to their talents and powers. ● Cut your coat according to your cloth. = 蟹は甲羅に似せて穴を掘る ◆ 入るを量りて出ずるを為す

## 取り道あれば抜く道あり

[If there is a road to take, there is a road (by which) to escape.] ● Whatever the law, people will always find a way to escape it; and the stricter a law is applied, the more cunning will be the methods by which people try to circumvent it. ● The more laws, the more offenders.

## 泥棒も十年

[Even a robber (needs) ten years (to learn his skills).] ● Whatever work one chooses it will take a long time before one will be proficient at it. ● Perseverance will win through. = 石の上にも三年 ♦ 雨垂れ石を穿つ ♦ 斧を研いで針にする ♦ ❷ 塵も積もれば山と成る ♦ 点滴石をも穿つ ♦ 千里の道も一歩より始まる ♦ 始めの一歩、末の千里

## 泥棒を捕らえて縄を綯う

[Twisting the rope after the robber has been caught.] ● To try to remedy a problem when it is too late. ● Lock the stable door after the horse is stolen. ● After death, the doctor. ● After meat, mustard. = 戦を見て矢を矧ぐ = 喧嘩過ぎての棒乳切り = 賊去って張弓 = 賊の後の棒乳切り = 敵を見て矢を矧ぐ = 難に臨んで兵を鋳る = 盗人を見て縄を綯う = 火を失して池を掘る ♦ 後の祭 ♦ 六日の菖蒲、十日の菊 ♦ 盆過ぎての鯖商い

## 呑舟の魚は枝流に泳がず

[Great (boat-swallowing) fish do not swim up brooks.] 📖 This proverb is attributed to the Chinese Daoist Liezi. ● Great people will not be found in the company of commoners nor meddling in trifling affairs. ● Great ships must have deep waters. ● Great would have none great, and the little all little. = 象は兎の小道に遊ばず = 大魚は小池に棲まず ♦ 大人は小目を遣わず ≠ 河海は細流を択ばず ≠ 大海は細流を択ばず

## 呑舟の魚を漏らす

[Let the great (boat-swallowing) fish escape.] ● Great criminals often manage to elude the law, while the petty criminals are caught. ● Little thieves are hanged, but great ones escape. ● Laws catch flies, but let hornets go free. ♦ 天網恢々疎にして漏らさず

## 富んでは驕る、貧しきは諂う

[The rich are haughty; the poor are obsequious.] ● Those who are rich look down on those who are not; those who are poor curry favor with the rich in the hope of thus improving their plight. ● Without favor none will know you, and with it you will not know yourself. = 人に受ける者は人を畏れ、人に予うる者は人に驕る ♦ 上交 諂わず下交驕らず

### 飛んで火に入る夏の虫

[The insects of summer that enter the flame.] ● Those who are drawn in by the lure of danger will eventually be consumed by it. • Like moths to the flame. = 秋の鹿は笛に寄る

# ナ

### 無い袖は振れない

[One cannot shake a sleeve one does not have.] ● Used when a lack of financial or material resources renders any plans impotent. • There comes nothing out of the sack but what was there.

### 長生きすれば恥じ多し

[The longer you live, the more shame you suffer.] ● A long life provides more opportunities to suffer indignities and opportunities for failure. • Long life has many miseries. • He that lives long suffers much. • The life of man is a winter way. = 命長ければ恥多し ♦ 命が辛き老後の恥 ≠ 命有れば海月も骨に会う ≠ 命有れば蓬莱山にも会う

な

### 泣かぬ猫は鼠を取る

[The cat that does not cry catches mice.] ● Shrewd people do not make a display of their talents, so that (when those around them have become complacent) they may use them to greater advantage. • Cats hide their claws. • Who knows most says least. • Still waters run deep. = 逸物の猫は爪を隠す = 獅子人を噛むに牙を露わさず = 鼠を取る猫は爪を隠す = 能ある鷹は爪を隠す = 猟ある猫は爪を隠す ♦ 浅瀬に仇波 ♦ 言葉多き者は品少なし ♦ 静かに流れる川は深い

### 流れを汲みて源を知る

[By drawing water from a stream one will know its source.] ● By observing someone's work one may know their character. • A tree is known by its fruits. • One may know the lion by its claws. = 実を見て木を知れ ♦ 虎豹の駒は食牛の気あり ♦ 栴檀は双葉より芳し ♦ 虎の子は地に落つれば牛を食う気あり ♦ 実の生る木は花から知れる

## 流れを汲みて源を濁す

[By drawing water from a stream one will pollute the stream.]
📖 This proverb is taken from the *Taiheiki*, a 14th-century Japanese historical epic. ● In one's desire to have a deeper understanding of something one may spoil it. ▸ 枝を矯めて花を散らす ▸ 枝を矯めんとして幹を枯らす ▸ 角を矯めて牛を殺す

## 泣き面に蜂が刺す

[Wasps sting the tear-stained face.] ● When calamity strikes it often strikes those who are already suffering. ● Misfortune seldom comes alone. = 弱り目に祟り目 ▸ 雨が降れば土砂降り ▸ 重き馬に上荷打つ ▸ 二度ある事は三度ある ▸ 不幸は重なるもの ▸❷ 目の寄る所へ玉が寄る

## 無くて七癖有って四十八癖

[Seven habits when none; forty-eight habits when some.] ● All people have their own peculiarities, be they many or few. ● Every man has his habits.

な

## 情けが仇

[Pity is a disservice.] ● Something that is done with the intention to help may in the end prove to have the opposite effect. ● A pitiful surgeon spoileth a sore. = 恩が仇 = 始めの情け今の仇

## 情けに刃向かう刃無し

[There is no sword that can resist kindness.] ● Kindness is a stronger force than enmity. ● Kindness is the noblest weapon with which to conquer.

## 情けは人の為ならず

[Kindness is not just for the sake of others.] ● Not only is a good deed often requited, but it is also beneficial for one's own conscience and peace of mind. ● He that pities others remembers himself. ▸ 愛出ずる者は愛返り、福往く者は福来る ▸ 愛は愛を生む ▸ 仇も情けも我が身より出る ▸ 魚心有れば水心 ▸ 旅は道連れ世は情け ▸ 問い声良ければいらえ声良い ▸ 人は情けの下に立つ

185

## 済す時の閻魔顔、借る時の地蔵顔

[The face of Emma when repaying; the face of Jizo when borrowing.] ✍ Emma is the King of Hell and has a square, scowling face; Jizo is the guardian deity of children and has a round, benign face. ● Asking someone for money is easy; repaying it is less easy. • When I lent I was a friend; when I asked I was unkind. • If you would make an enemy lend a man money, and ask it of him again. = 借りる時の地蔵顔、返す時の閻魔顔 = 用有る時の地蔵顔、用無き時の閻魔顔 ▶ 貸した物は忘れず、借りた物は忘れる

## 為せば成る

[If it is done it will take shape.] ☞ This proverb is taken from a poem written by the Edo-period *daimyō* Uesugi Yōzan (1751-1822). The complete poem runs: 為せば成る、為さねば成らぬ、何事も成らぬは、人の為さぬなりけり (What is done will do/ what is not done will not do/ whatever will not do is the undoing of man.) ● If one applies oneself to something wholeheartedly there is nothing that one cannot do. • Where there is a will there is a way. = 石に立つ矢 = 一念岩をも徹す = 一念天に通ず = 精神一到何事かならざらん = 為せば成る ▶ 石の上にも三年 ▶ 泥棒も十年

## 鉈を貸して山を伐られる

[Lend someone a hatchet and have one's mountain (forest) cut down.] ● What is granted as a concession is often interpreted as an invitation to take all. • Give someone an inch and they'll take a mile. = 寸を与えれば尺を望む = 庇を貸して母屋を取られる ▶ 有るが上にも欲しがるのが人情 ▶ 有るは嫌なり、思うは成らず ▶ 昨日に優る今日の花 ▶ 千石を得て万石を恨む ▶ 成るは嫌なり、思うは成らず ▶ 隴を得て蜀を望む

## 夏歌う者は冬泣く

[Those who sing in summer cry in winter.] ● Those who play in times of plenty must suffer in times of shortage. Similarly, those who waste away their youth in idle pursuits will have to reap bitter fruits in old age. • If you'll lie upon roses when young, you'll lie upon thorns when old. = 現在の甘露は未来の鉄丸なり = 楽しみは苦しみの

な

種 = 楽は苦の種 ▶ 苦有れば楽有り ▶ 喜び有れば憂い有り ▶ 楽有れば苦有り ≠ 苦は楽の種 ≠ 苦を知らぬ者は楽を知らぬ ≠ 楽しみは憂いに生ず

## 夏の虫氷を笑う

[The insect of summer does not know the ice.] ● An insect with a life-span that does not extend past autumn will have no knowledge of the hardships of winter. Similarly, those who lead secluded lives will never fully experience life, with all its potential for hardships and suffering. ● Home-keeping youth have ever homely wits. ● The frog in the well knows nothing of the great ocean. ▶ 井の中の蛙大海を知らず ▶ 燕雀は天地の高きを知らず ▶ 井蛙は以って海を語るべからず ▶ 井魚は共に大を語るべからず

## 七度尋ねて人を疑え

[Be doubtful of someone (only) after one has questioned them seven times.] ● One should not be unduly suspicious of other people. If something has gone wrong, one should give people ample opportunity to explain themselves before assigning blame. ● In trust is truth. ≠ 明日は雨人は泥棒 ≠ 人を見たら泥棒と思え

## 名は体を表わす

[The name displays the object.] ● By some remarkable law the names that people are given often give a real insight into their character. ● Names and nature do often agree. ● Nomen, omen.

## 怠け者の節句働き

[The labor of the lazy during festival times.] ● Those who are ashamed of having been idle when everyone else was hard at work try to make up for it by being ostentatiously busy when others rest. ● The lazy become industrious toward evening.

## 生兵法は大疵の基

[Unpolished military tactics are the foundation of great injuries.] 📖 This proverb is taken from Miyamoto Musashi's *Gorin no sho*. ● To undertake a major project whilst relying on only a rudimentary

な

knowledge or skill is a recipe for disaster. • A little knowledge is a dangerous thing. ♦ 敗軍の将は兵を語らず

### 生酔い本性違わず

[A little drunkenness does not change one's true character.] ● People's characters are fixed and not even alcohol will change them. • In wine there is truth. • In vino veritas.

### 蛞蝓にも角

[Even a slug has its horns.] ● Even the humblest of people have a way to show their pride, and thus one should treat everyone with the same respect. • Tread on a worm and it will turn. = 一寸の虫にも五分の魂 = 痩せ腕にも骨 ♦ 窮鼠猫を噛む ♦ ❶ 時に遭えば鼠も虎となる ♦ 鼠窮して猫を噛み、人貧しゅして盗みす ♦ ❶ 用いる時は鼠も虎となる

### 習い性と成る

[Habit will become second nature.] ● If one does something often enough it will become second nature. • Habit is second nature. ♦ 習うより慣れよ ♦ 門前の小僧習わぬ経を読む

### 習うより慣れよ

[Practice rather than learn.] ● Rather that learning a craft or a skill from books, one should acquire them through practice. • Practice makes perfect. • 習い性と成る ♦ 下手な鉄砲も数打ちゃ当たる ♦ 下手な鍛冶屋も一度は名剣 ♦ 門前の小僧習わぬ経を読む

### 成らぬうちが楽しみ

[There is pleasure as long as something is not completed.] ● One can derive pleasure from anticipating the outcome of a project; when it is completed, however, there is often a sense of anticlimax. = ❶ 成らぬうちが頼み = 待つ間が花

### 成らぬうちが頼み

[There is trust as long as something is not completed.] ❶ When one works on a project, there is a sense of anticipation; when it is com-

pleted, however, there is often a sense of anticlimax. = 成らぬうち
が楽しみ ❷ When something needs to be done, people will turn to
others for help; once it is done they will forget them. ◆ 借りる時の
地蔵顔、返す時の閻魔顔 ◆ 済す時の閻魔顔、借る時の地蔵顔 ◆ 用有
る時の地蔵顔、用無き時の閻魔顔

## 成らぬ堪忍するが堪忍

[True patience lies in bearing the unbearable.] ☞ This very
Japanese proverb was used by Emperor Hirohito during his
broadcast on August 15, 1945, in which he announced to the nation
Japan's surrender to the Allied Powers. ● Only those who have suffered what seems unendurable know what true endurance is.

## 成るは嫌なり、思うは成らず

[What materializes we come to dislike; what we think of does not
materialize.] ● It is part of the human condition that we get bored
with the things we can attain, while the things we dream about
never seem to be realized. ● Much would have more. = 有るは嫌な
り、思うは成らず ◆ 有るが上にも欲しがるのが人 ◆ 一生は尽くれど
も希望は尽きず ◆ 昨日に優る今日の花 ◆ 千石を得て万石を恨む ◆ 隴
を得て蜀を望む

## 何でも来いに名人無し

[There are no experts among those who would take on anything.]
● Those who profess mastery of many skills are usually expert at
none. ● They brag most that can do least. ● Jack of all trades and
master of none. ● He who commences many things finishes but few.
◆ 多芸は無芸 ◆ 百様を知って一様を知らず ◆ 万能足りて一心足らず

## 難に臨んで兵を鋳る

[Forging one's weapons in the face of danger.] ● To try to remedy a
problem when it is too late. ● Lock the stable door after the horse
is stolen. ● After death, the doctor. = 戦を見て矢を矧ぐ = 喧嘩過ぎ
ての棒乳切り = 賊去って張弓 = 賊の後の棒乳切り = 敵を見て矢を矧
ぐ = 泥棒を捕らえて縄を綯う = 盗人を見て縄を綯う = 火を失して池
を掘る ◆ 後の祭 ◆ 六日の菖蒲、十日の菊 ◆ 盆過ぎての鯖商い

な

# 二

## 憎まれっ子世に憚る

[Wicked boys are shunned by the world.] ● The cruel streak that causes one to be disliked as a child often helps one overcome difficulties and succeed in later life. • Ill weeds grow apace.

## 逃げる者は道を選ばず

[Those who (try to) escape do not choose the road (by which they can do so).] ● One in dire straits cannot be too particular in picking out the means of relief. • Any port in a storm. = 窮鳥 枝を選ばず ▶ 恋と戦は手段を選ばず ▶ 恋は手段を選ばず

## 錦は雑巾にならぬ

[Brocade makes for a bad mop.] ❶ People of high birth are not good at menial functions. ❷ Superior things, too, have their shortcomings.

## 日々是好日

[Day by day is a good day.] ● In life, it is important to live every day to the fullest, for each day may be our last. • Seize the day. Carpe diem. ▶ 明日の百より今日の五十 ▶ あの世千日この世の一日 ▶ 末始終 より今の三十 ▶ ❶ 近火で手を焙れ ▶ 後の千金より今の百文 ▶ 来年の 百両 より今年の一両

## 日光を見ずして結構と言う勿れ

[One cannot say one is contented until one has seen Nikkō.] ☞ Nikkō, a village some 150 kilometers north-west of Tokyo, houses a complex of temples and shrines, some of which date back to the Nara period (710-794). Nikkō is particularly known as the site of the Tōshōgu (東照宮), the magnificent shrine that was built on the death of Tokugawa Ieyasu in 1616, and houses his remains. The scenic beauty of the surrounding landscape and the splendor of the Tōshōgu amidst the dense and towering forests has caused Nikkō to become a hugely popular tourist destination. ● Only those who have seen the splendor of Nikkō are qualified to say they are satisfied with life. • See Naples and die.

## 二足の草蛙は履けぬ

[One cannot wear two pairs of straw sandals at once.] ● When one greedily pursues two goals, one risks obtaining neither. • Grasp all, lose all. • Between two stools one falls to the ground. = 虻蜂取らず = 一念は継ぐとも二念は継ぐな = 二兎を追う者は一兎をも得ず ♦ 大欲は無欲に似たり ≠ 一挙両得 ≠ 一石二鳥

## 似た者夫婦

[Those who are alike are man and wife.] ● People who have the same tastes and interests are often suitable marriage partners. Similarly, a husband and wife who get on well often have many things in common. • Like man, like wife. • Like marries like. ♦ 亭主の好きな赤鳥帽子

## 二度ある事は三度ある

[What happens twice happens thrice.] ● If something happens more than once, it is wise to anticipate that it may happen yet again. • What happens twice will happen thrice. = ❷ 目の寄る所へ玉が寄る ♦ 雨が降れば土砂降り ♦ 泣き面に蜂が刺す ♦ 不幸は重なるもの ♦ 弱り目に祟り目

## 二兎を追う者は一兎をも得ず

[He who runs after two hares will catch neither.] ● When one greedily pursues two goals, one risks obtaining neither. • He who runs after two hares will catch neither. • Grasp all, lose all. = 虻蜂取らず = 一念は継ぐとも二念は継ぐな = 二足の草蛙は履けぬ ♦ 大欲は無欲に似たり ≠ 一挙両得 ≠ 一石二鳥

## 女房は家の大黒柱

[A wife is the central pillar of a house.] ☞ Traditional Japanese houses were constructed with one massive central pillar, the *daikokubashira* (大黒柱), or "large black pillar," to support the roof and make the house more resilient to earthquakes. ● While the man of a house provides for the family's financial resources, it is the woman of the house who controls the money and holds the family together. • The wife is the key of the house. • A good wife is a

household treasure. A good wife is a goodly prize. ♦悪妻は六十年
の不作

### 人間万事金の世の中

[People and all things (exist) in a world of money.] ● In all human affairs money has its role to play, for better or for worse. • Money rules the world. • Money makes the mare go round. • All things are obedient to money. ♦金の世の中 ♦地獄の沙汰も金次第

# ヌ

### 糠に釘

[Nails into (rice) bran.] ● Used to describe a futile action. = 網の目に風たまらす = 籠で水を汲む ♦馬の耳に念仏 ♦蛙の面に水 ♦空吹く風と聞き流す ♦盗人に追い銭 ♦猫に小判 ♦馬耳東風 ♦豚に真珠

### 糟の中にも粉米

[There is crushed rice within the rice bran.] ❶ No matter how trivial a thing or an event may seem at first, on closer inspection, it may contain something of worth. ♦其の域に入らざれば之を知らず ❷ No matter how bad or evil someone may seem at first encounter, one may find a kernel of good in their hearts when one comes to know them better. ♦其の域に入らざれば之を知らず ≠ 外面女菩薩内心女夜叉

### 盗人に追い銭

[Additional payments to a robber.] ● Used in cases where money is spent on a venture that is bound to come to naught. • Throwing good money after bad. Throwing the handle after the blade. ♦馬の耳に念仏 ♦蛙の面に水 ♦籠で水を汲む ♦株を守りて兎を待つ ♦空吹く風と聞き流 ♦糠に釘す ♦猫に小判 ♦馬耳東風 ♦豚に真珠

### 盗人に鍵を預ける

[To entrust a thief with the safeguarding of one's key.] ● Used to

describe an act of complete folly. • Set the wolf to guard the sheep.
= 盗人に金の番 = 猫に鰹の番

## 盗人に金の番

[Have a thief watch the money.] ● Used to describe an act of complete folly. • Set the wolf to guard the sheep. = 盗人に鍵を預ける = 猫に鰹の番 ♦ 株を守りて兎を待つ

## 盗人にも三分の理

[Thieves, too, have their share of reason.] ● Even those who make their living through crime may operate along rational lines. • Give the devil his due. ♦ 乞食にも三の理屈 ♦ 盗人の昼寝も当てが有る

## 盗人の始まりは嘘から、嘘の始まりは身持ちから

[The thief begins with a lie; a lie begins with (bad) conduct.] ● Once one is capable of deceiving someone with a lie, one is capable of stealing without scruple. A lie starts with one's attempt to conceal one's bad conduct, and thus, bad conduct may lead one to commit a crime. • He that will lie will steal. A liar is worse than a thief. • Show me a liar and I will show you a thief. ♦ 嘘吐きは泥棒の始まり ♦ 嘘は盗みのもと

## 盗人の番には盗人を使え

[Employ a thief as a watchman for thieves.] ● To catch a thief, it is best to hire one, as only a thief knows when, how, and where thieves will strike. By extension, it is best to hire people with experience. • Set a thief to catch a thief. • A Thief knows a thief as a wolf knows a wolf. ♦ 毒を以て毒を制す

## 盗人の隙はあれども守り手の隙は無い

[Thieves may have their moments of leisure, yet watchmen have none.] ● Those who intend to commit a crime can bide their time and wait for the right moment. Those who have to prevent crime, however, have to be constantly vigilant. By extension, those who have the initiative always have the advantage. = 守り手の隙は無くとも盗人の隙あり

ぬ

## 盗人の昼寝も当てが有る

[The midday nap of a thief, too, has its purpose.] ● Even a seemingly purposeless event may be significant when seen within the proper context. ● A fox sleeps but counts his dreams. ◆ 乞食にも三の理屈 ◆ 盗人にも三分の理

## 盗人を見て縄を綯う

[Making a rope on seeing the robber.] ● To try to remedy a problem when it is too late. ● Lock the stable door after the horse is stolen. ● After death, the doctor. = 戦を見て矢を矧ぐ = 喧嘩過ぎての棒乳切り = 賊去って張弓 = 賊の後の棒乳切り = 敵を見て矢を矧ぐ = 泥棒を捕らえて縄を綯う = 難に臨んで兵を鋳る = 火を失して池を掘る ◆ 後の祭 ◆ 六日の菖蒲、十日の菊 ◆ 盆過ぎての鯖商い

## 塗箸で素麺を食う

[Eat *sōmen* with lacquered chopsticks.] ● *Sōmen* are a type of thin (and slippery) noodles. ● Used to describe something that is exceedingly difficult to do.

## 濡れぬ前の傘

[The umbrella before one gets wet.] ● Rather than wait until one encounters difficulties, one should prepare for contingencies. ● Look before you leap. = 転ばぬ先の杖 ◆ 明日は雨人は泥棒 ◆ 石橋を叩いて渡る ◆ 備え有れば憂い無し ◆ 人を見たら泥棒と思え ◆ 火を見れば火事と思え

# ネ

## 猫に鰹の番

[Set the cat to guard the bonito.] ● Used to describe an act of complete folly. ● Set the wolf to guard the sheep. = 盗人に鍵を預ける = 盗人に金の番

## 猫に小判

[*Koban* for the cat.] ✍ The *koban* (小判) is a oval Japanese gold coin that was first struck during the Tenshō era (1573-1592) and used up until the end of the Edo period (1600-1867). ● Used in instances where the recipient of aid does not appreciate its value and so renders it totally ineffective. ● Cast pearls before swine. ＝ 豚に真珠 ▶ 馬の耳に念仏 ▶ 蛙の面に水 ▶ 空吹く風と聞き流す ▶ 馬耳東風

## 猫は三年の恩を三日で忘れる

[Cats, even kept for three years, will forget (their owner's) kindness within three days.] ● Used to express the fickle nature of cats. ▶ 犬猫も三年飼えば恩を忘れず ≠ 犬は三日飼えば三年恩を忘れぬ

## 鼠 壁を忘る、壁鼠を忘れず

[The mouse forgets the wall; the wall does not forget the mouse.] ● Those who have been hurt or who are the victim of an injustice will continue to suffer the pain long after the event. Those who have caused someone pain or do someone an injustice tend to quickly forget the damage they have caused. ▶ 愛さ余って憎さ百倍

## 鼠 窮して猫を嚙み、人貧しゅして盗みす

[A mouse in distress will bite a cat; a human in distress will steal.] ● Like a mouse who seeks to bite a cat when driven into a corner, a human being when driven into poverty will resort to stealing. ● There is no virtue that poverty destroyeth not. ＝ 窮鼠猫を嚙む ▶ 一寸の虫にも五分の魂 ▶ ❶ 時に遭えば鼠も虎となる ▶ 蚰蜒にも角 ▶ 貧の盗みに恋の ▶ ❶ 用いる時は鼠も虎となる

## 鼠を取る猫は爪を隠す

[The cat that catches mice hides its claws.] ● Shrewd people do not make a display of their talents, so that (when those around them have become complacent) they may use them to greater advantage. ● Cats hide their claws. ＝ 逸物の猫は爪を隠す ＝ 獅子人を嚙むに牙を露わさず ＝ 泣かぬ猫は鼠を取る ＝ 能ある鷹は爪を隠す ＝ 猟ある猫は爪を隠す ▶ 浅瀬に仇波 ▶ 言葉多き者は品少なし ▶ 静かに流れる川は深い

## 熱し易いは冷め易し

[Easily heated things are easily cooled.] ● People who are easily

195

enthused about something tend to lose there interest with the same speed. • Soon hot, soon cold. ♦ 恋いたほど飽いた ♦ 近惚れの早飽き

# ノ

### 能ある鷹は爪を隠す

[A wise hawk hides its talons.] ● Shrewd people do not make a display of their talents, so that (when those around them have become complacent) they may use them to greater advantage. • Cats hide their claws. • Who knows most says least. • Still waters run deep. = 逸物の猫は爪を隠す = 獅子人を噛むに牙を露わさず = 泣かぬ猫は鼠を取る = 鼠を取る猫は爪を隠す ♦ 浅瀬に仇波 ♦ 言葉多き者は品少なし ♦ 静かに流れる川は深い

### 能書筆を択ばず

[A master calligrapher is not particular about his (writing) brush.] ● Those who are masters of their craft will be able to make a masterpiece even with inferior tools. • A poor craftsman quarrels with his tools. = 弘法は筆を択ばず = 名人は筆を択ばず = 名筆は筆を択ばず = 良工は材を択ばず ♦ 下手な番匠木の難を言う ♦ 下手の道具調べ

### 農民の息も天に昇る

[Even the vigor of farmers can reach the heavens.] ● When people with little power act in concert they can achieve great changes. • Union is strength. = 蟻の思いも天に届く = 蚤の息さえ天に上る = 蟇の息さえ天に上る

### 後の千金より今の百文

[Rather a hundred *mon* now than a fortune later.] The *mon* (文) was a currency unit that derived from the Chinese *wen*, and introduced to Japan during the Muromachi period (1333-1568). It was used up until 1870, when it was replaced with the *yen* (円). ● It is better to seize the opportunity of the moment and make a modest profit than to wait and risk making no profit at all. • A bird in the hand is worth two in the bush. • Better an egg today than a hen tomorrow. = 明日の百より今日の五十 = 末始終より今の三十 = ❶ 近火で手を焙れ = 来年の百両より今年の一両 ◆ あの世千日この世の一日 ◆ 大取りより小取り ◆ 聞いた百文より見た一文 ≠ 小節を規る者は栄名を成す能わず ≠ 小利を見れば則ち大事成らず

## 喉元過ぎれば熱さを忘れる

[Once (a hot drink) has passed the throat the heat is soon forgotten.] ● No sooner has the danger passed or people will have forgotten their fears. Similarly, as soon as the difficulties that caused one to turn to others for help have passed, one will forget the aid given. ● Vows made in storms are forgotten in calms. ● Danger past and God forgotten. ● The peril past, the saint mocked. = 暑さ忘れて蔭忘る = 雨晴れて笠を忘る = 病治りて薬師忘る ◆ 叶わぬ時の神叩き ◆ 苦しい時の神頼み ◆ 狡兎死して走狗烹らる ◆ 恐い時の仏頼み ◆ 災害は忘れた頃にやって来る ◆ 飛鳥尽きて良弓蔵る

## 蚤の息さえ天に上る

[Even the vigor of fleas can reach the heavens.] ● When people with little power act in concert they can achieve great changes. ● Union is strength. = 蟻の思いも天に届く = 農民の息も天に昇る = 蠹の息さえ天に上る

## 鈍間の一寸馬鹿の三寸

[The one *sun* of the dunce; the three *sun* of the idiot.] ✍ The Japanese *sun* (寸) is a traditional unit of measurement still used by Japanese craftsmen. One *sun* is roughly three centimeters. ● When a dunce passes through a Japanese sliding door, he will leave it open by one *sun*; if an idiot does so, he will leave it open by three *sun*. = 下衆の一寸鈍間の三寸馬鹿の開けっ放し

# ハ

## 敗軍の将は兵を語らず

[The general of a defeated army should not talk of tactics.] ● When one is unsuccessful in a certain discipline, one has no

197

authority to lecture others. ● A defeated general should not talk of battle. ◆ 生兵法は大疵の基

## 背水の陣

[To set up camp with one's back toward the water.] ☞ This proverb derives from a famous episode in Chinese military history. On the eve of battle with the forces of Zhao, the great general Han Xin abandoned the advantage of high terrain and instructed his men to set up camp on the banks of a river, thus forcing them to either win and live or retreat and drown—a tactic that won him the day. ● When one is utterly bent on success, the surest way to achieve it is to go about it in such a way that failure is not a viable option. ● Burn one's bridges behind one. = 糧を捨てて船を沈む = 清水の舞台から飛び降りる ◆ 死を先んずる者は必ず生ず ◆ 身を捨ててこそ浮かぶ瀬も有れ

## 馬鹿さしじがれば二がえ馬鹿

[Those who make fun of fools are twice fools.] ❶ Those who make fun of people with inferior mental faculties are below contempt. ◆ 踊る阿呆に見る阿呆 ❷ Those who make fun of those who are not in full control of their faculties—and may respond in unexpected ways—invite danger and are, therefore, twice as stupid since, though they are in full possession of their own faculties, they fail to use them. ● Fools rush in where angels fear to tread. ● What is not wisdom is danger. ● Danger is next neighbor to security. ◆ 君子は危うきに近寄らず ◆ 三十六計逃ぐるに如かず ◆ 重宝を抱く者は夜行せず ◆ 聖人は危うきに近寄らず ◆ 盲蛇に怖じず

## 馬鹿と鋏は使い様

[Idiots and a pair of scissors have their uses.] ● Even those of limited talents, when employed in the right way, may play useful roles in the greater scheme of things. ● A fool may give a wise man counsel. = 野郎と鋏が使い様 ◆ 門脇の姥にも用有り ◆ 枯れ木も山の賑わい ◆ 愚者も千慮に一得あり ◆ 癖ある馬に乗りあり ◆ 蹴る馬も乗り手次第 ◆❷ 時に遭えば鼠も虎となる ◆ 馬鹿も一芸 ◆ 貧乏人も三年置けば用に立つ ◆❷ 用いる時は鼠も虎となる ◆ 湯腹も一時、松の木柱も三年 ◆ 割れ鍋も三年置けば用に立つ

# 馬鹿に付ける薬無し

[There is no medicine for curing an idiot.] ● Fools are born as fools and no degree of good counsel or punishment will ever make them wise. ● He who is born a fool is never cured. = 阿呆に付ける薬無し ◆ 三十馬鹿と八月青田は治らない ◆ 惚れ病と馬鹿の治る薬は無い

# 馬鹿の一つ覚え

[The idiot's one-liner.] ● People of limited learning often harp on the same subject, as they have nothing else to say. ● He that knows little often repeats it. = 阿呆の一つ覚え ◆ 愚者の雄弁は沈黙なり ◆ 沈黙は愚者の機知である ◆ 知る者は言わず言う者は知らず ◆ 雀の千声鶴の一声

# 馬鹿も有ればこそ、利口も引き立つ

[Only because there are idiots do the wise look smart.] ● The wise are only so by virtue of the fools. ● Were there no fools there would be no wise men. = 下手があるので上手が知れる ◆ 自慢高慢馬鹿の内 ◆ 目明き千人、盲千人 ◆ 盲千人、目明き千人

# 馬鹿も一芸

[Idiots, too, may have their trade.] ● Even less talented people will be good at at least one skill or task, and thus be able to play a useful role. ● There is no play without a fool. = 愚者も千慮に一徳あり ◆ 門脇の姥にも用有り ◆ 癖ある馬に乗りあり ◆ 蹴る馬も乗り手次第 ◆ 馬鹿と鋏は使い様 ◆ 野郎と鋏が使い様

# 掃き溜めに鶴

[A crane in a dust-hole.] ● Among a crowd of mediocre people, one person with talent will stand out. ● Triton amongst the minnows. = 鶏群の一鶴 ◆ 一文は無文の師

# 白砂は泥に在りて之と皆黒し

[Among mud, all white sand will turn black.] ● Even good people will eventually be corrupted if they mingle with bad people. ● Better be alone than in bad company. ◆ 麻に連るる蓬 ◆ 朱に交われば赤くなる ◆ 善人の敵となるとも悪人を友とすな

199

### 白刃前に交われば流矢を顧みず

[When one comes across a drawn sword one has no eye for the flood of arrows.] ● When, in the thick of battle, one is engaged in man-to-man combat with the sword, one has no eye for the hail of arrows that fills the air. By extension, when one is confronted by a major obstacle one must put all one's efforts in surmounting that obstacle and ignore the minor problems that may arise. ≠ ❶ 大事の前の小事

### 馬耳東風

[The eastern wind in the ear of a horse.] ● Used in cases where good counsel or criticism is totally lost on someone. • Sing psalms to a dead horse. • Preaching to the wind. • In one ear and out the other. • Water on a duck's back. = 馬の耳に念仏 = 蛙の面に水 = 空吹く風と聞き流す ◆ 猫に小判 ◆ 豚に真珠

### 始めが大事

[The start is crucial.] ● To succeed in any venture it is important to make a good start and lay the foundation for success. • Well begun is half done. ◆ 一生の計は幼きにあり ◆ 一日の計は朝に在り ◆ 一年の計は元旦に在り ◆ 少年学ばざれば老後に知らず

### 始めから長老にはなれぬ

[One does not become a doyen overnight.] ● One cannot expect to achieve something in life overnight, but only through long and dedicated effort. = 沙弥から長老にはなれぬ ◆ 一朝一夕の故に非ず ◆ 馬に乗るまで牛に乗れ ◆ ❷ 将を射んと欲すれば先ず馬を射よ ◆ 千里の道も一歩より始まる ◆ 高きに登るは低きよりす ◆ 始めから長老にはなれぬ ◆ 始めの一歩、末の千里 ◆ ❷ 人を射んとせば先ず馬を射よ

### 始めの一歩、末の千里

[One step at the outset, a thousand *ri* at the finish.] ✍ The *ri* (里) is an ancient Chinese measurement of distance, the equivalent of 0.3 miles. With time, it came to denote the distance one could walk in an hour, and during the Edo period (1600-1867) it was officially defined as 36 *chō*, or about 2.44 miles. ● It may take many small efforts to accomplish a task, but once completed the result may be impressive.

• Learn to speak before you sing. • He who would climb a ladder must begin at the bottom. = 千里の道も一歩より始まる ♦ 一朝一夕の故に非ず ♦ 馬に乗るまで牛に乗れ ♦ 沙弥から長老にはなれぬ ♦ ❷ 将を射んと欲すれば先ず馬を射よ ♦ 高きに登るは低きよりす ♦ 始めから長老にはなれぬ ♦ ❷ 人を射んとせば先ず馬を射よ

## 始めの勝ちは糞勝ち

[The first victory is a hollow one.] ● Winning the war is more important than winning a battle. Similarly, in any contest, it is important to keep the final goal in sight and not get carried away by initial success. • He laughs best who laughs last. • All's well that ends well. = 先勝ちは糞勝ち ♦ 先勝ち ♦ 先にすれば人を制し、後るる時は制せらるる ♦ 先んずれば人を制す ♦ 早い者勝ち

## 始めの情け今の仇

[The good of the outset, the evil of now.] ● Something that is done with the intention to help may in the end prove to have the opposite effect. • A pitiful surgeon spoileth a sore. = 情けが仇 ♦ 恩が仇

## 走る馬にも鞭

[A whip even to a galloping horse.] ● Even very industrious people may require an incentive at times. ≠ 良馬は鞭影を見て行く

## 花一時人一盛り

[Flowers have their moment; people have their spell of prosperity.] ● Used to describe the fleeting nature of life. • Roses and maidens soon lose their bloom. • All that's fair must fade.

## 花多ければ実少なし

[When flowers are plentiful, fruits are few.] ❶ Those who are conspicuous in their ostentation are less so in their achievements. • Much cry, little wool. ❷ Those who make many promises often keep only few. • Much cry, little wool. ♦ 賄賂には誓紙を忘る

## 花は桜、人は武士

[Among flowers, the cherry tree; among people, the warrior.]

は

☞ Throughout Japanese history the blossom of the cherry tree and the life of a warrior have been admired for their ephemeral splendor. ● Amongst flowers the most splendid thing is the blossom of the cherry tree; amongst men the most splendid thing is the warrior.

## 花より団子

[Dumplings rather than flowers.] ● In life, practicality should be esteemed above elegance, substance over outward appearance, and profit over fame. ● Bread is better than song of birds. = 色気より食い気

## 花を見て枝を折る

[To break off the branch once one has seen the flower.] ● Used to describe the actions of someone who does not truly appreciate beauty.

## 祖母育ちは三百安い

[Those who are raised by their grandmother are a hundred (*mon*) cheaper.] ✐ The *mon* (文) was a currency unit that derived from the Chinese *wen*, and introduced to Japan during the Muromachi period (1333-1568). It was used up until 1870, when it was replaced with the *yen* (円). ☞ In traditional Japan it was normal for infants to be cared for by their grandparents while their parents labored. ● Those who are spoiled in childhood will make weak, self-indulgent adults. ● Mother's darlings make but milksop heroes. ♦ 可愛い子には旅をさせよ

## 鱧も一期、海老も一期

[One span of life to the eel; one span of life to the lobster.] ● No matter how they may differ in talent or temperament, all living things have a limited life span. ● Life is but a span.

## 早い者勝ち

[The quick win.] ● Those who make sure they are the first often gain the upper hand. ● First come, first served. ● The devil take the hindmost. = 先勝ち ♦ 始めの勝ちは糞勝ち

は

## 早起きは三文の得

[Three *mon* for those who rise early.] The *mon* (文) was a currency unit that derived from the Chinese *wen*, and introduced to Japan during the Muromachi period (1333-1568). It was used up until 1870, when it was replaced with the *yen* (円). ● Those who rise early will have a longer day to make their earnings. ● The early bird catches the worm. The first sweep finds the money lost at night. = 朝起きは三文の得 ▶ 宵寝朝起き長者の基

## 早く熟すれば早く腐る

[What ripens quickly rots.] ❶ Beauty that develops in early youth is lost early. ● Soon ripe, soon rotten. ❷ Talents that develop early in life are lost early. ● A man at five may be a fool at fifteen. ▶ 大器晩成

## 腹八分目に医者いらず

[An eight-tenths filled stomach needs no doctor.] ● Eating with moderation is the best way to stay healthy. ● Temperance is the best physic.

## 張り詰めた弓はいつか弛む

[A tightly strung bow will relax in time.] ● A state of tension cannot endure forever, nor can those who are on their guard remain so forever. ● A bow long bent at last waxeth weak.

## 盤根錯節に遭いて利器を知る

[One will only know the quality of one's tools by trying them on difficult wood.] ● Someone's hidden potential will only be revealed when they are tested by trying times. ● The school of adversity is the best school. ▶ 逸物の鷹も放さねば捕らず ▶ 大風吹けば古家の祟り ▶ 艱難汝を玉にす ▶ ❶ 千両の鷹も放さねば知れぬ ▶ 百貫の鷹も放さねば捕らず ▶ 雪圧して松の操を知る ▶ 瑠璃も玻璃も照らせば光る

## 万卒は得易く一将得難し

[It is easy to obtain ten thousand footmen, but difficult to obtain one general.] ● Though people with average talents can be found

は

easily, people with exceptional talents are hard to find. • Workmen are easier found than masters.

## 晩の虹は鎌を研げ、朝の虹は隣へ行くな

[A rainbow in the evening, sharpen your sickle; a rainbow in the morning, do not go next-door.] ● A rainbow in the evening is the harbinger of of fair weather (and a time of harvest); a rainbow in the morning is the harbinger of bad weather (when one should stay indoors). • A rainbow at morn, put your hook in the corn; a rainbow at eve, put your head in the sheave. = 朝虹は雨、夕虹は晴れ ▶ 朝焼けは雨、夕焼けは晴れ ▶ 夕焼けは晴れ、朝焼けは雨

## 判を貸すとも人請けするな

[Stand security for someone's debts but do not vouch for someone's character.] ● One may stand security for someone's debts, since one knows the risk, but to vouch for someone's character is to take on a risk that is impossible to estimate.

# ヒ

**ひ**

## 蟇の息さえ天に上る

[Even the vigor of toads can reach the heavens.] ● When people with little power act in concert they can achieve great changes. • Union is strength. = 蟻の思いも天に届く = 農民の息も天に昇る = 蚤の息さえ天に上る

## 庇を貸して母屋を取られる

[Let someone shelter under the eaves of your house and they will take the main building.] ● What is granted as a concession is often interpreted as an invitation to take all. • Who lets another sit on his shoulder will soon have him on his head. • Give someone an inch and they'll take a mile. = 寸を与えれば尺を望む = 鉈を貸して山を伐られる ▶ 有るが上にも欲しがるのが人情 ▶ 有るは嫌なり、思うは成らず ▶ 昨日に優る今日の花 ▶ 千石を得て万石を恨む ▶ 成るは嫌なり、思うは成らず ▶ 隴を得て蜀を望む

## 飛鳥尽きて良弓蔵る

[Putting away a good bow when one has run out of birds.] ● When there is no longer a need for something, even though it proved to be of great use in time of need, it is often neglected. • Vows made in storms are forgotten in calms. • Danger past and God forgotten. • The peril past, the saint mocked. = 魚を得て筌を忘る = 狡兎死して走狗亨らる ◆ 暑さ忘れて蔭忘る ◆ 雨晴れて笠を忘る ◆ 苦しい時の神頼 ◆ 恐い時の仏頼み ◆ 災害は忘れた頃にやって来る ◆ 喉元過ぎれば熱さを忘れる ◆ 病治りて薬師忘る

## 必要の前に法律無し

[In the face of necessity there is no law.] ● In emergencies it may be necessary to act in contravention to laws that have been drafted for normal conditions. • Necessity has no law.

## 必要は発明の母

[Necessity is the mother of invention.] 📖 This proverb is a direct translation from the equivalent found in Swift's *Gulliver's Travels*. It is often used and is a proverb that sits well with the Japanese, who throughout their history have displayed a remarkable capacity to adjust themselves to a changing world. ● When the need is there, people will find the means to meet it. • Necessity is the mother of invention. ◆ 窮すれば通ず

## 人おのおの楽しみ有り

[People have their various pleasures.] ● No person is exactly the same, and each and every one of us has their own tastes and interests. • There is no accounting for tastes. • Every man to his taste. • Some prefer nettles. Tastes differ. ◆ 人は好き好き

## 人肥えたるが故に尊からず

[People are not esteemed for their stoutness.] ● People are not judged on their outward appearance but on the content their of character. • Handsome is that handsome does. = 見目より心 = 山高きが故に貴からず ◆ 衣ばかりで和尚は出来ぬ ◆ 衣を染めんより心を染めよ ◆ 数珠ばかりで和尚が出来ぬ

## 人酒を飲み、酒酒を飲み、酒人を飲む

[A person drinks *sake*; *sake* drinks *sake*; *sake* drinks the person.]
● The more one indulges in alcohol, the more one loses the capacity to control one's drinking. • First glass for the thirst, the second for nourishment, the third for pleasure, and the fourth for madness. • Wine is a turncoat; first a friend, then an enemy. = 一杯は人酒を飲み、二杯は酒酒を飲み、三杯は酒人を飲む

## 人と屏風は曲がらぬと立たぬ

[People and *byōbu* won't stand unfolded.] ✍ The *byōbu* (屏風), or Japanese folding screen, will only stand up when slightly folded. Note that the verb *magaru* (曲がる) has the connotation of crookedness and corruption. ● In order to live in an imperfect world one must learn the art of compromise and, at times, even participate in life's injustices. • It is a wicked world and we make part of it. = 曲がれねば世が渡らぬ ♦ 商売と屏風は曲がらぬと立たぬ ♦ 正しき者は艱難多し

## 人に受ける者は人を畏れ、人に予うる者は人に驕る

[Those who receive (favors) from others fear others; those who bestow (favors) on others are haughty to others.] ● Those who receive favors from others easily become servile; those who grant favors easily become arrogant. • Without favor none will know you, and with it you will not know yourself. = 富んでは驕る、貧しきは諂う

## 人に鬼は無い

[Among people there is no devil.] ● As one goes through life it is not merely heartless people one encounters; at various stages of one's journey one is sure to encounter kind and compassionate people, too. • The devil is not so black as he is painted. = 地獄にも鬼ばかりではない = 浮き世に鬼は無い = 渡る世間に鬼は無い ≠ 人を見たら泥棒と思え

## 人に勝たんと欲する者は必ず先ず自ら勝つ

[Those who set out to conquer others must first of all conquer themselves.] ● Those who seek to win by exploiting the weaknesses of others, should first conquer their own weaknesses, so that they may not be exploited by others. • He that is master of himself will soon be master of others. = 山中の賊を破るは易く心中の賊を破るは難し ♦ 己れを責めて人を責むるな ♦ 五十歩をもって百歩を笑う ♦ 近くて見えぬは睫 ♦ 人の頭の蠅を追うより我が頭の蠅を追え ♦ 人の一寸我が一尺 ♦ 人の七難より我が十難 ♦ 我が頭の蠅を追え ♦ 我が身の上は見えぬ

## 人には添ってみよ、馬には乗ってみよ

[As for humans, try and accompany them; as for horses, try and ride them.] ● The only way to get to know someone really well is to be in their company over a protracted period. • Experience is the mother of wisdom. = 馬には乗ってみよ、人には添ってみよ

## 人の頭の蠅を追うより我が頭の蠅を追え

[Rather than pursue a fly on the head of others, pursue the fly on one's own (head).] ● Rather than pointing out the flaws and mistakes of others, one should first critically look at one's own shortcomings. • We see not what sits on our own shoulder. = 己れを責めて人を責むるな = 我が頭の蠅を追え ♦ 五十歩をもって百歩を笑う ♦ 猿の尻笑い ♦ 近くて見えぬは睫 ♦ ❷ 遠きを知りて近きを知らず ♦ 人の一寸我が一尺 ♦ 人の七難より我が十難 ♦ 目糞が鼻糞を笑う ♦ 目脂が鼻垢を笑う ♦ 我が身の上は見えぬ

## 人の一寸我が一尺

[The one *sun* in others, the one *shaku* in oneself.] ✍ The Japanese *sun* (寸) is a traditional unit of measurement still used by Japanese craftsmen. One *sun* is roughly three centimeters; a *sun* is ten *bu* (分) and a tenth of a *shaku* (尺). ● People are quick to notice minor flaws in others but slow to see the major flaws in themselves. • We see not what sits on our own shoulder. = 人の七難より我が十難 ♦ 己れを責めて人を責むるな ♦ 五十歩をもって百歩を笑う ♦ 猿の尻笑い ♦ 近くて見えぬは睫 ♦ 人の頭の蠅を追うより我が頭の蠅を追え ♦ 目糞が鼻糞を笑う ♦ 目脂が鼻垢を笑う ♦ 我が頭の蠅を追え ♦ 我が身の上は見えぬ

## 人の痛いのは三年でも辛抱する

[We can bear the pain of others for as long as three years.] ● People have a remarkable capacity to endure the suffering of others. ◆ 我が身を抓って人の痛さを知れ

## 人の噂も七十五日

[Even gossip about a person lasts but seventy-five days.] ● No matter how outrageous or sensational a rumor, with time, it will peter out like a spent candle. • A wonder lasts but nine days. = 世の取り沙汰も七十五日 ◆ 一犬虚を吠ゆれば万犬実を伝う ◆ 流言は知者に止まる ≠ 世間の口に戸は立てられぬ ≠ 人の口に戸は立てられぬ

## 人の口に戸は立てられぬ

[One cannot put a door in the mouth of the people.] ● People will talk without reserve or discretion on any subject. • People will talk. = 世間の口に戸は立てられぬ ◆ 阿呆の一つ覚え ◆ 愚者の雄弁は沈黙なり ◆ 知る者は言わず言う者は知らず ◆ 雀の千声鶴の一声 ◆ 馬鹿の一つ覚え ◆ 流言は知者に止まる

## 人の車に乗る者は人の患えに載る

[When one takes a ride in someone's cart one takes part in their sorrows.] ● When one gets involved in the affairs of others, one is often made to share in their difficulties too.

## 人の心は区々だ

[The hearts of people are multifarious.] ● All people are different and so the content of their hearts will differ. • So many men, so many minds. ◆ 人心の異なるその面の如し

## 人の七難より我が十難

[Rather than the seven defects of others, the ten defects of one's own.] ● People are quick to notice minor flaws in others but slow to see the major flaws in themselves. • We see not what sits on our own shoulder. = 人の一寸我が一尺 ◆ 己れを責めて人を責むるな ◆ 五十歩をもって百歩を笑う ◆ 猿の尻笑い ◆ 近くて見えぬは睫 ◆ ❷ 遠きを知りて近きを知らず ◆ 人の頭の蠅を追うより我が頭の蠅を追え ◆ 目糞が鼻糞を笑う ◆ 目脂が鼻垢を笑う ◆ 我が頭の蠅を追え ◆ 我が身の上は見えぬ

## 人の善悪はその交わりともによって知られる

[The goodness or badness of people can be known by the friends they keep.] ● Someone's character can often be told by the kind of company they keep. ● Tell me the company you keep and I will tell you what you are.

## 人のふり見て我がふり直せ

[Observe the behavior of others to adjust your own.] ● One should observe the mistakes made by others and correct one's own behavior accordingly so as to avoid making similar mistakes. ● One man's fault is another's lesson. ● Learn wisdom by the follies of others. ● It is good to learn at other men's cost. ● By other's faults wise men correct their own. = 前車の覆るは後車の戒め ✦ 木は規に依って直く人は人に依って賢し

## 人の行方と水の流れ

[The destiny of people and the drift of water.] ● In this life no one can tell where destiny will lead one. = 水の流れと人の末 ✦ 明日の事を言えば鬼が笑う ✦ 一寸先は闇 ✦ 三年先の事を言えば鬼が笑う ✦ 知者も面前に三尺の闇あり ✦ 三日先の事を言えば鬼が笑う ✦ 来年の事を言えば鬼が笑う

## 人は一代、名は末代

[People (last for only) one generation; fame (lasts) forever.] ● Though life is brief, the reputation built during one's lifetime, whether good or bad, lasts beyond the grave. ● Worthy men shall be remembered. = 身は一代、名は末代 ✦ ❷するは一時名は末代 ✦ 手形は残れど足形は残らず ✦ 虎は死して革を止め、人は死して名を残す

## 人は落ち目の志し

[As for people, resolution/kindness (is called for) when they are down on their luck.] ✍ This proverb has a double meaning, since the term *kokorozashi* (志し) can be translated both as aspiration or resolution, and as kindness or goodwill. ❶ It is especially when things do not go as one would hope that a spirited resolve to succeed will carry the day. ● He that hath no ill fortune is troubled with good. ♦ 艱難汝を玉にす ♦ 盤根錯節に遭いて利器を知る ♦ 雪圧して松の操を知る ♦ 瑠璃も玻璃も照らせば光る ❷ It is especially when one has hit on hard times that the kindness of others is most needed. • A friend in need is a friend indeed. ♦ 旅は道連れ世は情け ♦ 人は情けの下に立つ

## 人は好き好き

[People have different likes.] ● No person is exactly the same; each of us has their own tastes and interests. What is distasteful to one may be delightful to others. • There is no accounting for tastes. • Every man to his taste. • Some prefer nettles. • Tastes differ. ♦ 人おのおの楽しみ有り

## 人は情けの下に立つ

[People stand below compassion.] ● In life compassion is most important, since it is compassion that makes one human and without it humans cannot live. • There is a great deal of human nature in man. ♦ 旅は道連れ世は情け ♦ 愛出ずる者は愛返り、福往く者は福来る ♦ 愛は愛を生む ♦ 仇も情けも我が身より出る ♦ 魚心有れば水心 ♦ 問い声良ければいらえ声良い ♦ 情けは人の為ならず

## 人を射んとせば先ず馬を射よ

[If one would shoot someone shoot their horse first.] ❶ The best way to deal a decisive blow to an opponent is to destroy what they chiefly depend upon. = 将を射んと欲すれば先ず馬を射よ ❷ Those who want to achieve greatness should lay the foundation for success by honing their skills on less ambitious goals. • He that would the daughter win, must with the mother first begin. = 馬に乗るまで牛に乗れ = 将を射んと欲すれば先ず馬を射よ = 高きに登るは低きよりす ♦ 一朝一夕の故に非ず ♦ 沙弥から長老にはなれぬ ♦ 千里の道も一歩より始まる ♦ 始めから長老にはなれぬ ♦ 始めの一歩、末の千里

## 人を知る者は知なり、自ら知る者は明なり

[Those who know others are wise; those who know themselves are enlightened.] 📖 This proverb is attributed to the Chinese Daoist Laozi. ● Those who can tell the difference between intelligent and stupid people are wise, but those who can go a step further and see the wisdom or folly of their own thoughts have become enlightened. • Know thyself. ◆ 近くて見えぬは睫 ◆ 遠きを知りて近きを知らず ◆ 我が身の上は見えぬ ◆ ❶ 堤灯持ちの足元暗し ◆ ❶ 灯台下暗し

## 人を取る亀人に取られる

[Tortoises that seek to catch humans are caught by humans.] ● Those who wish to cause harm to others will eventually harm themselves. • They hurt themselves who wrong others. • Curses, like chickens, come home to roost. = 天を仰ぎて唾す = 狩人も罠に掛かる = 人を呪わば穴二つ ◆ 策士策に溺れる

## 人を呪わば穴二つ

[Curse someone and there will be two graves.] ● Those who wish to cause harm to others will eventually harm themselves. • They hurt themselves who wrong others. • Curses, like chickens, come home to roost. = 天を仰ぎて唾す = 狩人も罠に掛かる = 人を取る亀人に取られる ◆ 策士策に溺れる

## 人を見たら泥棒と思え

[When you see someone, consider them a robber.] ● In this dangerous world it is best to trust no one, so one will never be disappointed. • He who trusteth not is not deceived. • Trust is the mother of deceit. = 明日は雨人は泥棒 = 火を見れば火事と思え ◆ 石橋を叩いて渡る ◆ 石橋を叩いて渡る ◆ 転ばぬ先の杖 ◆ 備え有れば憂い無し ◆ 濡れぬ前の傘 ≠ 浮き世に鬼は無い ≠ 地獄にも鬼ばかりではない ≠ 七度尋ねて人を疑え ≠ 人に鬼は無い ≠ 渡る世間に鬼は無い

## 日に三度我が身を省みる

[Reflect on oneself three times a day.] ● In order to conduct oneself correctly, one should reflect on one's actions as often as possible. • He thinks not well that thinks not again. ◆ 人を知る者は知なり、自ら知る者は明なり

## 火の無い所に煙は立たない

[Smoke does not rise from a place where there is no fire.] ☞ This

211

proverb derives from its English equivalent. ● If rumors are rife, though they may not be wholly accurate, there is probably some factual basis for them. Similarly, when someone is frequently regarded with suspicion, there is probably an underlying reason for it. ● Where there's smoke there's fire. ● No smoke without fire. ♦ 火を見れば火事と思え ≠ 七度尋ねて人を疑え

## 百聞は一見に如かず

[A hundred hearsays do not equal a single sighting.] ● No matter how convincing the rumors, seeing something just once will settle any doubt. ● Seeing is believing. = 論より証拠

## 百様を知って一様を知らず

[Know all sorts yet know none.] ● The knowledge of those who profess to know about many things is often superficial. ● Jack of all trades and master of none. ● He who commences many things finishes but few. ♦ 何でも来いに名人無し ♦ 多芸は無芸 ♦ 万能足りて一心足らず

## 百里を行く者は九十を半ばとす

[To a traveler on a journey of one hundred *ri*, ninety *ri* is halfway.] ✍ The *ri* (里) is an ancient Chinese measurement of distance, the equivalent of 0.3 miles. With time, it came to denote the distance one could walk in an hour, and during the Edo period (1600–1867) it was officially defined as 36 *chō*, or about 2.44 miles. ● It is especially when one is on the verge of reaching a goal that one is likely to encounter unexpected problems and that one should be extra vigilant. ● Many things fall between the cup and the lip. ♦ 好事魔多し ♦ 勝って兜の緒を締めよ

## 百貫の鷹も放さねば捕らず

[Even a falcon of a hundred *kan* will not catch (any prey) unless it is set free.] ✍ The *kan* (貫) was a pre-war Japanese coin. One *kan* was worth ten thousand *yen* (円). ● No matter how much skill one has, it will be of no use without the opportunity to utilize it. ● A hooded falcon cannot strike the quarry. = 逸物の鷹も放さねば捕ら

ず = ❶ 千両の鷹も放さねば知れぬ ♦ 才有れども用いざれば愚人の如し ♦ 猿を檻に置けば豚と同じ ♦ 死を先んずる者は必ず生ず ♦ 身を捨ててこそ浮かぶ瀬も有れ ♦ 蒔かぬ種は生えぬ ♦ 物は試し

## 瓢箪から駒

[A chessman from a gourd.] ❶ Used in cases when the unexpected comes from an unexpected place. • It is the unexpected that often happens. ♦ 嘘から出た実 ❷ Used to describe a situation that is utterly unimaginable. • Pigs will fly. ♦ 朝日が西から出る ♦ 石が流れて木の葉が沈む ♦ 餅の中からの屋根石

## 病身者は長生きする

[Those with sickly constitutions live a long life.] ● Paradoxically, those who seem to have weak constitutions and are frequently afflicted by minor ailments often live to a ripe old age. • A cracked vessel often lasts longest. • Creaking doors hang the longest.

## 屏風と商人は真直ぐにては立たぬもの

[*Byōbu* and tradesmen will not stand up straight.] ✍ The *byōbu* (屏風), or Japanese folding screen, will only stand up when partially folded. As in English, the adjective *massugu* (真直ぐ), or "straight," has the connotation of honesty and being upright. ● Trade will only flourish with a slight degree of dishonesty. • There is knavery in all trades, but most in tailors. = 商人と屏風は曲がらねば世に立たぬ = 商売と屏風は曲がらぬと立たぬ ♦ 正しき者は艱難多し

## 火を避けて水に陥る

[Evade the fire, only to fall into the water.] ● No sooner do we think that we are out of trouble or we are enmeshed in more. • Out of the frying pan into the fire. = 一難去って又一難

## 火を失して池を掘る

[Digging a lake when the fire has died.] ● To try to remedy a problem when it is too late. • Lock the stable door after the horse is stolen. • After death, the doctor. • After meat, mustard. = 戦を見て矢を矧ぐ = 喧嘩過ぎての棒乳切り = 賊去って張弓 = 賊の後の棒

ひ

213

乳切り ＝ 敵を見て矢を矧ぐ ＝ 泥棒を捕らえて縄を綯う ＝ 難に臨んで兵を鋳る ＝ 盗人を見て縄を綯う ◆ 後の祭 ◆ 六日の菖蒲、十日の菊 ◆ 盆過ぎての鯖商い

## 火を見れば火事と思え

[When one sees a flame, consider it a fire.] ● In this dangerous world it is best to be prepared for the worst. In that way one will never be disappointed. • He who trusteth not is not deceived. • If you trust before you try, you may repent before you die. • Trust is the mother of deceit. ＝ 明日は雨人は泥棒 ＝ 人を見たら泥棒と思え ◆ 石橋を叩いて渡る ◆ 石橋を叩いて渡る ◆ 転ばぬ先の杖 ◆ 備え有れば憂い無し ◆ 濡れぬ前の傘

## 貧すれば鈍する

[When one is reduced to poverty one becomes dull-witted.] ● Those who are impoverished soon lose their airs and graces and become singularly devoted to the numbing task of day-to-day survival. • Poverty dulls the wit. ＝ 窮すれば鈍する

## 貧乏怖いもの無し

[The poor have nothing to fear.] ● Those who have no money need not fear that anyone will take it away from them. • A penniless traveler will sing in the presence of a robber.

## 貧の盗みに恋の歌

[The larceny of poverty; the poems of love.] ● A person driven into poverty will resort to stealing; a person in love will be inspired to write poems. That is to say, when driven to desperation, people will resort to any means to find relief. • There is no virtue that poverty destroyeth not. ＝ 窮鼠猫を噛む ◆ 一寸の虫にも五分の魂 ◆ ❶ 時に遭えば鼠も虎となる ◆ 蚯蚓にも角 ◆ 鼠窮して猫を噛み、人貧しゅして盗みす ◆ ❶ 用いる時は鼠も虎となる

## 貧乏人も三年置けば用に立つ

[Even a pauper may prove useful after three years.] ● No matter how insignificant the poor may seem, at the right moment, even they

214

may play a role of consequence. • There is no misfortune but has a redeeming feature. ＝割れ鍋も三年置けば用に立つ ◆ 門脇の姥にも用有り ◆ 枯れ木も山の賑わい ◆ 愚者も千慮に一徳あり ◆ 癖ある馬に乗りあり ◆ 蹴る馬も乗り手次第 ◆ ❷ 時に遭えば鼠も虎となる ◆ 馬鹿と鋏は使い様 ◆ 馬鹿も一芸 ◆ 禍も三年置けば用に立つ ◆ ❷ 用いる時は鼠も虎となる ◆ 野郎と鋏が使い様 ◆ 湯腹も一時、松の木柱も三年

## 貧乏暇無し

[The poor have no spare time.] ● The poor are constantly trying to stave off hunger and have no time for anything else. • Poor men have no leisure.

# フ

## 富貴にして苦あり、貧賎にして楽しみあり

[To the rich and famous (too) there is pain; to the poor and lowly (too) there is pleasure.] ● No matter one's station, pain and pleasure are two inseparable aspects of life, and all of us will have a fair share of both. • Fortune to one is mother, to another is stepmother.

## 富貴にして膳をなり易し、貧賎にして功をなし難し

[For the rich and famous it is easy to do good; for the poor and lowly it is difficult to distinguish oneself.] 📖 This proverb is taken from the *Soga monogatari*. ● If one has money it is easy to play the philanthropist; if one has none one will find it difficult to undertake anything. ◆ 富を為せば仁ならず、仁を為せば富まず ◆ 富む者仁ならず、仁なれば富まず

## 富貴には他人も集まり、貧賎には親戚も離れる

[To wealth and prestige even strangers gather; from poverty and ignominy even relatives flee.] ● When one is successful, people want to associate with you; when one is a failure people avoid you. • In time of prosperity, friends will be plenty; in times of adversity not one in twenty. ◆ 甘い物に蟻が付く

ふ

# 富貴は天にあり
ふうき　　　てん

[Wealth and prestige are (decided) in heaven.] ● Though one may desire riches and honors, ultimately, both are bestowed by fortune alone. ● No flying from fate. = 運は天にあり ▶ 運の神は屋根の上に住む
うん　てん　　　　　　　　うん　かみ　や　ね　　うえ　す

# 不義の富貴は浮雲の如し
ふ　ぎ　　ふうき　　ふうん　ごと

[Riches and honors gained unjustly are like floating clouds.] ● Wealth and honors gained by ruse or illegal means are fleeting and will sooner or later be lost. ● Ill-gotten goods seldom prosper. = 悪銭身に付かず
あくせんみ　　つ

# 覆水盆に返らず
ふくすいぼん　　かえ

[Spilt water will not return to the tray.] ☞ This proverb originates in an ancient Chinese folk tale about Tai Gong Wang, the private teacher of the Shu warlord Wu Wang. The scholar's incessant reading drives his wife to distraction and eventually causes her to sue for divorce. Not long after she has obtained it, Gong Wang's meritorious service earns him the governorship of the province of Qi. Upon hearing the news, his wife visits her former husband and appeals to him to take her back. In response, the governor spills water from a tray on purpose and tells her that he intends to remarry her when the water has returned to the tray. ● Words once spoken, or mistakes once made, cannot be undone. ● It is no use crying over spilt milk. What is done cannot be undone. = 流水源に返らず ▶ 死んだ子の年を数える ▶ 後悔先に立たず ▶ 提灯持ち後に立たず
りゅうすい　みなもと　かえ　　　　　　し　　こ　とし　かぞ　　　こうかいさき　た　　　ちょうちんも　　あと　た

# 河豚は食いたし命は惜しし
ふ　ぐ　　く　　　　いのち　お

[Blowfish are sweet, but so is life.] ☞ The Japanese blowfish, or *fugu* (河豚), is considered a delicacy. A special license, however, has to be obtained by chefs in order to prepare blowfish, as its liver contains a poison that causes muscles—including the heart—to contract, and thus lead to an agonizing death. ● In order to taste life's greatest pleasures one often has to put that very life at risk. ● Honey is sweet, but the bee stings. ● Every rose has a thorn.

ふ

## 不幸の裏には幸いが有る

[Behind misery lies happiness.] ● No matter how bitter the hardships there is always room for happiness. ● Every cloud has a silver lining. ● That which was bitter to endure may be sweet to remember. ♦ 禍も三年置けば用に立つ

## 不幸の際の伴侶は不幸を軽減す

[Company in times of misery makes the misery less.] ● When there is someone to console one in hard times it will make the going lighter. ● Company in distress makes it less. = 同病相憐れむ ♦ 牛は牛連れ ♦ 馬は馬連れ ♦ 鬼の女房に鬼神 ♦ 同気相求む ♦ 友は類をもって集まる = ❶ 目の寄る所へ玉が寄る ♦ 類は友を呼ぶ

## 不幸は重なるもの

[Misery is cumulative.] ● Calamities or hardships often strike at the same time. ● Misfortune seldom comes alone. = 雨が降れば土砂降り ♦ 痛い上の針 ♦ 重き馬に上荷打つ ♦ 泣き面に蜂が刺す ♦ 弱り目に崇り目 ♦ 二度ある事は三度ある ♦ ❷ 目の寄る所へ玉が寄る

## 武士に二言は無い

[A warrior does not have a double tongue.] ☞ Warriors of medieval Japan were expected to adhere to the Way of the Warrior, or *bushidō* (武士道) a military code of conduct. Among the five virtues of duty, manners, spirit, fidelity, and benevolence that were instilled in the medieval warrior, fidelity was perhaps the most highly valued, since a warrior's loyalty to his lord cemented the rigid yet fragile feudal social order. ● Those who live by the martial code of conduct will stand by their word. ● An honest man's word is as good as his bond. ♦ 七珍万宝の随一は人の命と人の誠

## 武士は食わねど高楊枝

[A warrior, though he has not eaten, will hold his toothpick high.] ● Though they may not have had anything to eat, warriors will act as if they have had a good meal, as it is beneath their dignity to complain. = 侍は食わねど高楊枝 ♦ 猿も食わねど高楊枝じ ≠ 兵法より食い方

ふ

## 豚に真珠

[Pearls before the swine.] ☞ This proverb derives from its English equivalent. ● Used when the recipient of aid or generosity does not appreciate its value. ● Cast pearls before swine. = 猫に小判 ◆ 馬の耳に念仏 ◆ 蛙の面に水 ◆ 空吹く風と聞き流す ◆ 糠に釘 ◆ 馬耳東風

## 踏まれた草にも花が咲く

[Even among the downtrodden grass flowers may blossom.] ● Sooner or later fortune will favor even the unfortunate. ● A man has his hour and a dog has his day. ● Every dog has its day. ● Fortune knocks once at least at every man's gate. ◆ 薊の花も一盛り ◆ 番茶も出花

## 振られて帰る果報者

[Those who return home jilted are fortunate.] ☞ Originally, this proverb was used with respect to those who had visited the licensed quarters but returned home without having succumbed to temptation, and were thus saved from losing large sums of money. ● Luck is on the side of those who are unlucky in love. ● When Venus does not smile on you Fortune does. ◆ 里の金には詰まるが習い

## 古木に手をかくるな若木に腰掛くるな

[Do not touch old wood; do not sit on young wood.] ● It is best to stay away from those without prospects and to not hinder those with bright prospects.

## 古きを温ねて新しきを知る

[Inquire into the old to know the new.] 📖 This proverb is taken from the *Analects* of Confucius. ● In order to understand current problems, one should study the circumstances leading to similar problems in the past. ● Things present are judged by things past. ● There is nothing new under the sun. = 来を知らんと欲する者は往を察す ◆ 現在の因果を見て過去未来を知る ≠ 昔は昔、今は今

## 文は人也

[The style (of writing) is the person.] 📖 This proverb is taken from the French philosopher George-Louis Leclerc de Buffon's maxim that *Le style est l'homme lui-même.* ● One's character will be revealed by one's style of writing. It sits well in Japanese (feudal) tradition in which, next to the acquisition of martial skills, much emphasis was placed on the acquisition of civil skills, something borne out by the expression 文武両道, emphasizing "the dual way of civil and martial accomplishments," a concept Chinese in origin. ● The style is the man. ▸ 文は武に優る ▸ 文武は車の両輪 ▸ 武を右にし文を左にす ▸ 馬子にも衣裳

## 文は武に優る

[The civil surpasses the martial.] ☞ This proverb seems to be somewhat at odds with the expression 文武両道, emphasizing "the dual way of civil and martial accomplishments," a concept Chinese in origin and popular during Japan's feudal era, when as much emphasis was placed on the acquisition of civil skills as martial skill. ● The power of civil accomplishments is superior to military accomplishments. ● The pen is mightier than the sword. ▸ 文は人也 ≠ 文武は車の両輪 ≠ 武を右にし文を左にす

## 文武は車の両輪

[Civil and martial (accomplishments are like the two wheels on a cart.] 📖 This proverb is taken from the *Nobunagaki*. It harkens back to the much older term of 文武両道, "the dual way of civil and martial accomplishments," a concept Chinese in origin. ● In order to become a well-rounded individual, it is vital that one develop both one's civil as well as one's martial skills. = 武を右にし文を左にす ▸ 文は人也 ≠ 文は武に優る

## 武を右にし文を左にす

[Have the martial on one's right and the civil on one's left.] ☞ During Japan's feudal era, much emphasis was placed on the acquisition of civil skills as well as martial skills, something borne out by the popular expression 文武両道, "the dual way of civil and martial accomplishments," a concept Chinese in origin. ● In order to become a well-rounded individual, it is vital that one develop

both civil and martial skills. = 士は文武を左右にす = 文武は車の両輪
♦ 文は人也 ♦ 馬子にも衣裳 ≠ 文は武に優る

# へ

## 平家を滅ぼす者は平家

[Those who destroy the Heike are Heike.] ☞ The Heike, or Taira, was a powerful military clan that rose to prominence during the 12th century, and whose decline is generally believed to have been brought about by their own arrogance. ● The demise of great people or dynasties is often caused by internal corruption and hubris rather than outside forces. Used when someone's failure can be attributed to their own follies. • As one sows, so one reaps. ♦ 亢竜悔い有り ♦ 驕る平家久しからず

## 瓶中の氷を見て天下の寒さを知る

[See the ice in the jug and know the cold of the land.] ● A wise person is able to infer the whole by knowing only one aspect. • One word is enough to a wise man. • Few words to the wise suffice. = ❷ 一葉落ちて天下の秋を知る = 一を聞いて十を知る = 一班を見て全豹を卜す ≠ 一を知って二を知らず ≠ 其の一を知りて其の二を知らず

## 兵法より食い方

[Rather than military tactics, a means to eat.] ● Soldiers need to eat and will have to concern themselves first with how to obtain food before they can turn to military affairs. • An army, like a serpent, travels on its belly. ≠ 侍は食わねど高楊枝 ≠ 武士は食わねど高楊枝

## 下手があるので上手が知れる

[The skilled are only known because of the unskilled.] ● Skilled people only manage to stand out by virtue of the unskilled. • Were there no fools there would be no wise men. = 馬鹿も有ればこそ、利口も引き立つ ♦ 自慢高慢馬鹿の内 ♦ 目明き千人、盲千人 ♦ 盲千人、目明き千人

## 下手な鍛冶屋も一度は名剣

[Even a poor blacksmith may make an excellent blade once.] ● Even those who lack the needed expertise may (accidentally) succeed at something if they attempt it many times. • He who shoots often, hits at last. = ❶ 下手な鉄砲も数打ちゃ当たる ♦ 習い性と成る ♦ 習うより慣れよ ♦ 盲のまぐれ当たり ♦ 門前の小僧習わぬ経を読む

## 下手な鉄砲も数打ちゃ当たる

[Even a bad marksman will hit (the target) if he shoots many times.] ☞ This proverb derives from its English equivalent. ❶ Even those who lack the needed expertise may (accidentally) succeed at something if they attempt it many times. • He who shoots often, hits at last. = 下手な鍛冶屋も一度は名剣 ♦ 習い性と成る ♦ 習うより慣れよ ♦ 盲のまぐれ当たり ♦ 門前の小僧習わぬ経を読む ❷ If one perseveres at something one may eventually succeed. • Practice makes perfect. ♦ 習い性と成る ♦ 習うより慣れよ ♦ 盲のまぐれ当たり ♦ 門前の小僧習わぬ経を読む

## 下手な番匠木の難を言う

[An unskilled carpenter blames the timber.] ● Those who lack the proper skills blame something else for their failures. • A bad workman quarrels with his tools. = 下手の道具調べ ♦ 弘法は筆を択ばず ♦ 能書筆を択ばず ♦ 名人は筆を択ばず ♦ 名筆は筆を択ばず ♦ 良工は材を択ばず

## 下手な棒銀休むに似たり

[A poor maneuver is tantamount to taking a rest.] ✍ A *bōgin* (棒銀) is a maneuver in Japanese chess, or *shōgi*, in which two pieces are used to tactical advantage. ● When amateurs resort to the methods of professionals the result will be the same as if they had done nothing at all. • Mickle fails that fools think. ♦ 蚌を煮て珠の爛るるを知らず

## 下手の長談義

[The long talk of the unskillful.] ● Those who are not skilled at talking often lose the attention of their audience by their longwindedness. • Brevity is the soul of wit.

## 下手の道具調べ

[The tool-inspection of the unskilled.] ☞ This proverb derives from its English equivalent. ● Those who blame others for making mistakes often lack the proper skills for a task themselves. ● A poor craftsman quarrels with his tools. = 下手な番匠木の難を言う ▸ 弘法は筆を択ばず ▸ 能書筆を択ばず ▸ 名人は筆を択ばず ▸ 名筆は筆を択ばず ▸ 良工は材を択ばず

## 蛇に噛まれて朽ち縄に怖ず

[Having been bitten by a snake one fears the rotten rope.] ✍ Another by now somewhat archaic meaning of *kuchinawa* (朽ち縄) is snake, in which case it is also rendered with the Chinese character for snake (蛇). ● Those who have experienced harm through failure will think twice before they try again. ● Once bitten, twice shy. = 羹に懲りて膾を吹く = 火傷した子供は火を恐れる

# ホ

## 坊主憎けりゃ袈裟まで憎い

[If one hates a Buddhist priest one hates even his robe.] ☞ A *kesaya*, *kesa* in Japanese, is the traditional Buddhist robe, worn over the shoulder. ● When one comes to dislike a person one is inclined to dislike everything even remotely connected to that person. ≠ 愛屋烏に及ぶ ≠ 可愛さ余って憎さ百倍

## 棒の下に回る犬は打てぬ

[One cannot hit a dog that lingers below the rod.] ● One cannot treat someone harshly who appeals for mercy. ● Mercy surpasses justice. = 杖の下に回る犬は打てぬ ▸ 窮鳥懐に入れば猟師も殺さず ▸ 飛ぶ鳥懐に入る時は狩人も助くる

## 法は人で無い、人は法で無い

[Law is not a person; a person is not the law.] ● Ultimately, law is an abstraction and those who exercise power should give ample scope to individual differences in its application. ▸ 悪法も亦法也

222

## 方便の愚は正、無方便の智は邪

[A foolish but pious fraud is good; a wise but unpious fraud is false.]
✍ The pious fraud (方便), or *upaya* in sanskrit, is a rhetorical device used to teach Buddhist doctrine to the masses. ● The truth, even spoken by a fool, is good; an untruth, even spoken by a wise person, is not good. ♦ 嘘も方便 ♦ 仏に方便聖人に権道

## 棒ほど願って針ほど叶う

[Wish for a club but be granted a needle.] ● The greater one's expectations, the greater the disappointment when they are not met. ● Ask for an ell and you get an inch. ● Ask much to have a little. ♦ 開けて悔しき玉手箱 ♦ 当て事と越中褌は向こうから外れる ♦ ❷ 大きい家に大きい風が吹く

## 蚌を煮て珠の爛るるを知らず

[Boil the gutter clam and spoil the pearl.] ● Used in instances where opportunities with great potentials are utterly misjudged and spoiled by using the wrong approach. ♦ 下手な棒銀休むに似たり

## 牡丹餅は棚から落ちて来ず

[*Botamochi* do not fall from shelves.] ✍ *Botamochi* (牡丹餅) are rice cake dumplings covered with bean jam. ☞ This proverb builds on the Japanese idiom 棚から牡丹餅, or "a *botamochi* from the shelf," which stands for a windfall or godsend. Rice cakes, or *mochi* (餅) are made by pounding steamed rice into cakes with a large and heavy wooden hammer, a time-consuming and and tiring process. ● No feat is accomplished without effort, and the greater the feat, the more effort is required. ● No pains, no gains. = 棚から牡丹餅は落ちてこない

## 蛍火をもって酒弥山を焼く

[To burn Mount Sumeru with the fire of a firefly.] ☞ Mount Sumeru, or Shumisen (酒弥山) in Japanese, is a legendary mountain from Buddhist lore that is said to stand at the center of the world and tower over all that surrounds it. ❶ If one used all one's ingenuity the greatest of enemies can be conquered with the simplest of means.

• Throw out a lobster and pull in a whale. • Throw a sprat to catch a herring. • Give an egg to gain an ox. • You may lose a fly to catch a trout. ♦ 海老で鯛を釣る ♦ ❶ 雁は八百、矢は三文 ❷ Great enterprises may come to naught through the tiniest of oversights. • A small spark makes a great fire. ♦ 蟻の穴から堤も崩れる ♦ 大山も蟻穴より崩る

### 仏作って魂を入れず

[To make an image of Buddha without consecrating it.] ☞ Traditionally, when a Buddhist image is completed a consecration ceremony is held to instill the image with the spirit of Buddha. ● Used in cases when something is completed, but the most important thing is forgotten. • Plowing the field and forgetting the seed.

### 仏に方便聖人に権道

[The pious fraud to Buddha; the expedient to the sage.] ✑ The pious fraud (方便), or *upaya* in sanskrit, is a rhetorical device used to teach Buddhist doctrine to the masses. ● Depending on one's position in life it may be necessary to use different means of obtaining a rightful goal. • Tell a lie and find the truth. • The end justifies the means. = 嘘も方便 ♦ 方便の愚は正、無方便の智は邪

### 仏の顔も三度まで

[Even Buddha's face (will have its effect only up to) three times.] ☞ This proverb is said to originate in an anecdote from Buddha's life and the fate of Sakya, the state over which his father had ruled. The ruler of a neighboring state, who felt he had been done an injustice by the Buddha's father, marched on Sakya to destroy it. En route he encountered the Buddha, who dissuaded him from attacking. This happened three times. The fourth time the army advanced, the Buddha was not there, and Sakya was destroyed. ● There are limits to the amount of injustice people can endure.

### 仏の沙汰も銭

[The judgment of Buddha, too, is (subject to) money.] ● In all walks of life money is a defining force. • Money makes the mare go round.

● Money is the best lawyer. = 地獄の沙汰も金次第 ▶ 愛は多能で有り、金は万能で有る ▶ 金の世の中 ▶ 金は世界の回り物 ▶ 金は天下の回り持ち ▶ 人間万事金の世の中 ▶ 欲の世の中

## 仏の光より金の光

[The luster of gold rather than the luster of Buddha.] ☞ Images of Buddha are often gilded, so that this proverb can be interpreted quite literally. ● The worldly power of money seems stronger than the spiritual power of Buddha. ● No penny, no paternoster. ▶ 阿弥陀の光も金次第 ▶ 金の光は阿弥陀ほど ▶ 地獄の沙汰も金次第 ▶ 釈迦も銭ほど光る

## 仏を直すとて鼻を欠く

[To break the nose by trying to mend the Buddha.] ● In attempting to correct minor errors in an area of little importance one may well cause irreparable damage in an area of great importance. ● To burn the house to frighten away the mouse. ● Throw out the baby with the bath water. = 枝を矯めて花を散らす = 枝を矯めんとして幹を枯らす = 角を矯めて牛を殺す ▶ 流れを汲みて源を濁す

## 誉れは謗りの基

[Fame is the foundation of slander.] ● The more one's name rises in the world, the more one will be envied by others and the greater will be the chance of incurring slander. ● After honor and state follow envy and hate. ● Envy is the companion of honor. ● The brighter the moon the more the dogs howl. ▶ ❶ 大きい家に大きい風が吹く ▶ 高山の巓には美木無し ▶ 高木風に妬まる ▶ 高木風に憎まる ▶ 高木は風に折らる ▶ 大木は風に折らる ▶ 大名の下には久しく居るべからず ▶ ❷ 出る杭は打たれる

## 誉められて唐辛子を食う

[Be praised and eat red pepper.] ● Those who are taken in by flattery and begin to think highly of themselves will eventually have to suffer the consequences of their folly. ● Trust not the praise of a friend, nor the contempt of an enemy. = 誉める人には油断すな ▶ 誉れは謗りの基

225

## 誉めるは毀る

[To praise is to malign.] ● One should be wary of excessive compliments, which may be intended to conceal scorn and jealousy. ● Trust not the praise of a friend, nor the contempt of an enemy. = 誉める人には油断すな ◆ 誉れは謗りの基

## 誉める人には油断すな

[Do not relax one's guard toward those who praise.] ● One should be wary of excessive compliments, which may be intended to conceal less friendly intentions. ● Trust not the praise of a friend, nor the contempt of an enemy. = 誉めるは毀る ◆ 誉れは謗りの基

## 誉める人は買わぬ

[Those who praise do not buy.] ● People who intend to buy something will point out its flaws to force the seller to lower the price. If they do not intend to buy, they can be generous with their compliments. ● Praise without profit puts little in the pot. = 品物を誉める人に買うた例なし

## 惚れた病に薬無し

[There is no medicine against love-sickness.] ● No amount of persuasion will cause someone who is infatuated to fall out of love. ● No herb will cure love. = 惚れ病と馬鹿の治る薬は無い ◆ 色は思案の外 ◆ 恋は思案の外 ◆ 愛屋烏に及ぶ ◆ 止めて止まらぬ恋の道

## 惚れた欲目

[The prejudice of infatuation.] ● One in love gives more credit to their loved one that others do. ● Love sees no faults. = 恋は盲目 ◆ 痘痕も靨

## 惚れて通えば千里も一里

[To the infatuated, a thousand *ri* are as one.] 🖾 The *ri* (里) is an ancient Chinese measurement of distance, the equivalent of 0.3 miles. With time, it came to denote the distance one could walk in an hour, and during the Edo period (1600-1867) it was officially defined as 36 *chō*, or about 2.44 miles. ● Distance will not affect the feelings between those who are deeply in love. • Absence makes the heart grow fonder. • Baghdad is not remote to a lover. ◆ 親は千里行くとも子を忘れず

## 惚れ病と馬鹿の治る薬は無い

[There is no medicine to cure the love-sick and the fool.] ● No amount of persuasion will cause someone who is infatuated to fall out of love, nor will any degree of good counsel ever make a fool wise. • No herb will cure love. = 阿呆に付ける薬無し = 惚れた病に薬無し ◆ 愛屋烏に及ぶ ◆ 色は思案の外 ◆ 恋は思案の外 ◆ 三十馬鹿と八月青田は治らない ◆ 止めて止まらぬ恋の道 ◆ 馬鹿に付ける薬無し

## 本貸す馬鹿、戻す大馬鹿

[The fool who lends a book, the greater fool who returns a book.] ● Once a book passes into the hands of someone else it tends not to return to its original owner. Hence, books should either be given away or kept. ◆ 愚は書を得て賢となり、賢は書に因って利あり

## 盆過ぎての鯖商い

[Sell mackerel after the festival has passed.] ● There is a right time and place to do things; when they are done too late or in the wrong place they may be pointless. • A day after the fair. • After meat, mustard. = 後の祭 = 六日の菖蒲、十日の菊 ◆ 戦を見て矢を矧ぐ ◆ 喧嘩過ぎての棒乳切り ◆ 賊去って張弓 ◆ 賊の後の棒乳切り ◆ 敵を見て矢を矧ぐ ◆ 泥棒を捕らえて縄を綯う ◆ 難に臨んで兵を鋳る ◆ 盗人を見て縄を綯う

## 煩悩有れば菩提有り

[If there are worldly passions there will be salvation.] ● Only when one knows what it is to have gone astray can one reach true enlightenment.

## 煩悩の犬は追えども去らず

[Even if one drives it away, the dog of worldly desires will not leave.] ● No matter how hard we try, as long as we live in an

ほ

imperfect world, we will be subject to its temptations. • The devil is never far off. = 煩悩は家の犬打ってども門を去らぬ

## 煩悩は家の犬打ってども門を去らぬ

[As for worldly desires, no matter how hard the dog of the house is beaten, it will refuse to leave the gate.] ● No matter how hard we try, as long as we live in an imperfect world, we will be subject to its temptations. • The devil is never far off. = 煩悩の犬は追えども去らず

# マ

## 参らすれば賜る

[Those who give will receive.] ● Those who are generous to others can expect to be treated generously in return. • He who gives to another bestows on himself. • The hand that gives gathers.• A generous man grows fat and prosperous. ◆ 取らんとする者は先ずあ与う

## 間男を知らぬは亭主ばかり

[The husband is the only one not to know the paramour.] ● The husband is the last one to find out about his wife's infidelity. • The goodman is the last to know what is amiss at home. • The cuckold is the last to know of it. = 町内で知らぬは亭主ばかりなり

## 曲がった木に曲がった矩

[A crooked ruler for crooked wood.] ● In order to carry out an extraordinary task one may need people with extraordinary talents or resort to extraordinary means.

## 蒔かぬ種は生えぬ

[An unsown seed will not sprout.] ● If one does not put assets or talents to good use, they will be of no benefit. • Nothing comes from nothing. • Nothing ventured, nothing gained. = 才有れども用いざれば愚人の如し ◆ 逸物の鷹も放さねば捕らず ◆ 猿を檻に置けば豚と同じ ◆ 死を先んずる者は必ず生ず ◆ ❶ 千両の鷹も放さねば知れぬ ◆ 百貫の鷹も放さねば捕らず ◆ 身を捨ててこそ浮かぶ瀬も有れ ◆ 物は試し

## 曲がれねば世が渡らぬ

[One can not travel through this world without bending.] ✍ The verb *magaru* (曲がる) has the connotation of crookedness and corruption. ● In order to live in this imperfect world one must learn the art of compromise. ◆ 人と屏風は曲がらぬと立たぬ ◆ 曲がれねば世が渡らぬ ◆ 正しき者は艱難多し

## 曲がれる枝に曲がれる影

[Crooked branches throw crooked shadows.] ✍ The verb *magaru* (曲がる) has the connotation of crookedness and corruption. ● The machinations of evil persons will be evil, and so will be the fruits of their labors. ● Ill sowers make ill harvests. ◆ 心正しければ事正し ◆ 歪み八石直ぐ九石

## 馬子にも衣裳

[Even a packhorse driver (wears) clothes.] ● Even people or things that are of no real importance will look impressive when they are dressed up nicely. ● Fine feathers make fine birds. ◆ 文は人也

## 貧しき者は書に因って富み、富める者は書に因って貴し

[The poor may become wealthy through books; the wealthy may become esteemed through books.] ● The poor may become wealthy by selling books; the wealthy may gain in prestige by acquiring the knowledge to be found in books. ● Reading maketh a full man, conference a ready man, and writing an exact man. ● Learning makes a good man better and an ill man worse. ◆ 愚者は書を得て賢に、賢者は書に因って利あり ◆ 愚は書を得て賢となり、賢は書に因って利あり

## 待つ間が花

[It is best while one waits.] ● One can derive pleasure from anticipating something enjoyable; when it is past, however, there is often a sense of anticlimax. ＝ 成らぬうちが楽しみ ＝ ❶ 成らぬうちが頼み

## 待てば海路の日和あり

[If one waits, there will be fair weather on the sea routes.] ● Even though conditions may be poor today, if one has the patience to wait,

ま

229

they will eventually turn favorable. • Everything comes to him who waits. = 果報は寝て待て ♦ 運は天にあり、牡丹餅は棚にあり ♦ 堪忍は無事長久の基 ♦ 辛抱する木に金がなる ≠ 株を守りて兎を待つ

## 学びて厭わざるは智なり、教えて倦まざるは仁なり

[To learn and not to dislike is wisdom; to teach and not to grow tired is benevolence.] 📖 This proverb is taken from the works of Mencius. ● To study and not to become envious of the stock of knowledge of one's teachers is the beginning of wisdom; to teach and not grow tired of the lack of understanding in one's pupils is the beginning of benevolence. ♦ 師の影は七尺下がって踏まず ♦ 弟子七尺去って師の影を踏まず

## 学で思わざれば則ち罔し、思いて学ばざれば則ち殆うし

[Learning without thinking is vacuous; thinking without learning is dangerous.] 📖 This proverb is taken from the *Analects* of Confucius. ● If one fails to reflect on what one has learned, studying is a fruitless effort; conversely, thinking deeply about something one does not truly understand may lead to dangerously erroneous conclusions. • Learning without thought is labor lost; thought without learning is perilous. ♦ 知徳は車の両輪の如し

## 儘にならぬが浮世の習い

[It is the way of the world that things do not turn out as expected.] ● Things usually do not turn out in the same way as one hoped or planned. • If wishes were horses, beggars would ride. = 然うは問屋が卸さない ♦ 有るが上にも欲しがるのが人情 ♦ 有るは嫌なり、思うは成らず ♦ 成るは嫌なり、思うは成らず

## 守り手の隙は無くとも盗人の隙あり

[Thieves may have their moment of leisure, yet watchmen have none.] ● Those who intend to commit a crime can bide their time and wait for the right moment. Those who have to prevent crime, however, have to be constantly on their guard. By extension, those who take the initiative always have the advantage. = 盗人の隙はあれども守り手の隙は無い

## 万能足りて一心足らず

[Suffice in talent yet lack in wholeheartedness.] ● Though one may have many talents, if one does not have the necessary dedication and commitment they will prove of little use. ● Jack of all trades and master of none. ● He who commences many things finishes but few. ♦ 多芸は無芸 ♦ 何でも来いに名人無し ♦ 百様を知って一様を知らず

# ミ

## 身有りて奉公

[While one has one's body one may serve (one's lord).] ● As long as one is healthy one is able to perform one's duties. ● While there is life there is hope. ♦ 命有っての物種 ♦ 命有っての物種、畑有って芋種

## 身から出た錆

[The rust from the body.] ✍ Rust is the product of impurities contained in a metal. ● In the same way as metal is consumed by its own impurities, so we are tormented and consumed by ours. ● An ill life, an ill end. = 刃の錆は刃より出でて刃を腐らす ♦ 悪人は畳の上では死なれぬ

## 水清ければ魚住まず

[Where the water is clear fish will not live.] ● Those who always behave in an upright way without ever indulging in a degree of merrymaking will find it hard to make friends.

## 水の流れと人の末

[The drift of water and the end of humans.] ● In this life no one can tell where destiny will lead. ● A man's destiny is always dark. = 人の行方と水の流れ ♦ 明日の事を言えば鬼が笑う ♦ 一寸先は闇 ♦ 三年先の事を言えば鬼が笑う ♦ 知者も面前に三尺の闇あり ♦ 三日先の事を言えば鬼が笑う ♦ 来年の事を言えば鬼が笑う

## 道は好む所によって安し

[The road is rendered easy by one's tastes.] ● One is more likely to

み

231

master an art or craft that one truly likes to do. ≠ ❷ 好きの道には薦被る ≠ 好く道より破る

## 三日乞食すれば一生止められぬ

[If one has been a beggar for three days one cannot give up for the rest of one's life.] ● Once one has grown used to begging for a living it is hard to give it up. Similarly, the slothful habit of a life of dependency is hard to shake off. • Once a beggar, always a beggar. = 三年乞食すれば生涯忘れられぬ = 乞食を三日すれば止められぬ

## 三日先の事を言えば鬼が笑う

[Talk of things three days ahead and the devil will laugh.] ● No one can predict what tomorrow may bring, so to talk of one's expectations for the future is to tempt providence. • Nobody knows what tomorrow may bring. • Nobody knows the 'morrow. = 明日の事を言えば鬼が笑う = 三年先の事を言えば鬼が笑う = 来年の事を言えば鬼が笑う ♦ 一寸先は闇 ♦ 知者も面前に三尺の闇あり ♦ 人の行方と水の流れ ♦ 水の流れと人の末

## 三日見ぬ間の桜

[The cherry (blossoms) that cannot be seen for more than three days.] ● Life is short and its pleasures are fleeting. • Life is a shuttle. • Life is half spent before we know what it is. ♦ 会うは別れの始め ♦ 門松は冥途の旅の一里塚

## 三つ子の魂百まで

[The spirit of a three-year-old will last until a hundred.] ● A person's character does not change; traits that are displayed in early youth will endure till one dies. • The child is the father of the man. • As a boy, so the man. ♦ 老いたる馬は路を忘れず ♦ 雀百まで踊り忘れず

## 満つれば欠くる世の習い

[As the moon waxes, so it wanes.] ● Life has its ups and downs, and if something is on the rise today, it may decline tomorrow. • Every flow has its ebb. = 月は満つれば欠ける = 世は七下がり七上がり

## 源 清ければ流れ清し

[If the wellspring is clear, the stream will be clear.] ● If someone has a good heart, their actions and the fruits of their labors will be good, too. ● Muddy springs will have muddy streams. = 心正しければ事正し ♦ 巧言 令色 鮮し仁 ♦ 見目より心

## 実の生る木は花から知れる

[A fruit-bearing tree is known by its blossom.] ● Even at an early age, people with exceptional talents will stand out. ● A tree is known by its fruits. = 栴檀は双葉より芳し ♦ 虎豹の駒は食牛の気あり ♦ 虎の子は地に落つれば牛を食う気あり ♦ 流れを汲みて源を知る ♦ 実を見て木を知れ ≠ 大器晩成 ≠ ❷ 早く熟すれば早く腐る

## 実る稲田はは頭垂る

[Ripening rice plants hang their heads.] ● The more learning and experience one accumulates, the more one becomes aware of one's shortcomings and the minor role one plays in the greater scheme of things—an awareness that, in turn, will lead one to conduct oneself with more modesty and humility. ● The boughs that bear most hang lowest. = 学問は置きどころによりて善悪分かる、臍の下良し鼻の先悪し ♦ 大賢は愚なるが如し ♦ 大巧は拙なるが如し ♦ 大知は愚の如し

## 身は一代、名は末代

[The body (lasts but) one generation; fame (lasts) forever.] ● Though life is brief, the reputation built up during one's lifetime, whether good or bad, lasts beyond the grave. ● Worthy men shall be remembered. = 人は一代、名は末代 ♦ ❷ するは一時名は末代 ♦ 手形は残れど足形は残らず ♦ 虎は死して革を止め、人は死して名を残す

## 耳の楽しむ時は慎むべし

[When the ears are having fun one should be careful.] ● Especially when one finds oneself enraptured by the praise and flattery of others one should be on guard. ● Trust not the praise of a friend, nor the contempt of an enemy. ♦ 甘言が愚人を喜ばしむ ♦ 口に蜜有り腹に剣有り ♦ 信言は美ならず、美言は信ならず ♦ 追従する者陰にて誹る ♦ 天子将軍の事でも陰では言う ♦ 天子将軍も障子の内

み

## 見目より心

[The heart, rather than features.] ● It is better to have a good heart than good features. Similarly, the essence of things is more important than their outward appearance. ● Handsome is that handsome does. = 人肥えたるが故に尊からず = 山高きが故に貴からず ▶ 巧言令色鮮し仁 ▶ 衣ばかりで和尚は出来ぬ ▶ 衣を染めんより心を染めよ ▶ 心正しければ事正し ▶ 鞘が無くても身は光る ▶ 数珠ばかりで和尚が出来ぬ ▶ 源清ければ流れ清し

## 見るに目の欲触るに煩悩

[Visual passions for what one can see; worldly passions for what one can touch.] 📖 This proverb is taken from the *Tōkaidō meishoki*. ● All that can be seen and touched is nourishment to the senses and may help to stir up one's worldly desires. ▶ 一寸嘗めたが身の詰まり

## 身を殺して仁を為す

[Sacrifice oneself to do good (to others).] 📖 This proverb is taken from the *Analects* of Confucius. ● Those who seek to do good to others often sacrifice themselves to do so. ● A candle lights others and consumes itself.

## 身を捨ててこそ浮かぶ瀬も有れ

[Only when one throws oneself (into the water) will one find the shoals that may lift one up.] ● Only when one is willing to abandon the security of one's current situation will one find ways to improve one's predicament. ● Nothing ventured, nothing gained. ● To dive in at the deep end. = 死を先んずる者は必ず生ず ▶ 糧を捨てて船を沈む ▶ 清水の舞台から飛び降りる ▶ 虎穴に入らずんば虎子を得ず ▶ 背水の陣

## 実を見て木を知れ

[Know the tree by its fruit.] ● One should never be too hasty to judge people, but wait to observe the fruit of their labors. ● A tree is known by its fruits. ● One may know the lion by its claws. = 流れを汲みて源を知る ▶ 虎豹の駒は食牛の気あり ▶ 栴檀は双葉より芳し ▶ 虎の子は地に落つれば牛を食う気あり ▶ 実の生る木は花から知れる

# ム

### 六日の菖蒲、十日の菊

[Sixth-day irises, tenth-day chrysanthemums.] ✍ In Japan, irises are used to liven up the Boy's Festival (端午の節句), which is held on May 5; chrysanthemums are celebrated on the Chrysanthemum Festival (重陽の節句), which is held on September 9. ● There is a right time and place for most actions; when done at the wrong time or place they may lose their effect. ● A day after the fair. ● After meat, mustard. = 後の祭 = 盆過ぎての鯖商い ♦ 戦を見て矢を矧ぐ ♦ 喧嘩過ぎての棒乳切り = 賊去って張弓 = 賊の後の棒乳切り ♦ 敵を見て矢を矧ぐ ♦ 泥棒を捕らえて縄を綯う ♦ 難に臨んで兵を鋳る ♦ 盗人を見て縄を綯う

### 昔の剣は今の菜刀

[The sword of former days is the sickle of today.] ❶ With age the faculties and talents wither and cause people to become obsolete. ❷ It is better to turn an old and outdated object of beauty into a modern tool with practical use. ● From swords to plowshares.

### 昔は昔、今は今

[The old days are the old days; the present is the present.] ● The past and the present belong to different realms and cannot be compared. Thus it is useless to argue that things should be as they were in the old days. ● Let bygones be bygones. ≠ 現在の因果を見て過去未来を知る ≠ 古きを温ねて新しきを知る ≠ 来を知らんと欲する者は往を察す

### 無常の風は時を選ばず

[The wind of mutability does not single out the moment.] ● No matter what one's age is, death may call at any door and at any time. ● Death keeps no calender.

### 無駄無ければ不足無し

[If there is no wastefulness, there will be no need.] ● If one is sparing in the use of one's resources, they will last and there will be no dearth. ● Waste not, want not.

## 無知は傲慢の元

[Ignorance is the source of arrogance.] | ● Those who are not aware of the diversity of human talents will not be aware of their own limits and thus see no cause to be humble. ● Ignorance is the mother of impudence.

## 棟折れて垂木く崩る

[When the ridge of a roof breaks, the rafters will give way.] ● When those who lead break under the pressure of a crisis, those who are placed below then will give up hope, too. ◆ 強将の下に弱卒無し

## 無理が通れば道理が引っ込む

[Where force passes, reason retreats.] ● When brute force rules a society, right and reason will inevitably be eclipsed. ● Where might is master, justice is servant. ● Drums beat where laws are silent.

# メ

## 目明き千人、盲千人

[One thousand seers, one thousand blind.] ● There are as many intelligent people in the world as there are fools; for each person who can tell right from wrong, there is one who cannot. ● Some are wise and some are otherwise. = 盲千人、目明き千人 ◆ 馬鹿も有ればこそ、利口も引き立つ ◆ 下手があるので上手が知れる

## 名将は名将を知る

[A great commander knows a great commander.] ● It takes a person with exceptional talent to recognize the exceptional talents in someone else. ● It takes a great man to understand one. ● Great minds think alike. = 燕雀安んぞ鴻鵠の志を知らんや ◆ 英雄人を欺く ◆ 大巧を成す者は衆に謀らず

## 名人の子に名人無し

[There are no masters among the children of masters.] ☞ During the Edo period (1600-1867), Japanese society was strictly divided

め

into the four hereditary classes of samurai, farmer, artisan, and merchant. The lack of mobility between classes forced those whose sons did not have requisite talent to adopt disciples who did, so as to ensure the continuation of the family tradition. ● A great artist's or craftsman's gift is not hereditary. Similarly, great families do not necessarily produce great offspring. • Great men's sons seldom do well. ◆ 蛙の子は蛙 ◆ 父も父なら子も子だ ◆ 瓜の蔓に茄子はならぬ ◆ 子は生むも心は生まぬ

## 名人は筆を択ばず

[A master is not particular about his (writing) brush.] ● Those who are masters of their craft will be able to make a masterpiece, even with inferior tools. • A poor craftsman quarrels with his tools. = 弘法は筆を択ばず = 能書筆を択ばず = 名筆は筆を択ばず = 良工は材を択ばず ◆ 下手な番匠木の難を言う ◆ 下手の道具調べ

## 冥途の道に王無し

[On the road to Hades there are no kings.] ● No matter how rich, influential or elevated one's position in life, all people are mortal. • Death is the grand leveller. ◆ 下駄も仏も同じ木の切れ

## 名筆は筆を択ばず

[A master-calligrapher is not particular about his (writing) brush.] ● Those who are masters of their craft will be able to make a masterpiece, even with inferior tools. • A poor craftsman quarrels with his tools. = 弘法は筆を択ばず = 能書筆を択ばず = 名人は筆を択ばず = 良工は材を択ばず ◆ 下手な番匠木の難を言う ◆ 下手の道具調べ

め

## 目糞が鼻糞を笑う

[Eye-mucus laughing at nasal mucus.] ● Laughing at the mistakes of others is folly, since no one is above reproach and sooner or later one is apt to make a mistake oneself. • The pot calling the kettle black. = 五十歩をもって百歩を笑う = 猿の尻笑い = 目脂が鼻垢を笑う ◆ 己れを責めて人を責むるな ◆ 近くて見えぬは睫 ◆ ❷ 遠きを知りて近きを知らず ◆ 人の頭の蠅を追うより我が頭の蠅を追え ◆ 人の七難より我が十難 ◆ 我が頭の蠅を追え ◆ 我が身の上は見えぬ

## 盲千人、目明き千人

[One thousand seers, one thousand blind.] ● There are as many intelligent people in the world as there are fools; for each person who can tell right from wrong, there is one who cannot. • Some are wise and some are otherwise. = 目明き千人、盲千人 ♦ 馬鹿も有ればこそ、利口も引き立つ ♦ 下手があるので上手が知れる

## 盲のまぐれ当たり

[The accidental hit of the blind.] ● Even those with no expertise in a certain field may occasionally get it right. • A blind man may sometimes shoot a crow. ♦ ❶ 犬も歩けば棒に当たる ♦ 下手な鉄砲も数打ちゃ当たる ♦ 下手な鍛冶屋も一度は名剣

## 盲蛇に怖じず

[The blind do not fear snakes.] ● Those who are not aware of danger are not restrained by fear and so able to act with boldness. • Fools rush in where angels fear to tread. • Danger is next neighbor to security. • What is not wisdom is danger. ♦ 危ない事は怪我の内 ♦ 君子は危うきに近寄らず ♦ 三十六計逃ぐるに如かず ♦ 重宝を抱く者は夜行せず ♦ 聖人は危うきに近寄らず ♦ ❷ 馬鹿さしじがれば二がえ馬鹿

## 目の寄る所へ玉が寄る

[Where the eye wanders the pupil follows.] ❶ People in similar circumstances or with the same personalities tend to be drawn together. • Birds of a feather flock together. • Like attracts like. = 牛は牛連れ = 馬は馬連れ = 鬼の女房に鬼神 = 同気相求む= 友は類をもって集まる = 類は友を呼ぶ ♦ 同病相憐れむ ♦ 不幸の際の伴侶は不幸を軽減す ❷ An event of a certain nature is likely to be followed by an even that is similar in nature. • What happens twice will happen thrice. = 二度ある事は三度ある ♦ 雨が降れば土砂降り ♦ 泣き面に蜂が刺す ♦ 不幸は重なるもの ♦ 弱り目に崇り目

## 目脂が鼻垢を笑う

[Eye mucus laughing at nasal mucus.] ● Laughing at the mistakes of others is folly, since no one is above reproach and sooner or later one is apt to make a mistake oneself. • The pot calling the kettle black. = 五十歩をもって百歩を笑う = 猿の尻笑い = 目糞が鼻糞を笑う ♦ 己れを責めて人を責むるな ♦ 近くて見えぬは睫 ♦ ❷ 遠きを知りて近きを知らず ♦ 人の頭の蠅を追うより我が頭の蠅を追え ♦ 人の七難より我が十難 ♦ 我が頭の蠅を追え ♦ 我が身の上は見えぬ

# モ

## 儲けぬ前の胸算用

[The mental arithmetic prior to the making of profit.] ● Refers to those who make plans solely based on their expectations of outcomes that are uncertain. • Sell the lion's skin before one has caught the lion. • Don't count your chickens before they are hatched. = 捕らぬ狸の皮算用 = 空飛ぶ雁を吸い物に当てる

## 鵙が鷹を生む

[A shrike begets a hawk.] ● Used when someone from a humble background attains greatness. • A black hen lays white eggs. = 鳶が鷹を生む ≠ 瓜の蔓に茄子はならぬ ≠ 蛙の子は蛙 ≠ 鳶の子鷹にならず

## 用いる時は鼠も虎となる

[In times of need, even a mouse becomes a tiger.] ❶ In times of crisis even small people may rise to the occasion and perform heroic feats. Similarly, even seemingly insignificant people may play a role of importance when given a chance. • Put a coward on his metal and he will fight the devil. = 時に遭えば鼠も虎となる ♦ 窮鼠猫を噛む ♦ 鼠窮して猫を噛む、人貧しゅして盗みす ♦ ❷ 門脇の姥にも用有り ❷ Even those whose presence seems of no consequence may have their part to play in the greater scheme of things. • For the want of a nail the shoe was lost, for the want of a shoe the horse was lost, for the want of a horse the battle was lost. = 時に遭えば鼠も虎となる ♦ 枯れ木も山の賑わい ♦ 愚者も千慮に一得あり ♦ 癖ある馬に乗りあり ♦ 蹴る馬も乗り手次第 ♦ 鴎目大なれど観ること鼠に若かず ♦ 馬鹿と鋏は使い様 ♦ 馬鹿も一芸 ♦ 貧乏人も三年置けば用に立つ ♦ 野郎と鋏が使い様 ♦ 湯腹も一時、松の木柱も三年 ♦ 割れ鍋も三年置けば用に立つ

### 餅の中からの屋根石

[A roof stone out of a rice cake.] ☞ Where the winds blow hardest in Japan, heavy stones are placed on the roofs of houses to prevent them from being lifted by the winds. ● Used to describe a situation that is utterly unimaginable. • Pigs will fly. = 朝日が西から出る ◆ 石が流れて木の葉が沈む ◆❷ 瓢箪から駒

### 餅は餅屋

[For rice cakes, the rice cake shop.] ● In all trades there are professionals and it is best not to dabble in their fields but to rely on their expertise. • Every man to his trade. = 海の事は漁父に問え = 酒は酒屋に茶は茶屋に = 田作る道は農に問え ◆ 海老踊れども川を出でず ◆ 鴉が鵜の真似 ◆ 芸は道に依りて賢し ◆ 鹿つきの山は猟師知り、魚つきの浦は網人知る

### 本木に勝る末木無し

[There are no branches that surpass the stem.] ● In the friendships and loves one has throughout one's life the earliest and oldest are often the best. • Old love will not be forgotten. • Old friends and old wine and old gold are best. ◆ 焦げたる木には火が付きやすい ◆ 友と酒は古い程良し ◆ 焼け木杭に火が付く

### 物も言い様で角が立つ

[Something may cause offense by the way it is said.] ● Even when there is no real cause for offense people may be hurt simply by the way in which things are said. ✍ This proverb builds on the idiom 角が立つ, the literal meaning of which is "the edge stands up," yet the idiomatic meaning of which is "to arouse bitterness" or "to have a rough going." • Harsh words make the going rough.

### 物は試し

[As for things, try them.] ● The only way one will know whether one's ideas are feasible is by putting them into practice. • The proof of the pudding is in the eating. • Nothing comes from nothing. • Nothing ventured, nothing gained. ◆ 逸物の鷹も放さねば捕らず ◆ 才有れども用いざれば愚人の如し ◆ 猿を檻に置けば豚と

同じ ◆ 死を先んずる者は必ず生ず ◆ ❶ 千両の鷹も放さねば知れぬ ◆ 百貫の鷹も放さねば捕らず ◆ 蒔かぬ種は生えぬ ◆ 身を捨ててこそ浮かぶ瀬も有れ

## 貰う物なら夏も小袖

[When it is a gift, even a *kosode* is welcome in summer.] ✍ A *kosode* (小袖) is a traditional padded, warm silk garment that dates back to the Heian period (794-1185). ● Even when a gift does not exactly suit one's requirements one should accept it with grace. ● Do not look a gift horse in the mouth. ◆ 長者の万灯より貧者の一灯

## 門前の小僧習わぬ経を読む

[A young Buddhist monk at a temple will read the untaught sutra.] ● When one is constantly exposed to the practices of others, one will, with time, acquire them as a matter of course. ● A saint's maid quotes Latin. ＝ 勧学院の雀は蒙求を囀る ◆ 朱に交われば赤くなる ◆ 習い性と成る ◆ 習うより慣れよ ◆ 下手な鉄砲も数打ちゃ当たる ◆ 下手な鍛冶屋も一度は名剣

# ヤ

## 刃の錆は刃より出でて刃を腐らす

[The rust on a blade comes from the blade and destroys the blade.] ● In the same way that metal is consumed by its own impurities, so we are tormented and consumed by ours. ● An ill life, an ill end. ＝ 身から出た錆 ◆ 悪人は畳の上では死なれぬ

や

## 火傷した子供は火を恐れる

[A scalded child fears the fire.] ☞ This proverb derives from its English equivalent. ● Those who have experienced the disappointment of failure will think twice before they undertake a similar adventure again. And when they do, they may go to extraordinary lengths to avoid the same experience twice. ● A burnt child fears the fire. ＝ 羹に懲りて膾を吹く ＝ 蛇に噛まれて朽ち縄に怖ず

## 焼け木杭に火が付く

[A charred pile easily takes fire.] ● Love between those who have been separated by fate easily blazes anew. • Old pottage is sooner heated than made anew. = 焦げたる木には火が付きやすい ♦ 本木に勝る末木無し

## 安物買いの銭失い

[Cheap articles are a waste of money.] ● Cheap articles often last the shortest time and will only cause one to buy the better and more expensive article the second time round. • Buy cheap and waste your money. = 良い物に安い物無し

## 痩せ腕にも骨

[Even in a thin wrist there is bone.] ✍ In Japan the wrist is synonymous with skill, as, for instance, in the idiomatic expression 腕が有る: to have skill, or be a good hand at something. ● Even the humblest of people will have some skill or ability in which they may take pride, and thus one should treat everyone with the same respect. • A little body often harbors a great soul. = 一寸の虫にも五分の魂 = 蛞蝓にも角 ♦ 窮鼠猫を噛む ♦ ❶ 時に遭えば鼠も虎となる ♦ 鼠窮して猫を噛む、人貧しゅして盗みす ♦ ❶ 用いる時は鼠も虎となる

## 雇う乞食は冷や飯を食わず

[Employed beggars will turn up their nose at cold rice.] ● Even the lowliest person may become impudent when given too much credit. Hence, when one hires someone, one should take care not to overindulge them, lest they become haughty. • Set a beggar on horseback and he'll ride a gallop. = 乞食も雇えば冷や飯を食わず = 雇う法師は味噌を嫌う ♦ 門脇の姥にも用有り ♦ 枯れ木も山の賑わい ♦ 癖ある馬に乗りあり ♦ 蹴る馬も乗り手次第 ♦ 馬鹿と鋏は使い様 ♦ 野郎と鋏が使い様

## 雇う法師は味噌を嫌う

[An employed bonze will dislike *miso*.] ✍ *Miso* (味噌) is a condiment of fermented *soya* bean paste widely used in Japanese cuisine. ● Even the lowliest person may become impudent when

242

given too much credit. Hence, when one hires someone, one should take care not to overindulge them, lest they become haughty. ● Set a beggar on horseback and he'll ride a gallop. ＝ 乞食も雇えば冷や飯を食わず ＝ 雇う乞食は冷や飯を食わず ◆ 門脇の姥にも用有り ◆ 枯れ木も山の賑わい ◆ 癖ある馬に乗りあり ◆ 蹴る馬も乗り手次第 ◆ 馬鹿と鋏は使い様 ◆ 野郎と鋏が使い様

## 柳に風折れなし

[Willows do not lose their branches in strong winds.] ● People with pliant characters are better able to endure heavy trials than strong persons with rigid characters. ● Willows are weak, yet they bind other wood. ● Oaks may fall when reeds stand the storm. ＝ 木強ければ折れ易し ＝ 強き木はむず折れ ＝ 柳の枝に雪折れ無し ◆ 柔能く剛を制する、弱能く強を制する ◆ 茶碗を投げば綿で抱えよ

## 柳の枝に雪折れ無し

[Willows do not lose their branches through heavy snow.] ● People with pliant characters are better able to endure heavy trials than strong persons with rigid characters. ● Willows are weak, yet they bind other wood. ● Oaks may fall when reeds stand the storm. ＝ 木強ければ折れ易し ＝ 強き木はむず折れ ＝ 柳に風折れなし ◆ 柔能く剛を制する、弱能く強を制する ◆ 茶碗を投げば綿で抱えよ

## 柳の下に何時も泥鰌は居らぬ

[Loaches are not always found under willows.] ☞ The loach, a small fish that dwells in wet rice paddies and muddy streams, is used in Japanese cuisine (loach soup). In the old days loaches were a supplement in the diet of poor farmers. ● One cannot expect to be lucky a second time round by the same means. ● The fox is not caught twice in the same snare. ＝ 株を守りて兎を待つ ◆ 網の目に風たまらす ◆ 籠で水を汲む ◆ 糠に釘 ≠ 果報は寝て待て ≠ 辛抱する木に金がなる ≠ 待てば海路の日和あり

## 柳は緑、花は紅

[Willows are green; flowers are crimson.] ❶ Used to convey the beauty of nature—unaffected by human artifice. ❷ Used to convey the splendor of spring. ❸ There is a great diversity of life in the world, yet each species has its own innate value and beauty.

## 薮を突いて蛇を出すな

[Do not poke the bush to call forth the snake.] ● Unless absolutely necessary, it is better not to raise a sensitive issue or to meddle in other people's affairs. ● Let sleeping dogs lie. ♦ 触らぬ神に祟り無し ♦ 触らぬ蜂は刺さぬ ♦ 知らぬ神に祟り無し

## 病治りて薬師忘る

[Once the ailment has mended the doctor is forgotten.] ● No sooner has the danger passed than will people have forgotten their fears. Similarly, as soon as the difficulties that caused one to turn to others for help have passed, one will forget the aid given. ● Vows made in storms are forgotten in calms. ● Danger past and God forgotten. ● The peril past, the saint mocked. = 暑さ忘れて蔭忘る = 雨晴れて笠を忘る = 喉元過ぎれば熱さを忘れる ♦ 叶わぬ時の神叩き ♦ 苦しい時の神頼み ♦ 狡兎死して走狗烹らる ♦ 恐い時の仏頼み ♦ 災害は忘れた頃にやって来る ♦ 飛鳥尽きて良弓蔵る

## 病は気から

[Illness comes from the mind.] ● The degree to which one suffers from an affliction depends on one's frame of mind; one day the illness will be severe, the next day it will be light. = 万の病は心から ♦ 病は気で勝つ

## 病は気で勝つ

[Illnesses are conquered by the spirit.] ● The degree to which one suffers from an affliction depend on one's frame of mind, so the route to good health is a positive attitude. ♦ 病は気から

## 病は口より入り禍は口より出づ

[Illnesses enter through the mouth; calamities exit through the mouth.] ● Illnesses arise from people eating the wrong things; calamities arise from people saying the wrong things. ♦ 口は災いの元 ♦ 舌は禍の根 ♦ 禍は口から

や

### 病を知れば療ゆるに近し

[When an illness is known, recovery is near.] ☞ This proverb derives from its English equivalent. ● Once one recognizes one's faults, one can begin to mend one's ways. • A disease known is half cured.

### 山高きが故に貴からず

[Do not esteem the mountain because of its height.] ● It is not appearance that counts in life but character. • Do not judge a book by its cover. = 人肥えたるが故に尊からず = 見目より心 = 山高きが故に貴からず ♦ 巧言令色鮮し仁 ♦ 衣ばかりで和尚は出来ぬ ♦ 衣を染めんより心を染めよ ♦ 心正しければ事正し ♦ 数珠ばかりで和尚が出来ぬ ♦ 源清ければ流れ清し

### 野郎と鋏が使い様

[A fellow and a pair of scissors have their uses.] ● Even people of limited talent, when employed in the right way may play their role in the greater scheme of things. • A fool may give a wise man counsel. = 馬鹿と鋏は使い様 ♦ 門脇の姥にも用有り ♦ 枯れ木も山の賑わい ♦ 愚者も千慮に一徳あり ♦ 癖ある馬に乗りあり ♦ 蹴る馬も乗り手次第 ♦ ② 時に遭えば鼠も虎となる ♦ 馬鹿も一芸 ♦ 貧乏人も三年置けば用に立つ ♦ ② 用いる時は鼠も虎となる ♦ 湯腹も一時、松の木柱も三年 ♦ 割れ鍋も三年置けば用に立つ

# ユ

### 勇将の下に弱卒無し

[There are no weak soldiers under a brave general.] ● Talented leaders will make sure that they have talented people at their command. Equally, the example set by courageous leaders will bring out the best in those under their command. • A good general makes good men. • A good officer will make good men. = 強将の下に弱卒無し = 良将の下に弱卒無し ♦ 麻に連るる蓬 ♦ 大木の下に小木育つ

### 雄弁は銀、沈黙は金

[Eloquence is silver; silence is gold.] ● Though eloquence requires

ゆ

great intelligence and skill, silence when one is tempted to speak requires total self-control. ● Speech is silver, silence is golden. ● No wisdom like silence. = 沈黙は金、雄弁は銀 = 言わぬが花 ♦ 一寸の舌に五尺の身を損ず ♦ 愚者の雄弁は沈黙なり ♦ 口数の多い者は襤褸を出す ♦ 口は災いの元 ♦ 君子は九度思いて一度言う ♦ 言葉多ければ恥多し ♦ 三寸の舌に五尺の身を亡ぼす ♦ 舌は禍の根 = 禍は口から

## 夕焼けは晴れ、朝焼けは雨

[Evening glow, clear weather; morning glow, rain.] ● A red sky in the morning is a sign of bad weather to come; a red sky in the evening is a sign of fair weather to come. ● Red sky in the morning, shepherd's warning; red sky at night, shepherd's delight. = 朝焼けは雨、夕焼けは晴れ ♦ 朝虹は雨、夕虹は晴れ ♦ 晩の虹は鎌を研げ、朝の虹は隣へ行くな

## 幽霊の正体見たり枯れ尾花

[Withered stalks of eulalia grass may take on the shape of a ghost.] ● What at first site inspires terror may, on closer scrutiny, be quite harmless. ● The Devil is not so black as he is painted. ♦ 大きい大根は辛く無い

## 歪み八石直ぐ九石

[The warped eight *koku*, the straight nine *koku*.] ✍ A *koku* (石) is the traditional Japanese measure for rice yields, equivalent to approximately 180 liters, considered an average person's annual consumption. ● Rice stalks that lean will produce less rice than those that stand straight. Similarly, people who are upright in conduct will be more fruitful than those who have crooked characters. ● Ill sowers make ill harvests. ♦ 心正しければ事正し ♦ 曲がれる枝に曲がれる影

**ゆ**

## 雪圧して松の操を知る

[Under the weight of snow one will know the fidelity of the pine's branches.] ● Someone's hidden potentials will only be revealed when they are tested by trying times. ● The school of adversity is the best school. ♦ 逸物の鷹も放さねば捕らず ♦ 大風吹けば古家の祟り ♦ 艱難

汝を玉にす ▶ ❶千両の鷹も放さねば知れぬ ▶ 盤根錯節に遭いて利器を知る ▶ 百貫の鷹も放さねば捕らず ▶ 瑠璃も玻璃も照らせば光る

## 油断大敵

[Negligence (is a) great enemy.] ● More than anything else, lack of due attention lies at the root of failure and defeat. ● Take heed is a good thing. = 油断は怪我の元 ▶ 警戒は警備なり ▶ 治に居て乱を忘れず

## 油断は怪我の元

[Negligence is the source of injury.] ● More than anything else, lack of due attention lies at the root of failure and defeat. ● Take heed is a good thing. = 油断大敵 ▶ 警戒は警備なり ▶ 治に居て乱を忘れず

## 湯腹も一時、松の木柱も三年

[Even hot water may stay hunger for a time; even pine wood may serve as a post for three years.] ● No matter how insignificant or inferior something may seem, at the right moment, it may play a useful role. ● There is no misfortune but has a redeeming feature. ▶ 門脇の姥にも用有り ▶ 枯れ木も山の賑わい ▶ 愚者も千慮に一徳あり ▶ 癖ある馬に乗りあり ▶ 蹴る馬も乗り手次第 ▶ ❷時に遭えば鼠も虎となる ▶ 馬鹿と鋏は使い様 ▶ 馬鹿も一芸 ▶ 禍も三年置けば用に立つ ▶ 貧乏人も三年置けば用に立つ ▶ ❷用いる時は鼠も虎となる ▶ 野郎と鋏が使い様 ▶ 割れ鍋も三年置けば用に立つ

# ヨ

## 夜揚がりの天候は長持ちせぬ

[Evening clearings do not last.] ● Spells of fair weather that come late in the day usually do not last. ▶ 朝曇りば晴れ、夕曇りは雨

## 良い中には垣をせよ

[Put up a fence between close friends.] ● No matter how close one's friendship, one should always maintain a degree of reserve. ● A hedge between keeps friendship green. = 親しき中にも垣を作れ ▶ 遠きは花の香 ▶ 隣りの花は赤い

### 宵寝朝起き長者の基

[Sleeping early and rising early is the foundation of the rich.] ● To be successful, one should get to bed early to get a good sleep, and get up early to take advantage of the day. ● Early to bed and early to rise makes a man healthy, wealthy and wise. ● The early bird catches the worm. = 朝起きは三文の得 = 早起きは三文の得

### 用有る時の地蔵顔、用無き時の閻魔顔

[The face of Jizo when one has business; the face of Emma when one has none.] ☞ Jizo is the guardian deity of children and has a round, benign face; Emma is the King of Hell and has a square, scowling face. ● When people require help they will go out of their way to please; if they have no need of help they act badly or indifferently. ● When I lent I was a friend; when I asked I was unkind. ● If you would make an enemy lend a man money, and ask it of him again. = 借りる時の地蔵顔、返す時の閻魔顔 = 済す時の閻魔顔、借る時の地蔵顔 ♦ 貸した物は忘れず、借りた物は忘れる ♦ ❷ 成らぬうちが頼み

### 善く戦い者は怒らず、善く勝つ者は争わず

[Those who fight well do not lose their temper; those who win well do not quarrel.] 📖 This proverb is attributed to the Chinese Daoist Laozi. ● Those who are strong do not get into fights over trifling affairs; those who are always victorious do not make enemies without good reason. ♦ 良将は戦わずして勝つ

### 欲の深い鷹は爪を抜ける

[An avaricious falcon loses its talons (by seizing too large a prey).] ● Those who in their greed, ambition, or desire, set their sights too high often overreach themselves and come to grief. ● Grasp all, lose all. = ❷ 大欲は無欲に似たり ♦ 虻蜂取らず ♦ 一念は継ぐとも二念は継ぐな ♦ 二足の草蛙は履けぬ ♦ 二兎を追う者は一兎をも得ず

### 欲の世の中

[Amid a world of avarice.] ● We live in a world in which greed is a defining force. ● Money makes the mare go round. ● Money is the best lawyer. = 仏の沙汰も銭 ◆ 愛は多能で有り、金は万能で有る ◆ 金の世の中 ◆ 金は世界の回り物 ◆ 金は天下の回り持ち ◆ 人間万事金

## 善く泳ぐ者は溺れ、善く騎る者は堕つ

[Those who swim well drown; those who ride well fall.] ● In the field where one feels most confident one tends to become complacent—a complacency that may be the cause of failure.

## 予言者故郷に容れられず

[Prophets are not welcome in their home towns.] 📖 This proverb is taken from the *New Testament*. ● The qualities of those who stand out from the rest are often not recognized by those immediately around them. • A prophet is not accepted in his own country.

## 世の取り沙汰も七十五日

[Worldly rumors last but seventy-five days.] ● No matter how outrageous or sensational, with time a rumor will peter out like a spent candle. • A wonder lasts but nine days. = 人の噂も七十五日 ◆ 一犬虚を吠ゆれば万犬実を伝う ◆ 流言は知者に止まる ≠ 世間の口に戸は立てられぬ ≠ 人の口に戸は立てられぬ

## 世は七下がり七上がり

[The world has seven ups and seven downs.] ● In life there are ups and downs, and if something is on the rise today, it may decline tomorrow. • Every flow has its ebb. = 月は満つれば欠ける = 満つれば欠くる世の習い

## 読み書き算用は世渡りの三芸

[Reading, writing, and arithmetic are the three arts of making a living.] ● To get on in life, one at least has to learn to read, write, and do arithmetic. • Reading maketh a full man, conference a ready man, writing an exact man. ◆ 愚は書を得て賢となり、賢は書に因って利あり ◆ 貧しき者は書に因って富み、富める者は書に因って貴し

## 由らしむべし知らしむべからず

[One should make the people act (according to one's will), but not

よ

inform them (of one's intentions).] 📖 This proverb is taken from the *Analects* of Confucius. ❶ It is possible to make people do what is right, but to make them understand what is right is difficult. ❶ One should make the people comply by way of order, but one need not expound the underlying policies. = 民は之に由らしむべし、之を知らしむべからず

## 喜び有れば憂い有り

[When there is joy there is grief.] ● Joy and grief are inseparable aspects of life. Consequently, if there is joy at present, there will be grieving in the future. Similarly, the comfort one enjoys at present may well come at the price of suffering in the future. • After pleasure comes pain. • Every pleasure has a pain. = 苦有れば楽有り = 楽有れば苦有り ▶ 苦は楽の種 ▶ 苦を知らぬ者は楽を知らぬ ▶ 現在の甘露は未来の鉄丸なり ▶ 楽しみは憂いに生ず ▶ 楽しみは苦しみの種 ▶ 夏歌う者は冬泣く ▶ 楽は苦の種

## 万の病は心から

[All illnesses come from the heart.] ● The degree to which one suffers from an affliction depends on one's frame of mind; one day the illness will be severe, the next day it will be light. = 病は気から ▶ 病は気で勝つ

## 弱り目に祟り目

[Calamity to the weakling.] ● When calamity strikes it often strikes those who are already suffering. • Misfortune seldom comes alone. = 泣き面に蜂が刺す ▶ 雨が降れば土砂降り 痛い上の針 ▶ 重き馬に上荷打つ ▶ 二度ある事は三度ある ▶ 不幸は重なるもの ▶ ❷ 目の寄る所へ玉が寄る

# ラ

## 来を知らんと欲する者は往を察す

[Those who desire to know the future must observe the past.] ● In order to understand and tackle current problems, one should study the actions and outcomes of similar problems in the past. • Things present are judged by things past. • There is nothing new under the sun. = 古きを温ねて新しきを知る ♦ 現在の因果を見て過去未来を知る ≠ 昔は昔、今は今

## 来年の事を言えば鬼が笑う

[Talk of next year and the devil will laugh.] ● No one can predict what tomorrow may bring, and to talk of one's expectations for the future is to tempt providence. • Nobody knows what tomorrow may bring. • Nobody knows the 'morrow. = 明日の事を言えば鬼が笑う = 三年先の事を言えば鬼が笑う = 三日先の事を言えば鬼が笑う 一寸先は闇 ♦ 知者も面前に三尺の闇あり ♦ 人の行方と水の流れ ♦ 水の流れと人の末

## 来年の百両より今年の一両

[Rather this year's one *ryō* than tomorrow's one hundred.] ✍ The *ryō* (両) is an ancient Japanese unit of measurement for weighing silver and gold. During the Meiji period (1868-1912) the *ryō* became synonymous with the *yen* (円). ● It is better to seize the opportunity of the moment and make a modest profit rather than wait for great gains and make no profit at all. • A bird in the hand is worth two in the bush. • Better an egg today than a hen tomorrow. = 明日の百より今日の五十 = 末始終より今の三十 = ❶ 近火で手を焙れ = 後の千金より今の百文 ♦ あの世千日この世の一日 ♦ 大取りより小取り ♦ 聞いた百文より見た一文 ≠ 小節を規る者は栄名を成す能わず ≠ 小利を見れば則ち大事成らず

## 楽有れば苦有り

[When there is pleasure there is pain.] ● Pain and pleasure are inseparable aspects of life: if there is pleasure at present, there will be suffering in the future; if there is suffering today, there will be pleasure in the future. • After pleasure comes pain. • Every pleasure has a pain. = 苦有れば楽有り = 喜び有れば憂い有り ♦ 苦は楽の種 ♦ 苦を知らぬ者は楽を知らぬ ♦ 現在の甘露は未来の鉄丸なり ♦ 楽しみは憂いに生ず ♦ 楽しみは苦しみの種 ♦ 夏歌う者は冬泣く ♦ 楽は苦の種

ら

## 楽は一日苦は一年

[Pleasure for a day, pain for a year.] ● Pleasure is usually short-lived; suffering usually lasts for long periods. Similarly, giving way to the temptations of the moment may lead to life-long regrets. ● Short pleasure, long pain. ● From short pleasures, long repentance. = 一年の快楽、百年の後悔を残す ◆ 一寸嘗めたが身の詰まり

## 楽は苦の種

[Pleasure is the seed of pain.] ● Pain and pleasure are inseparable aspects of life: if there is pleasure at present, there will be pain in the future. Similarly, the pleasure one has today may be come at the cost of pain in the future. ● Unrest comes from rest. = 現在の甘露は未来の鉄丸なり = 楽しみは苦しみの種 = 夏歌う者は冬泣く ◆ 苦有れば楽有り ◆ 楽有れば苦有り ≠ 苦は楽の種 ≠ 苦を知らぬ者は楽を知らぬ ≠ 楽しみは憂いに生ず

# リ

## 李下に冠を正さず

[Do not adjust one's crown when below a plum tree.] ● Even a king, when sitting below a plum tree, should not raise his hand to adjust his crown lest he is suspected of pinching a plum. By extension, when one is in a position of responsibility or a position that is subject to public scrutiny one should always act with integrity and circumspection so as to avoid the least suspicion. ● Leave no room for scandal. = 瓜田に靴を納れず

## 流言は知者に止まる

[Wild rumors stop with the wise.] 📖 This proverb is taken from the works of the Chinese Confucianist Xunzi. ● Rumors without foundation will be passed on unquestioned among fools, but wise people will question their foundation and refrain from giving them any credence by passing them on. ◆ 一犬虚を吠ゆれば万犬実を伝う ◆ 世間の口に戸は立てられぬ ◆ 人の噂も七十五日 ◆ 人の口に戸は立てられぬ ◆ 世の取り沙汰も七十五日

り

## 流水 源に返らず

[Running water will not return to the source.] ● Words once spoken or mistakes once made cannot be undone. ● It is no use crying over spilt milk. ● What is done cannot be undone. = 覆水盆に返らず ◆ 死んだ子の年を数える ◆ 後悔先に立たず ◆ 提灯持ち後に立たず

## 竜馬の躓き

[The stumbling of a stallion.] ● Even those who seem complete master of their craft may sometimes get it wrong. ● Homer sometimes nods. ● A good marksman may miss. = 王良も時として馬車を覆す 河童の川流れ = 賢者も千慮の一失 = 弘法にも筆の誤り ◆ 猿も木から落ちる = 知者にも千慮の一失 = 上手の手から水が漏れる

## 猟ある猫は爪を隠す

[A cat with a prey will hide its claws.] ● Shrewd people do not make a display of their talents, so that (when those around them have become complacent) they may use them to greater advantage. ● Cats hide their claws. ● Who knows most says least. ● Still waters run deep. = 獅子人を噛むに牙を露わさず = 泣かぬ猫は鼠を取る = 鼠を取る猫は爪を隠す = 能ある鷹は爪を隠す ◆ 浅瀬に仇波 ◆ 言葉多き者は品少なし ◆ 静かに流れる川は深い

## 良禽は木を択んで棲む

[A shrewd bird selects the tree in which to build its nest.] ● A clever person carefully chooses a wise master, so that their services may not go unrewarded. ◆ 忠臣を孝子の門に求む ◆ 忠臣は二君に仕えず

## 両虎相闘えば勢い倶に生きず

[When two tigers fight the vigor will not live on in both.] ● When two brave people meet each other in a contest only one will emerge victorious. ◆ 英雄並び立たず ◆ 英雄人を忌む ◆ 両雄並び立たず

## 良工は材を択ばず

[Master craftsmen do not single out the materials (with which to work).] ● Those who are masters of their craft will be able to make a masterpiece regardless of the inferior quality of the materials. ● A

り

253

poor craftsman quarrels with his tools. = 弘法は筆を択ばず = 能書筆を択ばず = 名人は筆を択ばず ♦ 下手の道具調べ ♦ 下手な番匠木の難を言う

### 良工は人に示すに朴を以てせず

[Master craftsmen do not use coarse wood to display (their work) to others.] ✍ Though *boku* (朴) is one of the terms used to refer to the magnolia tree, here it is used to refer to rough, unrefined wood, or unfinished materials in general. ● Great craftsmen will wait until the fruit of their labor is completed before they reveal it to the world.

### 良将の下に弱卒無し

[There are no weak soldiers under a good general.] ● Talented leaders will make sure that they have talented people at their disposal. Similarly, by setting an example courageous leaders will bring out the best in those under their command. • A good general makes good men. • A good officer will make good men. = 強将の下に弱卒無し = 勇将の下に弱卒無し ♦ 麻に連るる蓬 ♦ 大木の下に小木育つ

### 良将は戦わずして勝つ

[A good general wins without fighting.] 📖 This proverb is taken from *The Art of War* by the Chinese general Sunzi. ● Great leaders will settle a conflict by force of authority and efficacy of diplomacy. • He is the best general who makes the fewest mistakes. ♦ 善く戦い者は怒らず、善く勝つ者は争わず

### 良馬は鞭影を見て行く

[A good horse will run on seeing the whip's shade.] ● Wise people do not have to be guided in order to do what is right, nor do they have to be warned to refrain from doing what is wrong. • A nod for a wise man, and a rod for a fool. ♦ 小人閑居して不善をなす ≠ 走る馬にも鞭

### 良薬口に苦し

[Good medicine is bitter in the mouth.] ● Good counsel or an experience that improves one's character may not be pleasant to hear or undergo. • Bitter pills may have wholesome effects. • That is not always good in the maw that is sweet. ♦ 諫言耳に逆らう ♦ 口に甘き物かならずしも腹を養わず ♦ 忠言耳に逆らう

## 両雄 並び立たず

[Two heroes cannot stand together.] ● Two great individuals with strong personalities find it hard to cooperate. Sooner or later they will vie for supremacy and only one will win out. • Two cooks in one yard do not agree. • Diamond cuts diamond. = 英雄並び立たず ♦ 英雄人を忌む ♦ 両虎相闘えば勢い倶に生きず

## 悋気は恋の命

[Envy is the life of love.] ✍ *Koi* (恋) stands for romantic love, which is often selfish, whereas *ai* (愛) stands for emotional love, which is usually altruistic. ● It is difficult to love without envy. • Love being jealous makes a good eye asquint. • Love is never without jealousy.

# ル

## 類は友を呼ぶ

[A species calls its mate.] ● People in similar circumstances or people with similar personalities tend to be drawn together. • Birds of a feather flock together. • Like attracts like. = 牛は牛連れ = 馬は馬連れ = 同気相求む = 友は類をもって集まる = ❶ 目の寄る所へ玉が寄る ♦ 鬼の女房に鬼神 ♦ 同病相憐れむ ♦ 不幸の際の伴侶は不幸を軽減す

## 類を以て類を度る

[Judge matters by (similar) matters.] ● One should always compare things or issues within the same category. Similarly, as long as one uses a similar situation or event to assess another, the same principles will apply, even if they are set in a different time. • Things present are judged by things past. ♦ 現在の因果を見て過去未来を知る ♦ 古きを温ねて新しきを知る ♦ 来を知らんと欲する者は往を察す ≠ 昔は昔、今は今

る

## 瑠璃の光も磨きがら

[Lapis lazuli, too, shines to the extent it has been polished.] ● No matter how talented one may be, without the proper training and discipline one will not become a person of fine character. ● An uncut gem does not sparkle. = 玉磨かざれば光なし ◆ 逸物の鷹も放さねば捕らず ◆ 瓦も磨けば玉となる ◆ 才有れども用いざれば愚人の如し ◆ ❶ 千両の鷹も放さねば知れぬ ◆ 百貫の鷹も放さねば捕らず ≠ 瓦は磨いても玉にはならぬ

## 瑠璃も玻璃も照らせば光る

[Lapis lazuli as well as glass will shine when lit.] ● People with talent, major or minor, will stand out from the rest (when given the opportunity). ◆ 氏より育ち ◆ 艱難汝を玉にす ◆ 盤根錯節に遭いて利器を知る ◆ 雪圧して松の操を知る ◆ 若い時の苦労は買うてもよせ

# レ

## 礼勝てば則ち離る

[The victory of etiquette is tantamount to detachment.] ● Etiquette is often a cold reminder of one's social position (and the difference between one's social status and that of others), and may result in emotional alienation. ◆ 礼繁きの者は実心衰うるなり

## 礼儀は富足より生り、盗賊は飢寒より起こる

[Good manners are born in wealth; robbers are brought forth by hunger and cold.] ● The degree of politeness people are willing to display toward each other is very much subject to the conditions under which they live. ● Other times, other manners. ◆ 鹿を死するや音を択ばず

## 礼繁きの者は実心衰うるなり

[Those with much etiquette have little sincerity.] ● Those who are excessively polite are often so only to hide their lack of sincerity. ● Much eloquence, little conscience. ◆ 七珍万宝の随一は人の命と人の誠 ◆ 礼勝てば則ち離る

れ

### 礼過ぐれば諂いとなる

[Excessive etiquette turns to flattery.] ● A too generous use of etiquette will soon seem unnatural and be interpreted as an attempt to ingratiate oneself. ✦ 礼も過ぎれば無礼となる

### 礼も過ぎれば無礼となる

[Excessive etiquette turns to insolence.] ● A too generous use of etiquette will soon seem unnatural, causing the other party to suspect that it is intended to hide contempt. ✦ 礼過ぐれば諂いとなる

# ろ

### 隴を得て蜀を望む

[Attain Long and covet Shu.] ☞ This proverb derives from an episode in ancient Chinese history in which Zhongda, a famous general of the Wei forces, set his eyes on the province of Shu as soon as he had conquered the province of Long, an act that elicited the above words from his lord Cao Cao. ● Those who obtain what they have set their eyes on are often tempted to acquire yet more. ● Avarice knows no bounds. = 千石を得て万石を恨む ✦ 有るが上にも欲しがるのが人情 ✦ 有るは嫌なり、思うは成らず ✦ 昨日に優る今日の花 ✦ 成るは嫌なり、思うは成らず

### 論語読みの論語知らず

[Those who read yet do not know the *Analects*.] ☞ The *Analects*, or *Lun-yu* (論語), are a collection of Confucius' sayings and doings which were compiled by his pupils shortly after his death. ● Said of those who read and study the works of the sages but fail to act on what they have learned. ● Practice what you preach. ● Folly and learning often dwell together. ✦ 一を知って二を知らず ✦ 其の一を知りて其の二を知らず ✦ 遠きを知りて近きを知らず ✦ 百様を知って一様を知らず ✦ 万能足りて一心足らず

### 論より証拠

[Proof rather than argument.] ● Rather that be swayed by (hearing)

a theory, however plausible, most people will only be convinced by (seeing) concrete proof. • The proof of the pudding is in the eating. = 百聞は一見に如かず

# ワ

## 賄賂には誓紙を忘る

[In corruption one forgets (even) one's written pledges.] ● It is easy to declare one's integrity, but only few are able to resist the temptation of illegal gain when offered. • Corruption of the best becomes the worst. • A bribe will enter without knocking. ♦❷ 花多ければ実少なし

## 我が頭の蠅を追え

[Pursue the fly on one's own head (first).] ● Rather than pointing out the flaws and mistakes of others, one should first critically look at one's own shortcomings. • We see not what sits on our own shoulder. = 己れを責めて人を責むるな = 人の頭の蠅を追うより我が頭の蠅を追え ♦ 五十歩をもって百歩を笑う ♦ 猿の尻笑い ♦ 近くて見えぬは睫 ♦❷ 遠きを知りて近きを知らず ♦ 人の一寸我が一尺 ♦ 人の七難より我が十難 ♦ 目糞が鼻糞を笑う ♦ 目脂が鼻垢を笑う ♦ 我が身の上は見えぬ

## 若い時の苦労は買うてもよせ

[Hardships in young age, buy them if you have to.] ● Character will only be developed when put to the test under adverse conditions. Therefore one should subject oneself to hardships as early as possible, so that one may grow into a mature adult. • The school of adversity is the best school. • Adversity makes a man wise. = 艱難汝を玉にす ♦ 盤根錯節に遭いて利器を知る ♦ 雪圧して松の操を知る ♦ 瑠璃も玻璃も照らせば光る

## 若い時の遊芸が用に立つ

[The light accomplishments of youth may be of use.] ☞ This is a parody on the proverb 芸は身を助ける. ● Those who have mastered

わ

a skill in their merrymaking during times of plenty, may find that it is the only skill that will earn them a living during times of need. • Art brings bread. ▶ 芸は身を助けぬ籠の鶉 ▶ 芸は身を助ける

## 若い時は二度無い

[One is not young twice.] ● A person is only young once, and to miss the opportunities of youth is to have missed them forever. • Time and tide wait for none. = 盛年重ねて来たらず = 若きは二度と無し ▶ 光陰に関守無し ▶ 光陰人を待たず ▶ 歳月人を待たず ▶ 月日に関守無し

## 我が門にて吠えぬ犬無し

[There are no dogs that do not bark at the gate of their own house.] ● When within the safety of their own homes, even the most timid tend to lord it over those around them. • A lion at home, a mouse abroad. = 我が家に鳴かぬ犬無し ▶ 家に居ちゃ蛤貝、外へ出ちゃ蜆貝

## 若きは二度と無し

[There is no second youth.] ● One is only young once, and to miss the opportunities of youth is to have the window of life closed on one forever. • Time and tide wait for none. = 盛年重ねて来たらず = 若い時は二度無い ▶ 光陰に関守無し ▶ 光陰人を待たず ▶ 歳月人を待たず ▶ 月日に関守無し

## 我が寺の仏は尊し

[The Buddha in one's own temple is (most) revered.] ● People value things they own and people closest to them the most.

## 我が身の上は見えぬ

[One cannot see above one's head.] ● It is easy to see the shortcomings of others, but to see one's own shortcomings is exceedingly difficult. • We see not what sits on our own shoulder. = 近くて見えぬは睫 ▶ 己れを責めて人を責むるな ▶ 局に当たる者は惑う ▶ 五十歩をもって百歩を笑う ▶ 猿の尻笑い ▶ 堤灯持ちの足元暗し ▶ 灯台下暗し ▶ ❷ 遠きを知りて近きを知らず ▶ 人の頭の蠅を追うより我が頭の蠅を追え ▶ 人の一寸我が一尺 ▶ 人の七難より我が十難 ▶ 目糞が鼻糞を笑う ▶ 目脂が鼻垢を笑う ▶ 我が頭の蠅を追え

わ

## 我が身を抓って人の痛さを知れ

[Pinch oneself to know the pain of others.] ● When considering the suffering of others one should try to imagine how one would feel in similar circumstances. ● Do as one would be done by. = 己が身を抓みて痛さを知れ

## 我が家に鳴かぬ犬無し

[There are no dogs that do not howl in their own house.] ● When within the safety of their own homes, even the most timid tend to lord it over those around them. ● A lion at home, a mouse abroad. = 我が門にて吠えぬ犬無し ♦ 家に居ちゃ蛤貝、外へ出ちゃ蜆貝

## 禍 慎家の門に入らず

[Calamity does not enter the gate of a cautious house.] ● Those who are cautious in everything and prepare for the worst will escape calamities. ● Providing is preventing. ♦ 備え有れば憂い無し ♦ 濡れぬ前の傘

## 禍 も三年置けば用に立つ

[Even a calamity may prove useful after three years.] ● Though one may initially be able to see only the disadvantages of one's misfortune, in time the lessons learned may be of great value. ● Ill luck is good for something. ● There is no misfortune but has a redeeming feature. ♦ 貧乏人も三年置けば用に立つ ♦ 不幸の裏には幸いが有る ♦ 割れ鍋も三年置けば用に立つ

## 禍 は口から

[The mouth is the origin of disaster.] ● A rumor or a remark made in an unguarded moment may be the cause of irreparable damage. ● Little said is soon amended. = 一寸の舌に五尺の身を損ず = 口は災いの元 = 舌は禍の根 ♦ 言わぬが花 ♦ 愚者の雄弁は沈黙なり ♦ 口数の多い者は襤褸を出す ♦ 君子は九度思いて一度言う ♦ 言葉多ければ恥多し ♦ 沈黙は金、雄弁は銀

## 渡る世間に鬼は無い

[In the world through which we pass there is no devil.] ● As one goes

**わ**

260

through life, it is not merely heartless people one encounters, but also kind and compassionate people. • The devil is not so black as he is painted. = 地獄にも鬼ばかりではない = 浮き世に鬼は無い = 人に鬼は無い ≠ 人を見たら泥棒と思え

## 笑う顔に矢立たず

[Arrows do not strike those who laugh.] ● Fortune is on the side of those who have a positive outlook on life. • Laugh and be fat. • Laugh and the world laughs with you, weep and you weep alone. ▶ 笑う門には福来たる

## 笑う門には福来たる

[Fortune comes to a laughing gate.] ● In households filled with laughter and mirth fortune will need no invitation. • Laugh and be fat. • Laugh and the world laughs with you, weep and you weep alone. ▶ 笑う顔に矢立たず

## 割れ鍋に綴じ蓋

[The fitting lid on a cracked pan.] ● No matter how eccentric one may be, there is always someone of the other sex that is attracted. • Every Jack has his Jill. • Let beggars match with beggars. = ❷ 合わぬ蓋有れば合う蓋有り ▶ 女に廃りがない

## 割れ鍋も三年置けば用に立つ

[Even a cracked pan may prove useful after three years.] ● No matter how insignificant something may seem, at the right moment, it may play a role of consequence. • There is no misfortune but has a redeeming feature. = 貧乏人も三年置けば用に立つ ▶ 門脇の姥にも用有り ▶ 枯れ木も山の賑わい ▶ 愚者も千慮に一得あり ▶ 癖ある馬に乗りあり ▶ 蹴る馬も乗り手次第 ▶ ❷ 時に遭えば鼠も虎となる ▶ 馬鹿と鋏は使い様 ▶ 馬鹿も一芸 ▶ 禍も三年置けば用に立つ ▶ ❷ 用いる時は鼠も虎となる ▶ 野郎と鋏が使い様 ▶ 湯腹も一時、松の木柱も三年

わ

# Index

Floating World Editions publishes books that contribute to a deeper understanding of Asian cultures. Editorial supervision: Ray Furse. Japanese text editing: Kyoko Suzuki. Book and cover design: Chōkei Studios. Printing and binding: IngramSpark. The typefaces used are Osaka and Trebuchet MS.